Complexity at the Frontier

Integrating Systems Thinking, AI, and Quantum Computing

Tom Sparrow CAPM, PMP, MBA, MSc, DBA(c)

PMP Services Ltd.

Published by PMP Services Ltd.

Calgary, Alberta, Canada

ISBN 978-1-0697874-0-8

First Edition, 2025

Printed in Canada/United States of America

To my Sparrow family — Sally, Kate, Bobby, Cole, Kelsea, and Igor.

This book belongs to you as much as to me.

With special love to my parents, Bob and Bobbie — whose spirit and determination shaped the path that led me here.

Acknowledgements

I wish to express my deepest appreciation to the institutions and educators who have shaped my academic and professional journey. My graduate studies at **Athabasca University, the University of Victoria, and Golden Gate University** provided the foundation and opportunities to grow, challenge ideas, and expand perspectives.

I am especially grateful to the professors whose guidance and mentorship have left a lasting impact: **Professor Andre Kushniruk, Professor Elizabeth Borycki, and Professor Sandy MacIver** at the University of Victoria; **Professor Rocky Dwyer** at Athabasca University; **and Professor Sreerama Murthy** at Golden Gate University. Each, in their own way, has inspired me to strive for excellence in both scholarship and practice.

I also extend sincere thanks to my doctoral colleague, **Michelle Freer**, whose insights and stimulating discussions pushed me to deeper levels of thought and reflection. I am equally grateful to **Dustin Karsin**, whose thoughtful discussions and manuscript reviews provided clarity and enriched the work presented here. And finally, **Michael Frahm**, whose work "Concepts of Complexity" kick started this initiative.

To all who have contributed to this journey, directly and indirectly, your support has been invaluable.

Preface: A Guide to Engaging with this Book

As you begin your journey through Complexity at the Frontier: Integrating Systems Thinking, AI, and Quantum Computing, you are embarking upon a rich and rewarding exploration of ideas that deeply influence our rapidly changing world. This book is intended not simply as an academic resource but as an invitation that showcases a thoughtful dialogue about complexity, technology, and ethics, crafted to resonate with readers from diverse backgrounds and perspectives.

To fully appreciate and gain insight from this work, consider approaching each chapter with openness and curiosity. The topics discussed, from chaos theory and quantum mechanics to artificial intelligence and adaptive governance, might initially appear challenging or abstract. However, these chapters have been thoughtfully structured to guide you through complex ideas clearly and reflectively. Take your time with each section, allowing the concepts to resonate, and sink-in. Consider the practical and philosophical implications as they relate to your experiences and understandings of the world.

As you engage with the historical and contemporary insights of pioneers such as Henri Poincaré, Edward Lorenz, Norbert Wiener, Donella Meadows, Herbert Simon, and many others, you may find it beneficial to reflect periodically on how their theories and ideas intersect with your personal observations or professional challenges in life. Doing so can transform your reading experience from passive absorption into an active, dynamic exploration of your own intellectual and practical landscape.

Throughout the book, complexity is presented not as an obstacle to overcome, but rather as a dynamic space that offers profound opportunities for adaptive governance, responsible innovation, and continuous learning, initiatives near and dear to me personally. To best harness the insights provided reflect upon your own decision-making processes, organizational structures, or the societal frameworks you interact with regularly. Consider how these complexity-informed strategies might practically and ethically enhance your own approach to technology, innovation, or policy.

Engaging actively with the provided examples, analogies, and case studies will also enrich your experience and viewpoint. These narratives serve as relatable illustrations, bridging complex theoretical frameworks with real-world situations. Feel encouraged to identify similar complexities within your own professional or personal environment, applying these insights practically to situations you understand deeply.

You will notice consistent themes of adaptability, reflection, transparency, and ethical responsibility woven throughout the chapters. Let these themes guide your thinking and provide a reflective lens through which you can examine and understand each topic. Pause regularly to contemplate questions such as, "How do these concepts **influence** my decisions and actions, and those of my organization? A related question is: 'How might these insights **guide** the development of technology that is both ethically responsible and genuinely responsive to societal needs?'" As we stand at this pivotal moment in the evolution of artificial intelligence and quantum computing, thoughtful reflection on such matters becomes increasingly crucial.

Above all, allow yourself to approach this book with an openness to seeing complexity not merely as abstract theory, but as something integral to our everyday lives, influencing how we connect, make choices, and respond ethically to change. By engaging with this work reflectively and practically, you are not just absorbing knowledge, you are actively participating in a thoughtful exploration of ideas that hold significant potential for meaningful change.

Enjoy your exploration. May this journey into complexity, systems thinking, artificial intelligence, and quantum innovation inspire thoughtful reflection, innovative actions, and responsible stewardship in the increasingly interconnected world we all share.

Table Of Contents

Acknowledgements v

Preface A Guide to Engaging with this Book vi

Introduction 1

Chapter 1: Chaos Theory and the Evolution of Artificial Intelligence A Poincaréan Analysis of Deep Learning, Machine Learning, Generative AI, and Quantum Computing 3

- Abstract 3
- Introduction 3
- Fundamental Concepts of Chaos Theory 4
- Chaos Theory in the Context of AI 5
- Generative AI: Emergence and Algorithmic Chaos 10
- Quantum Computing and Chaotic Dynamics 11
- Ethical and Regulatory Challenges 19
- Continuous Learning and Adaptive Oversight 22
- Applying Chaos Theory to AI and Quantum Computing Governance 33

Chapter 2: From Planck to Lorenz – Quantum Foundations and Chaotic Complexity 43

- Abstract 43
- Lorenz and the Butterfly Effect 45
- Chaos, Entropy, and Complexity 49
- Bridging Chaos Theory and Quantum Computing 52
- Conceptual Synergy and Relevance to Complexity 61
- Philosophical Convergence 62

Chapter 3: Holland and Kauffman – Genetic Algorithms, Adaptive Systems, and the Emergence of Self-Organization in Complexity 67

Abstract 67
John Holland 68
Applications to Real-World Problems 78
Stuart Kauffman and Self-Organization 80
Synthesis and Reflection 86

Chapter 4: Bateson and Prigogine – Systems Thinking, Dissipative Structures, and Complexity at the Edge of Chaos 89

Introduction 89
Gregory Bateson: Systemic Thinking and Feedback Loops 90
Ilya Prigogine: Dissipative Structures and Irreversibility 95

Chapter 5: Murray Gell-Mann and Claude Shannon – Complexity, Information, and Adaptive Systems 109

Introduction 109
Murray Gell-Mann: Complexity and Adaptive Systems 111
Claude Shannon: Information, Entropy, and Uncertainty 122

Chapter 6: Norbert Wiener and Heinz von Foerster—Cybernetics, Communication, and Observing Complexity .. 139

Introduction 139
Norbert Wiener: Cybernetics and Communication 141
Heinz von Foerster: Second-Order Cybernetics and Observing Systems 151
Conclusion 167

Chapter 7: Warren McCulloch and Ross Ashby—Neural Networks, Cybernetics, and the Complexity of Cognition ... 171

Introduction 171
Warren McCulloch 173
Ross Ashby 186

Conclusion 201

Chapter 8: Stafford Beer and Niklas Luhmann—Managing Organizational and Social Complexity 203

Introduction 203

Stafford Beer 205

Niklas Luhmann 218

Conclusion 232

Chapter 9: Systems, Rationality, and Sustainability—Insights from Donella Meadows, John von Neumann, and Herbert A. Simon 235

Introduction 235

Donella Meadows 237

John von Neumann 250

Herbert A. Simon 266

Conclusion 279

Chapter 10: Integrating Complexity—Navigating the Future through AI and Quantum Computing 283

Introduction: Reflecting on Our Complex Journey 283

Complexity as the Foundation of Contemporary AI 285

Cybernetic Principles in Modern AI Governance and Decision-making 291

Complexity, Natural Language Processing, and Large Language Models 297

Quantum Computing: Expanding Computational Complexity and Possibilities 303

Ethical Stewardship and Humanistic AI Innovation 309

Synergy and Future Directions: Navigating Complexity with AI and Quantum Innovation 314

Conclusion: Complexity as an Invitation to Ethical Innovation and Adaptation 319

Glossary of Key Terms and Acronyms 323

References **327**

Figure References **335**

Index **339**

Introduction

The journey from early visionary thinkers to today's advanced technologies in artificial intelligence and quantum computing is far more than a historical timeline, it's a profound narrative about human curiosity, creativity, and the relentless pursuit of understanding complexity. At its core, this journey owes a great debt to Michael Frahm's insightful exploration in "Concepts of Complexity." Frahm masterfully weaves together the intellectual legacies and personal narratives of pioneering minds such as Henri Poincaré, Norbert Wiener, Warren McCulloch, Ross Ashby, and Heinz von Foerster, whose foundational theories continue to guide our most innovative computational breakthroughs.

Yet, Frahm's work also brings attention to other transformative figures whose ideas significantly enrich our understanding of contemporary complexity. Visionaries such as John Holland, whose pioneering concepts around genetic algorithms and adaptive systems underscore the evolutionary and emergent nature of generative AI models; Stuart Kauffman, whose insights into self-organization help illuminate the spontaneous complexity inherent in deep neural networks; Gregory Bateson, whose work on feedback loops and systems thinking clarifies the intricate interactions within AI-driven ecosystems; Ilya Prigogine, whose revelations on dissipative structures and irreversibility inform the dynamics of chaotic neural network landscapes; Murray Gell-Mann, whose concept of complex adaptive systems provides essential perspectives on adaptive learning methodologies; and Claude Shannon, whose foundational work on information entropy illuminates the probabilistic and uncertain terrain navigated by machine learning and generative AI.

Today's sophisticated technologies, such as deep learning architectures, machine learning frameworks, and generative AI systems, reflect these foundational ideas by leveraging immense computational resources to interpret and harness complexity, turning theoretical insights into tangible innovations. Quantum computing takes us even further into uncharted territories, engaging quantum phenomena such as superposition, entanglement, and coherence, thus opening computational possibilities unimaginable to earlier theorists yet deeply rooted in their visionary work.

Profoundly inspired by Frahm's narrative approach, his compelling storytelling, depth of historical context, and focus on placing each thinker's contributions within their broader circumstances. This work aims not only to reveal the theoretical foundations underpinning modern computational systems but also to bring the humanity of their creators vividly to life. By connecting the wisdom of these remarkable minds from the past to today's dynamic technological frontiers, this work strives to offer readers an engaging, insightful, and deeply human journey through complexity at the frontier.

Chapter 1: Chaos Theory and the Evolution of Artificial Intelligence A Poincaréan Analysis of Deep Learning, Machine Learning, Generative AI, and Quantum Computing

Abstract

Henri Poincaré greatly advanced our understanding of chaos theory by highlighting that even algorithmic systems designed with strict rules can behave erratically, with small parameter shifts magnified into divergent pathways in AI training and quantum modeling. In this chapter, I explore how chaos theory remains incredibly relevant today, especially as we navigate the complexities of deep learning, machine learning, generative AI, and quantum computing. By drawing clear connections between the principles of chaos theory and these cutting-edge AI technologies, in Chapter One I show how chaos theory offers us both valuable insights and practical tools that can be applied at many levels and industry. These tools can help us build smarter, more robust, and more transparent systems and governance frameworks, and develop adaptable ways to manage and oversee the powerful but often unpredictable computational systems that are shaping our future.

Introduction

In the late 1800s and early 1900s, Henri Poincaré shared ground-breaking ideas that would eventually become the backbone of what we now call chaos theory. He recognized something fascinating, that even when systems follow clear, logical rules, tiny variations at the start can lead to dramatically different and unexpected outcomes. Today, this insight continues to shape our understanding of complex systems, especially in fields like artificial intelligence. Modern AI technologies, including deep learning, machine learning, generative AI, and quantum computing, embrace this complexity. They reflect precisely the kind of unpredictable, yet patterned behaviors Poincaré first observed, reminding us that even the most advanced technologies still echo the wisdom of earlier thinkers.

Fundamental Concepts of Chaos Theory

Chaos theory revolves around three core principles:

- ✓ **Fragility of starting parameters:** Minute variations at the start of a system can drastically alter outcomes (Lorenz, 1963).
- ✓ **Nonlinearity and Deterministic Behavior:** Chaotic systems, while governed by deterministic rules, exhibit behaviors that appear random and unpredictable.
- ✓ **Emergent Complexity:** Systems display complex and novel patterns of behavior emerging from simple underlying rules.

These foundational concepts directly correspond to modern AI architectures and quantum computing operational dynamics.

A simple visual representation illustrating how small initial differences evolve into large divergent outcomes over time. The graphic typically shows two initially closely aligned trajectories diverging dramatically as they evolve.

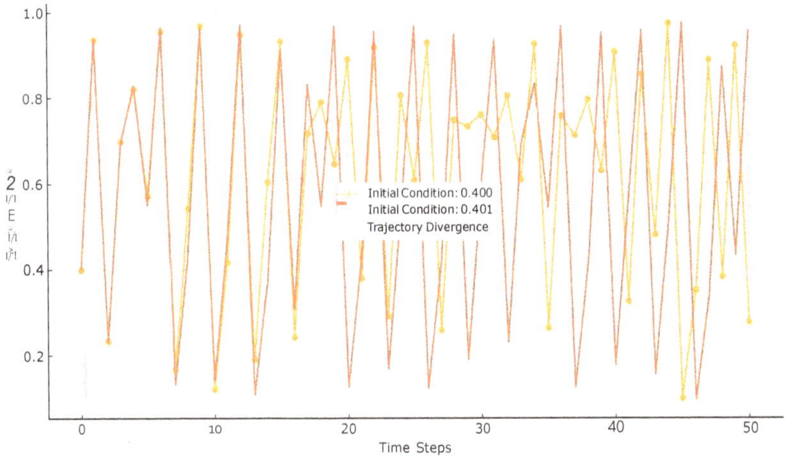

Figure 1.1. *Sensitivity to initial conditions demonstrates divergence in trajectories of chaotic systems with slightly different starting values (0.400 vs. 0.401). Adapted from Gleick (1987).*

Note. This figure highlights the defining feature of chaos theory: rule-based yet practically unforecastable outcomes due to exponential sensitivity to initial conditions. Although governed by precise rules, even infinitesimal variations at the start yield increasingly divergent results, a phenomenon commonly known as the butterfly effect. This concept underscores why chaotic systems—ranging from weather forecasting to AI model training—are inherently limited in their long-term predictability.

Chaos Theory in the Context of AI

Initial Condition Sensitivity in Model Training

In the world of machine learning and deep learning, it often feels like navigating through a delicate ecosystem, where even the smallest decisions made early on can have surprisingly large ripple effects down the line. For instance, something as subtle as the initial weights assigned randomly to neurons, the specific data samples chosen for training, or minor tweaks to hyperparameters can drastically influence the model's eventual performance and behavior. This sensitivity mirrors the principles of chaos theory, famously described as the "butterfly effect," where tiny variations in initial conditions can create dramatically different outcomes (Lorenz, 1963; Gleick, 1987).

Recent research underscores this chaotic dynamic, revealing how seemingly trivial choices at the outset of model training can profoundly impact the reliability and repeatability of results (Bouthillier, Laurent, Vincent, & Goyal, 2021). Such insights remind us that managing complexity in AI isn't just about controlling algorithms, it's also about appreciating and carefully navigating the subtle uncertainties inherent in their foundational settings.

Nonlinear Dynamics and Optimization

Training deep neural networks can be likened to charting a course through a vast, intricate landscape filled with peaks and valleys, each representing possible solutions or outcomes. This optimization landscape, characterized by extremely high-dimensional spaces, poses a profound challenge (Goodfellow, Bengio, & Courville, 2016). Within these expansive terrains, countless nonlinear interactions occur among the neurons and layers of the network. These interactions can lead training paths to become unexpectedly twisted and unpredictable. Even slight variations in initial configurations such as starting weights or learning rates can drastically alter the journey, leading the model toward entirely different destinations (Bouthillier, Laurent, Vincent, & Goyal, 2021).

This inherent unpredictability echoes the dynamics observed in chaotic systems, where seemingly straightforward rules and interactions give rise to astonishingly complex and unforeseen behaviors (Lorenz, 1963; Gleick, 1987). As a result, each training session in deep learning can unfold in unique ways, underscoring the critical importance of thoughtful initialization, adaptive methods, and robust frameworks to effectively navigate these complex and uncertain computational landscapes (Choromanska et al., 2015).

When navigating the intricate optimization landscapes of deep neural networks, human oversight becomes critically important not merely as passive observers, but as active participants ensuring alignment with ethical and social responsibilities. Given the inherent unpredictability and complexity within these powerful computational systems, there exists a tangible risk that models may behave in unintended ways, reflecting biases, producing misinformation, or generating outputs not anchored to factual realities, a phenomenon often described as "hallucinations" (Ji et al., 2023; Bender et al., 2021).

From an ethical standpoint, the deployment of deep learning models requires vigilant monitoring to uphold principles such as fairness, transparency, accountability, and privacy (Floridi & Cowls, 2019). Human oversight provides the crucial check-and-balance necessary to identify and rectify ethical issues before they propagate, thus ensuring that AI outcomes align closely with human values and societal expectations.

Moreover, the potential for models to "hallucinate," creating plausible yet incorrect information, underscores the necessity for continuous human engagement. This engagement involves actively interpreting outputs, fact-checking, and validating real-time data to preserve trust and accuracy (Ji et al., 2023). Incorporating real-time validation frameworks, such as those involving dynamic data checks or robust interpretability methods like SHAP and LIME, can further strengthen the reliability and credibility of model predictions (Lundberg & Lee, 2017; Ribeiro, Singh, & Guestrin, 2016).

Integrating thoughtful human judgment into AI training and deployment enhances our capacity to anticipate and manage unforeseen behaviors, mitigate ethical risks, ensure truthful representations, and maintain public confidence in these advanced technological systems.

Deployment and Model Drift

When we deploy AI systems into the real world, we send them into environments that are constantly evolving and full of surprises much like ships setting sail into unpredictable seas. As these AI systems begin interacting with live, dynamic contexts, they inevitably encounter changing circumstances that differ from the conditions under which they were originally trained. This phenomenon, often referred to as "model drift," describes the gradual yet continuous shift in the environment's data patterns, behaviors, or user interactions, which can significantly alter the model's effectiveness over time (Quiñonero-Candela, Sugiyama, Schwaighofer, & Lawrence, 2009).

Further complicating matters, AI systems often become entangled in unforeseen feedback loops, where their own decisions influence the environment in ways that feed back into subsequent decisions, sometimes creating self-reinforcing cycles that amplify errors, biases, or instability (Sculley et al., 2015). For instance, recommender systems in social media platforms can create feedback loops by continually suggesting similar content, shaping users' preferences and behaviors, which then reinforce the system's future recommendations, potentially leading to echo chambers or polarization (Pariser, 2011).

These dynamics closely resemble the unpredictable and sensitive nature of chaotic systems in complexity science, where small changes can lead to disproportionately large outcomes (Lorenz, 1963; Gleick, 1987). Thus, maintaining effective and trustworthy AI systems demands vigilant monitoring and adaptive management strategies such as regular retraining, continuous model validation, and real-time monitoring to identify shifts quickly and respond proactively (Gama et al., 2014).

Recognizing and managing the inherent unpredictability of deployed AI systems requires not only technical vigilance but also careful human oversight, ensuring these powerful technologies continue to function effectively, ethically, and beneficially in the face of constant change (Floridi & Cowls, 2019).

The following is a clear visual representation of a multi-layer neural network highlighting input layers, hidden layers, activation functions, and output layers. This should help the reader visualize the non-linear complexity inherent in neural networks.

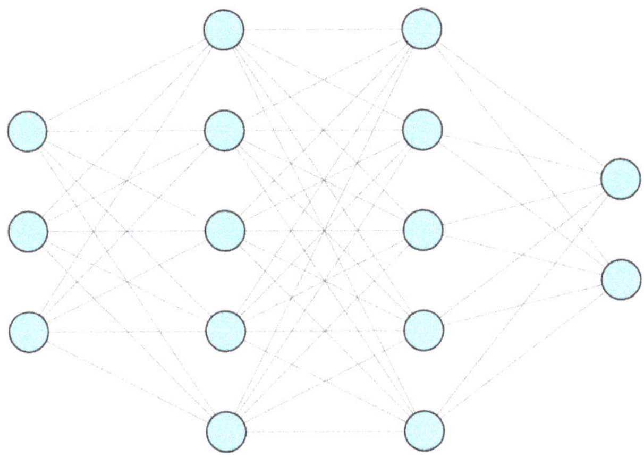

Figure 1.2. *Simplified diagram of a deep neural network showing layers, nodes, and activation functions. Adapted from Goodfellow et al. (2016)*

Note. Each circle represents a node where inputs are weighted and transformed through activation functions. The layers collectively contribute to the non-linear decision-making capacity of the network.

Generative AI: Emergence and Algorithmic Chaos

Generative AI models can be thought of as digital artists or storytellers capable of producing genuinely novel, creative outputs. Rather than simply retrieving stored responses, these sophisticated systems transform input prompts into entirely new creations through complex, probabilistic, and nonlinear data interactions. Much like human creativity, their outputs often defy precise prediction or straightforward control, echoing the unpredictability found in natural processes (Goodfellow, Bengio, & Courville, 2016).

This unpredictable creativity resonates deeply with principles from chaos theory, originally articulated by Henri Poincaré, which emphasize how small, seemingly insignificant changes in initial conditions can lead to vastly different outcomes (Poincaré, 1890; Gleick, 1987). In generative AI, this manifests vividly as "prompt sensitivity," where slight alterations in user inputs, even just changing a word or two, can drastically shift the entire nature and style of the AI's output (Ji et al., 2023).

Generative models often exhibit what we might call "emergent behaviors," wherein unexpected and novel patterns, concepts, or even errors spontaneously arise. These behaviors emerge organically during interactions within the deep-layered, nonlinear neural architectures of the models. Notably, these outcomes are often not explicitly programmed by developers, representing the inherent creativity and complexity of these systems (Bommasani et al., 2021).

A significant challenge presented by this creative complexity is "opacity," where the deeply interconnected, multi-layered structure of generative models makes it extraordinarily difficult for humans to interpret exactly how and why specific outputs emerge (Rudin, 2019). Like navigating through a dense fog, the internal decision-making processes of these AI systems are often obscured, posing important implications for interpretability, transparency, trustworthiness, and ethical governance (Floridi & Cowls, 2019).

Together, these attributes prompt sensitivity, emergent behaviors, and opacity highlighting the deep parallels between generative AI and the dynamics of chaos theory. By embracing this connection, developers, researchers, and regulators alike can better appreciate and manage the powerful yet unpredictable nature of generative AI, ensuring that it is deployed responsibly, transparently, and in alignment with human values (Mitchell, 2019; Floridi & Cowls, 2019).

Quantum Computing and Chaotic Dynamics

Quantum computing takes us into an entirely different realm of computational thinking, one characterized by unpredictability, subtlety, and intriguing complexity. Unlike classical computing, which operates largely through predictable, deterministic logic, quantum computing embraces probability and uncertainty at its core. Quantum systems engage with phenomena such as superposition and entanglement, which significantly increase their sensitivity to small changes in initial quantum states or environmental conditions. This heightened sensitivity introduces unique forms of chaotic behavior, a phenomenon known as "quantum chaos," where quantum systems display unpredictable behaviors similar to classical chaotic systems, making precise predictions extraordinarily challenging (Nielsen & Chuang, 2010).

Quantum algorithms, including variational quantum algorithms and quantum neural networks, explicitly incorporate elements of chaos theory, particularly their extreme sensitivity to initial conditions and nonlinear interactions. This complexity demands thoughtful approaches, rigorous interpretability methods, and dynamic regulatory frameworks designed to handle the inherent uncertainty and unpredictability of quantum computational outcomes (McClean et al., 2016; Farhi, Goldstone, & Gutmann, 2014; Preskill, 2018).

Understanding the complexity of quantum computing means appreciating three remarkable quantum properties that profoundly influence how these systems behave:

Quantum superposition (multiple states at once).

Quantum particles, such as electrons or photons, can occupy multiple states simultaneously until they're measured (Nielsen & Chuang, 2010). A useful image is a dimmer set to several brightness levels at once rather than a single on/off position. Quantum computers exploit this to examine many possibilities in parallel, which can dramatically expand computational reach.

Quantum entanglement (correlations across distance).

When particles become entangled, measuring one immediately constrains the possible outcome for the other, no matter how far apart they are. The effect is non-classical correlation, not signal sending, but it still reshapes how we think about cause and effect (Horodecki et al., 2009). Think of paired readouts that always reveal related values the instant you check either screen, even if the devices are in different cities.

Sensitivity to perturbations (small changes, big effects).

Quantum states are exquisitely sensitive to tiny disturbances. Minute shifts in the environment or initial conditions can lead to large, sometimes surprising changes in outcomes—echoing ideas from chaos theory (Lorenz, 1963; Zurek, 2003). Picture a pencil balanced on its tip: the faintest breeze is enough to send it one way or another.

Together, superposition, entanglement, and sensitivity open extraordinary computational possibilities and introduce real challenges. They call for ongoing human oversight, good interpretability tools, and adaptive ethical governance to manage the unpredictability and creative power of quantum technologies (Floridi & Cowls, 2019; Preskill, 2018).

A human-centred approach to effective oversight

Treat quantum systems as socio technical: their outputs affect people, institutions, and communities. Effective oversight is less about control for its own sake and more about care, clarity, and accountability.

Purpose & proportionality. Be explicit about why quantum is truly needed. Appoint a named risk owner. Require a proportionality check (prefer classical methods when they suffice).

Practice at the console. Keep a human in the loop for high impact actions; set intervention thresholds; use a two-person rule for sensitive runs; conduct pre-mortems and red team exercises; estimate variability via ensemble runs; keep a quantum run ledger (inputs, hardware context, and rationale); and ensure reversibility with rollbacks/kill switches when outcomes are uncertain.

Public accountability. Explain decisions in plain language; invite affected stakeholders into design reviews; provide an appeal channel to challenge outcomes; and commission periodic, independent audits.

Anchor these steps in recognized AI ethics principles including beneficence, non-maleficence, autonomy, justice, and explicability, so deployments demonstrate a real duty of care (Floridi & Cowls, 2019). Given today's noise prone, probabilistic hardware, treat unpredictability as a design constraint: monitor drift, document near misses, and update guardrails through continuous learning and post incident reviews (Preskill, 2018). In short: clear purpose, reversible decisions, rigorous logging, independent scrutiny, and meaningful voice for those affected.

Plain language version

Quantum computing processes information in ways that feel closer to nature, powerful, but not always predictable.

1. **Superposition**
   Imagine a coin spinning in the air. While it spins, it isn't simply heads or tails; in a sense, it carries both possibilities. That's how quantum bits can explore many options at once (Nielsen & Chuang, 2010).
2. **Entanglement**
   Picture two magical dice that stay linked: when you read one, the other instantly shows a correlated result—even if it's far away (Horodecki et al., 2009).
3. **Sensitivity**
   Think of a house of cards; a tiny nudge can change everything (Lorenz, 1963; Zurek, 2003).

Because of these features, people need to stay involved. We should be able to explain what systems are doing, pause or reverse when needed, and listen to those affected. With thoughtful oversight and plain language accountability, we can explore quantum's promise without losing sight of human values (Floridi & Cowls, 2019; Preskill, 2018).

Why This Matters:

These quantum effects mean quantum systems don't behave predictably like classical systems (everyday objects).

Quantum computing can harness these chaotic behaviors for extraordinary computational power, solving problems beyond traditional computers.

Understanding and managing these behaviors are crucial for developing stable, reliable quantum technologies.

The following figure illustrates how chaotic dynamics emerge in both quantum states and AI computational states when subjected to small perturbations. This provides a comparative view of sensitivity across different systems.

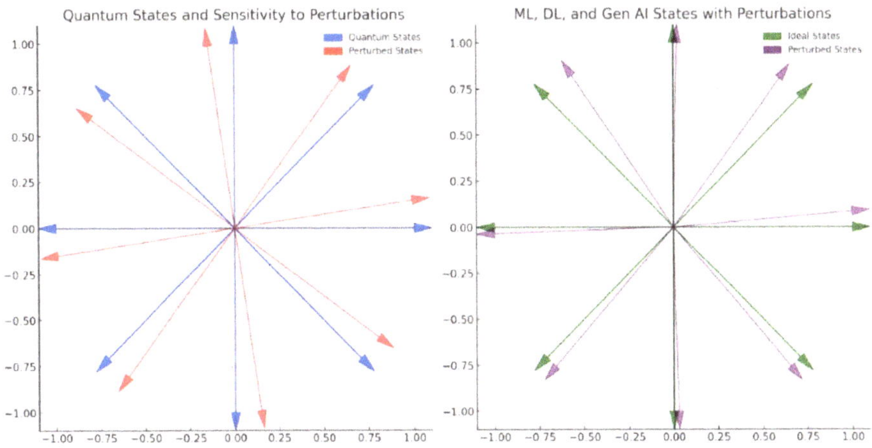

Figure 1.3. *Graphical representation of chaotic dynamics in quantum and AI computational systems. Adapted from Nielsen & Chuang (2010).*

Note. The left panel illustrates quantum states and their sensitivity to perturbations, while the right panel shows analogous sensitivity in machine learning and generative AI systems. Both highlight how small changes in state lead to divergent trajectories, emphasizing the role of chaotic dynamics across computational paradigms.

The left diagram in Figure 1.3 illustrates the concept of sensitivity to initial conditions in quantum states. It visually demonstrates how quantum states (shown in blue) can diverge dramatically when small perturbations (shown in red) occur. These perturbations highlight the inherent instability and unpredictability within quantum systems, characteristic of chaotic dynamics.

The right diagram in Figure 1.3 extends this principle to Machine Learning (ML), Deep Learning (DL), and Generative AI models. It shows ideal computational states (green) and how minor disturbances from noise or data variability (purple) can lead to significantly different outcomes, emphasizing the necessity of stability and robustness in AI-driven computational models.

Both diagrams illustrate the fundamental principle that small initial differences or perturbations can amplify into considerable divergences, a critical aspect in understanding and managing complexity in various computational domains.

Why the quantum plot looks stable

The left panel is effectively drawing qubit like states on a **unit circle** (a 2 D slice of the Bloch sphere). In this idealized view, small perturbations are modeled as **rotations**. Rotations are length preserving, they change direction but not magnitude. So, every arrow keeps the same distance from the origin even when "nudged."

That matches the math: **unitary** evolution in quantum mechanics preserves norms and inner products. As long as you perturb coherently (e.g., tiny phase or angle errors), the picture stays neat, same lengths but slightly different angles.

The fragility you expected—**decoherence, dephasing, amplitude damping, measurement collapse**—is non unitary. Those effects would **shrink** or blur the arrows and introduce discontinuities. They simply aren't depicted in this visualization.

Why the ML/DL/Gen AI plot stretches

Most learned models are **not norm preserving**. Each layer applies non orthogonal weight matrices and non linear activations. Small input changes can be **amplified** as they propagate, so layer-by-layer updates compound distortions, where small changes become stretched disproportionately across different model pathways, similar to tension accumulating in fabric under uneven pulls.

Training itself often encourages expansion along some directions (e.g., margin making, confidence calibration). The result is **anisotropy**:

some vectors get longer faster than others, which is why the purple arrows lengthen.

Reconciling expectation with reality

- In theory space, quantum looks calm because we're showing its **coherent** side.
- In hardware space, quantum is famously temperamental: noise channels would shorten arrows and smear directions. If we plotted those non unitary effects, the quantum panel would look less stable than the ML one in a hurry.

Take away

The left image shows how quantum ought to behave when we keep it perfectly coherent; the right shows how learning systems often behave when small nudges compound. For teams and stakeholders, the message is practical: **treat quantum fragility as a design constraint** (monitor for decoherence and add rollback paths) and **treat ML drift as a safety concern** (regularize, calibrate, and watch for amplification of small changes). Different technologies, different failure modes, but both need steady human hands on the controls.

If you want the figure to match live behavior more closely

- Add **decoherence** to the quantum plot (radial shrink toward the center, random phase jitter).
- Compare using **state fidelity** (or the Fubini–Study distance) on the quantum side, rather than Euclidean radius, to make sensitivity visible.
- On the ML side, fix the scale per step (or use **cosine similarity**) to separate "true drift amplification" from mere length growth.

The following figure compares perturbations in quantum states and AI states, illustrating how drift is measured differently in each system

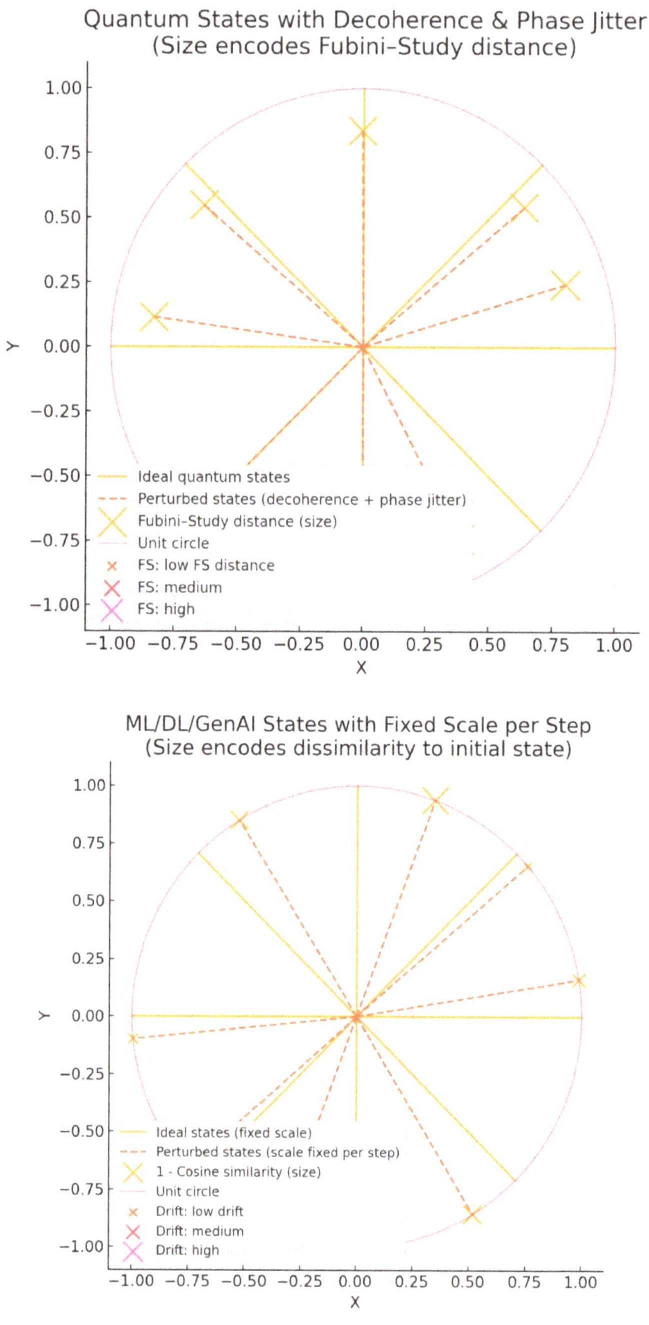

Figure 1.4. *Comparing perturbations: Quantum states with decoherence and phase jitter (left) versus ML/DL/GenAI states with fixed scale per step (right). Author's illustration (2025).*

Note. The left panel encodes decoherence and phase jitter in quantum states, with marker size showing Fubini–Study distance. The right panel illustrates AI states under fixed scale, where marker size reflects true directional drift (1–cosine similarity) rather than length growth.

Ethical and Regulatory Challenges

Alignment and Uncertainty

When dealing with advanced AI and quantum systems, we often find ourselves facing scenarios that feel somewhat unpredictable, similar to managing a project under shifting stakeholder priorities and market shocks. Because these systems can behave chaotically rapidly evolving in ways we can't easily foresee. It's challenging to ensure they are consistent with the expectations of project sponsors, regulators, and communities. As these technologies continuously learn from new data and complex quantum interactions, maintaining control and stability becomes progressively more difficult (Preskill, 2018; Bommasani et al., 2021).

To tackle this complexity, it becomes crucial to integrate thoughtful, responsible practices into the very foundation of how we design, monitor, and manage these systems. Here are several key approaches that help ensure our AI and quantum technologies remain safe, ethical, and closely aligned with human goals:

Transparency and practical interpretability

Transparency is about giving people a legible account of what the system looked at, how it weighed those inputs, and how confident it was. Post hoc tools such as **SHAP** and **LIME** help here in different ways: tools like LIME approximate what drove a single prediction, while SHAP distributes credit across features more systematically, together giving practitioners complementary ways to unpack black-box AI. Used together, they surface **why** an output was produced and **how sensitive** it is to small changes—information that researchers, policymakers, and the public can act on (Lundberg & Lee, 2017; Ribeiro, Singh, & Guestrin, 2016).

From explanations to accountability

Explanations should not live only in notebooks. For high stakes uses, pair them with plain language summaries, uncertainty indicators (e.g., confidence or calibration), and **counterfactuals** that answer, "What minimal change would flip the decision?" Publish model cards and data documentation so stakeholders can see training data scope, known limitations, and performance across groups. Keep an **explanation log** outlining the model version, inputs, parameters, and attribution results so external reviewers can reproduce decisions later.

Choosing and stress testing methods

Interpretability is not one size fits all.

- Use **local** methods (LIME/SHAP) to justify individual decisions; use **global** tools (partial dependence, accumulated local effects, interaction scores) to understand overall behavior.
- Stabilize results: fix random seeds, select appropriate background data for SHAP, and check robustness by repeating runs under small input jitters.
- Evaluate **faithfulness**: if you remove the top attributed features, does model performance drop as predicted? If not, treat the explanation with caution.

Person-centric delivery

Different audiences need different views. Front line staff may prefer a traffic light summary (key drivers, confidence, recourse steps). Regulators need audit trails and error bounds. Affected individuals deserve accessible narratives that explain what influenced an outcome and what lawful steps exist to seek review or remedy.

Guardrails and trade offs

Transparency can expose sensitive data or invite gaming. Mitigate this with differential privacy or aggregation, rate limit explanation access in adversarial settings, and document what cannot be disclosed and why. Above all, remember that an explanation is evidence, not a moral warrant. Pair interpretability with fairness testing, red team evaluations, and clear escalation paths when explanations reveal problems.

Risk Management and Accident Mitigation

Given their inherent unpredictability, it's essential to anticipate and manage potential risks proactively. This involves adopting structured layers of oversight and embedding continuous vigilance into system operations. By clearly defining escalation procedures and maintaining regular training for human reviewers, we can quickly spot and respond to unexpected behaviors or errors, thereby minimizing potential harm or disruption (Perrow, 1999; Reason, 2016). This kind of proactive approach is especially valuable when chaotic dynamics might amplify small mistakes into larger systemic problems.

Ethical and Fairness Considerations

Chaotic and unpredictable AI systems can inadvertently introduce bias or act unfairly, potentially harming people or groups. To prevent this, institute **closed loop governance**: ongoing fairness audits and drift monitoring tied to user and community feedback, defined trigger thresholds, and clear remediation paths providing data correction, feature or threshold changes, and scheduled or event driven retraining followed by post fix verification and audit logging. These feedback loops make oversight continuous rather than episodic, ensuring the system adapts as contexts shift while avoiding unintended discrimination or unethical outcomes (Binns, 2018; Mehrabi et al., 2021; O'Neil, 2016).

Loop stages:

Measure → compare to thresholds → diagnose → mitigate → verify → document → redeploy → monitor

Guard against **harmful self reinforcing loops** (e.g., feedback that over samples already surveilled groups) by using sampling controls, reweighting, exploration policies, and periodic human review.

Why this is a problem.

- You measure **exposure** (who gets observed) more than **ground truth** (what really happens).
- The loop **reinforces** and **magnifies** initial biases.
- Under observed groups contribute little feedback, so the model may be **less accurate** for them and miss harms they experience.

Continuous Learning and Adaptive Oversight

Because AI and quantum systems naturally evolve over time, our approach to governing them must evolve as well. Rather than relying on static rules or rigid frameworks, organizations need adaptive, iterative governance processes that can dynamically respond to new insights, changing data, and evolving system behaviors in real-time. This approach emphasizes ongoing learning, flexibility, and responsiveness, helping to ensure these powerful systems continue to serve humanity's best interests and adapt safely to changing environments (Cohen, Kolt, Bengio, Hadfield, & Russell, 2024; Floridi & Cowls, 2019).

By embedding these responsible AI strategies into our management and operational practices, organizations can effectively navigate and mitigate the complexity and unpredictability posed by the chaotic nature of advanced AI and quantum computing systems. In doing so, we not only harness the incredible potential of these technologies but also uphold ethical standards, trustworthiness, and societal wellbeing (Floridi & Cowls, 2019; Mitchell, 2019).

Systemic Risk and Feedback Loops

When we apply AI and quantum computing to high-stakes environments such as financial trading systems, healthcare diagnostics, or cybersecurity measures we need to approach these technologies thoughtfully and carefully. These systems aren't just isolated tools; they're active participants within their environment, constantly influencing and being influenced by their surroundings. This interplay can inadvertently create complex feedback loops, where the system's actions ripple outward and loop back, sometimes magnifying small mistakes into significant and unpredictable consequences (Sculley et al., 2015; Perrow, 1999).

Imagine a financial algorithm intended to make quick trading decisions. If the model makes a minor misjudgment, it could trigger an unexpected chain of reactions in the market. Other automated systems, responding to these signals, might amplify this initial misstep, potentially leading to large-scale market instability similar to the "flash crashes" we've occasionally seen in financial markets (Kirilenko et al., 2017).

In healthcare, a subtle error or bias embedded in a quantum-enabled AI diagnostic tool could lead to incorrect treatment recommendations. If healthcare providers rely heavily on these recommendations without adequate human oversight, these initial inaccuracies could rapidly amplify, resulting in systemic medical errors that endanger patient safety (Topol, 2019).

Below are plain language examples of how a small error or bias in a **quantum enabled AI diagnostic** could snowball in healthcare—plus why **false positives in cancer detection** matter so much.

Examples of error → amplification in care

Breast cancer screening (mammography).

If an AI slightly over weights benign features (e.g., calcifications in dense breasts), it can raise the callback rate. In routine screening, about **10% of mammograms lead to callbacks**, yet only a small fraction of those is cancer; **over 10 years, more than half of women screened annually will experience at least one false positive**, often requiring extra imaging or biopsy. These events create stress, costs, and most importantly can **reduce future screening participation**, which harms population health. If a hospital leans on the model's output without human review, those callbacks (and anxiety) multiply system wide.

Lung cancer screening (low dose CT):

In the National Lung Screening (NLST) trial, **~24%** of CT screens were flagged positive per round, and **~96%** of those positives were **false positives**. Most led to more imaging; a smaller share led to invasive follow up with risks (pneumothorax, bleeding). An over sensitive quantum/AI reader could push these already high false positive rates even higher, straining clinics and exposing patients to more procedures and worry.

Dermatology triage across skin tones:

If training data under represent darker skin, a skin lesion model may over or under flag lesions for some groups. Over flagging means extra referrals and biopsies (false positives); under flagging means delayed cancer detection (false negatives). Either way, bias compounds when clinician trust and workflow begin to depend on the model's triage cues.

Treatment recommendation engines:

Topol documents how an oncology decision aid trained on limited/synthetic cases issued unsafe drug suggestions; scale that error through order sets, auto populated notes, and clinician automation bias, and a local flaw becomes a systemic hazard. A quantum accelerated recommender with the same upstream bias would amplify the problem faster.

"Liquid biopsy" / multi cancer early detection (MCED):

Even with high specificity, screening a low prevalence population can yield many false positives, triggering scans, biopsies, and anxiety. Policymakers are urging caution until mortality benefit is proven at scale—an impatient rollout, especially with aggressive AI triage, risks large numbers of healthy people being labeled "possibly cancer."

Why false positives in cancer detection are so significant

- **Patient impact:** extra imaging, invasive biopsies, procedure complications, time off work, and months of uncertainty; distress can persist for years in some studies.
- **Behavioral impact:** false positives can discourage return to screening, reducing life saving early detection later.
- **System impact:** scarce diagnostic capacity gets consumed by follow ups for people without cancer, delaying care for those who do.
- **Math of low prevalence (illustrative):** suppose we screen 100,000 people where true cancer prevalence is 0.5% (500 cases). If sensitivity is 90% and specificity 99% (1% false positive rate):

→ True positives: 0.90 × 500 = 450

→ False positives: 0.01 × 99,500 = 995

→ Share of positives that are false: 995 / (450 + 995) ≈ 69%

Most "positive" results are false, yet each can set off a costly and stressful cascade. (This is why thresholds, confirmatory tests, and careful deployment matter.)

Where "quantum enabled" changes the risk profile

Quantum models can be stochastic and noise sensitive (decoherence, readout errors). If not carefully calibrated and monitored, small hardware or data shifts can mis-calibrate risk scores nudging a borderline "watch and wait" case into "biopsy now" across thousands of patients. Preskill's Noisy Intermediate-Scale Quantum or NISQ assessment underscores that noise limit's reliability without strong error mitigation, which is critical before embedding quantum components in clinical pathways.

Practical guardrails (keep humans in the loop)

- Double read + adjudication: require a human second reader (and, for positives, consensus) before invasive steps.
- Calibrate and monitor: track PPV/NPV (Positive Predictive Value/Negative Predictive Value), callback rates, and biopsy yield by site, device, and demographic; alert on drift.
- Confirm before treatment: mandate orthogonal confirmation (e.g., pathology) before initiating therapy.
- Bias checks: evaluate performance across subgroups; rebalance training data; add exploration sampling to avoid over monitoring the same populations.
- Accountability: log model version, inputs, and rationale; enable rapid rollback; audit recommendations regularly.

Bottom line: False positives are not benign "false alarms." They carry psychological, clinical, and system level costs. Any quantum enabled AI that touches diagnosis needs calibrated thresholds, confirmatory testing, continuous bias/stability monitoring, and explicit human sign off—so small errors don't cascade into avoidable harm.

Similarly, in cybersecurity, small misalignments or overlooked vulnerabilities within quantum-based encryption or AI-driven threat detection systems could lead to catastrophic security breaches. The consequences might cascade, potentially compromising sensitive information and critical infrastructure, thereby posing severe risks on a global scale (Brundage et al., 2018).

Here are concrete, real world cases that illustrate how small misalignments or overlooked vulnerabilities in quantum era cryptography and AI driven threat detection can cascade into serious risk and how similar slips have already produced system wide consequences.

Quantum and "quantum safe" cryptography

Tricking quantum key hardware (Quantum Key Distribution or QKD).

"Some commercial quantum key systems were fooled by shining bright light at their detectors, letting attackers steal the secret key without setting off alarms. The science wasn't broken; the hardware design was".

Lesson: "Quantum based" ≠ "unbreakable." You still must secure the devices and their side channels (indirect clues like light or timing that can leak secrets).

A "quantum safe" algorithm that wasn't (SIKE, 2022).

Supersingular Isogeny Key Encapsulation or SIKE was proposed to resist future quantum attacks, but researchers showed a regular (non quantum) method could recover the keys. Anyone who deployed it early would have lost their "quantum safe" protection overnight.

Lesson: A candidate in testing is not the same as production ready security.

Tiny timing leaks in a standard (KyberSlash, 2023–2024).

Kyber (standardized as ML KEM) had implementations where small differences in response time could reveal secret keys in certain patterns of use. Libraries were patched quickly.

Lesson: Even strong math can be undone by small coding details; write constant time code (runs in the same time no matter what the secret) and test for leaks.

AI driven threat detection

Padding malware to look harmless (2019).

Attackers showed that adding chunks of "good" content to malware could trick a popular AI based antivirus into calling it safe. The vendor patched, but it proved a point.

Lesson: AI detectors can be gamed if features aren't chosen and tested carefully; small model blind spots can enable large scale evasion until systems are retrained.

How small slips can snowball (recent, non quantum examples)

Colonial Pipeline (2021): one password → fuel disruptions.

A single compromised VPN account helped ransomware spread, leading to a major pipeline shutdown and regional fuel shortages.

Lesson: Minor access gaps can cause major real world consequences when systems are tightly connected.

SolarWinds (2020): trusted updates → thousands exposed.

The Solar Winds breach revealed how trusted software updates can themselves become attack vectors, a parallel to governance blind spots when project assurances are accepted at face value without layered verification.

Lesson: "Trusted" channels can become blind spots without layered checks.

Ukraine power grid (2015): cyber operations → power outages.

Coordinated attacks cut electricity to about 225,000 customers.

Lesson: Digital intrusions can directly impact critical infrastructure and public safety.

Why this matters for "quantum + AI" security

Quantum based encryption can fail quietly due to implementation mistakes (hardware quirks, timing leaks) even when the underlying math is sound. Some post quantum algorithms may be retired quickly if new attacks are found.

AI based detectors can be poisoned or bypassed if they aren't stress tested against clever tricks and changing data.

In critical infrastructure, these small cracks can cascade into outages, data exposure, or strategic access for adversaries.

Practical guardrails (in plain language)

Build and test crypto code to be constant time; review for side channels (timing, power, light).

For quantum gear, do hardware security reviews—don't assume physics will save you.

For AI detectors, run adversarial tests and regularly retrain on fresh, representative data.

Use layered defenses: code signing with transparency logs, independent telemetry, and kill switches.

Keep continuous red teaming and have fast patch/rollback processes so small issues don't become big incidents.

From technical chaos to organizational practice.

These examples show that AI and quantum systems can behave like chaotic processes in complexity science: small missteps don't fade, they can snowball into large scale disruption. That's why governance must go beyond box ticking. Effective oversight means continuous monitoring, real time risk sensing, human checkpoints at decision points, clear transparency about model limits, and periodic ethical audits so teams can spot and correct misalignments before they spiral (Floridi & Cowls, 2019; Cohen et al., 2024).

The same pattern holds in project management.

Complex projects are tightly coupled systems. A tiny estimation error, a late design change, or a supplier delay can cascade into cost blowouts and schedule slippage if feedback is slow or siloed. To keep small issues small:

Risk (keep signals live): Maintain a risk register with triggers (early warning indicators such as RFI aging, submittal cycle time, change order backlog). Run pre-mortems and scenario drills; track a risk burndown so exposure falls over time, not just on paper.

Price escalation (stabilize inputs): Use index linked contracts and escalation clauses, place long lead orders early, diversify vendors, and set aside contingency tied to commodity indices. Review budgets monthly against market movements and hedge critical items where appropriate.

Scheduling (see drift early): Monitor critical path drift, float consumption, and earned schedule trends; use rolling wave look aheads and Monte Carlo schedule risk analysis to quantify slippage risk. Gate high impact decisions through an Integrated Change Control board to curb scope creep.

Closed loop governance (catch → fix → verify): When thresholds are breached, escalate quickly to a named risk owner, apply the remedy (data or design correction, resequencing, contract adjustment), and verify the fix before resuming normal operations.

Bottom line

Whether you're tuning a model or delivering a hospital, small deviations can compound. Build closed feedback loops, keep metrics visible, and empower people to pause, question, and correct. That is how organizations translate complex system insight into everyday safety and reliability (Floridi & Cowls, 2019; Cohen et al., 2024).

Managing these powerful but inherently unpredictable technologies responsibly requires a dynamic, proactive, and human-centered approach, carefully balancing innovation with vigilance and accountability.

Governance and Adaptive Regulation

Considering the rapid pace and unpredictable nature of AI and quantum computing technologies, traditional regulatory approaches and those fixed rules designed for predictable scenarios often fall short. Much like trying to steer a boat through constantly changing currents, effectively managing these dynamic and complex technologies demands a governance approach that's flexible, responsive, and adaptive to real-time developments (Floridi & Cowls, 2019; Wallach & Marchant, 2018).

Modern AI and quantum computing systems evolve continuously, adapting to new data inputs, environmental interactions, and unforeseen feedback loops. Because of this fluid and sometimes chaotic environment, a static, rigid framework quickly becomes outdated, losing relevance and effectiveness almost as soon as it's implemented (Cohen et al., 2024). Instead, regulatory frameworks need to resemble living systems themselves capable of learning, adjusting, and evolving as circumstances change.

This type of adaptive governance emphasizes continuous monitoring, feedback-driven improvements, and iterative policy adjustments. It proactively incorporates the latest scientific insights, ethical considerations, and societal values into decision-making processes, allowing regulatory bodies and organizations to stay ahead of risks and challenges as they arise (Floridi & Cowls, 2019; Mitchell, 2019).

Adaptive governance frameworks also involve active collaboration between policymakers, technologists, ethicists, and the broader community. Engaging diverse stakeholders ensures that governance remains inclusive, responsive, and better aligned with society's evolving expectations and needs (Stilgoe, Owen, & Macnaghten, 2013).

From a practical standpoint, build closed loop governance rather than one off checks. Start with regulatory sandboxes, safe testbeds with clear entry/exit criteria, so high risk features can be trialed under guardrails. Pair this with dynamic risk assessments and real time oversight dashboards that track drift, bias, and performance; define thresholds that auto escalate to a named risk owner, require a two person rule for high impact actions, and enable pause/rollback when results look unsafe. Make the loop explicit by the following process:

measure → compare → intervene → verify → document and support it with plain language transparency (model cards, decision rationales) and audit logs. Keep policies agile, updating controls as evidence accumulates and contexts change (Wallach & Marchant, 2018; Armstrong et al., 2019).

The same pattern applies in project management: use early warning risk triggers, manage price escalation with index linked controls and contingencies, and watch critical path drift through integrated change control so small issues are caught, corrected, and confirmed before they compound. Embracing adaptive governance frameworks not only enhances the safety and reliability of AI and quantum technologies but also fosters greater trust and public confidence, ensuring these powerful innovations remain ethically responsible, human-centered, and aligned with broader societal interests.

Applying Chaos Theory to AI and Quantum Computing Governance

Managing sophisticated computational systems, particularly AI and quantum technologies operating within chaotic and unpredictable environments requires a thoughtful and nuanced approach. Rather than striving for complete control, which is often impossible due to their inherent complexity, we should instead embrace strategies that enhance our ability to respond and adapt effectively as situations evolve.

To achieve this, several key practical principles emerge as especially valuable:

Emphasize Resilience

In unpredictable settings, our best defense is to create systems designed for resilience systems capable of absorbing shocks, adapting to surprises, and recovering quickly from unexpected behaviors or errors (Taleb, 2012; Hollnagel, Woods, & Leveson, 2007). Resilient design prioritizes flexibility and adaptability, recognizing that some level of uncertainty and chaos is inevitable. Instead of rigidly controlling every aspect, resilient systems can adjust dynamically, thereby effectively managing unforeseen scenarios and ensuring long-term stability and effectiveness.

Here's what that idea looks like in practice—not as theory, but as day to day habits, roles, and tools that make a system bend without breaking.

The shape of a resilient system

Anticipate (before things go wrong).

- Run pre-mortems ("It's six months later and we failed—why?").
- Do scenario drills for rare but plausible shocks (data drift, supplier failure, sudden demand spikes).
- Keep a living risk register with clear owners and early warning indicators (triggers).

Monitor (see trouble early).

- Real time dashboards for health (latency, error rates), drift (data, model calibration), and capacity (buffers, inventory, qubits available).
- Alert thresholds that escalate to a named human (and backup) when crossed.
- For quantum/AI: watch fidelity, FS - Fubini-Study – Distance/metric or distance/cosine similarity, and false positive/negative trends, not just accuracy.

Respond (graceful under stress).

- Fail safely: circuit breakers, rate limits, and timeouts to stop cascading failure.
- Fallback modes: if the fancy path falters, drop to a simpler, proven one (e.g., hybrid quantum classical, older model version, manual review).
- Feature flags and canary releases so risky changes affect 1% before 100%.
- Kill switch/rollback that a human can trigger in seconds, not hours.

Learn (get better because of stress).

- Blameless post incident reviews within 72 hours: what happened, why defenses didn't catch it, what we'll change.
- Track near misses (not only outages) and update playbooks.
- Retire brittle practices; standardize what worked under pressure.

These four abilities, anticipation, monitor, respond, learn, are the backbone of resilience (Hollnagel, Woods & Leveson). Taleb's insight adds a stretch goal: when possible, design elements that improve under variability (e.g., regular chaos drills, diverse model ensembles).

What you would see in the organization

Dashboards that show operational health and ethical risk side by side (performance, bias, drift, data quality).

Runbooks & playbooks that on call teams actually use (who does what at minute 5, 15, 60).

Redundancy and diversity by design: multiple data sources, vendor options, and "champion–challenger" models.

Buffers: slack in schedules, inventory for long lead items, and error budgets for services.

Clear roles: a designated risk owner for each major hazard and a two person rule for high impact actions.

Transparent logs: versioned models/configs, decision rationales, and audit trails for later review.

Concrete mini scenarios

AI clinical triage: When the model's confidence drops or data distribution shifts, the system auto routes those cases to a human reviewer, slows throughput (notifies clinics), and rolls back to a previous model if thresholds are exceeded while logging everything for a next day review.

Quantum workload: If qubit fidelity degrades, jobs defer to classical/hybrid solvers, and the platform spins up a quarantine sandbox to test fixes without risking production; a single button pauses new quantum runs until metrics recover.

Project management: A commodity price spike hits steel. Early warning triggers fire, the team switches to index linked pricing in pending change orders, re-sequences tasks to protect the critical path, and draws from a dedicated escalation contingency avoiding a schedule domino effect.

Quick checklist (use this to audit a design)

- [ ] Early-warning indicators with named owners
- [ ] Canary/feature-flag deployment path (A **canary** is a small, low-risk trial of a change in production)
- [ ] Fallback/"safe mode" and manual override

- Circuit breakers, timeouts, backoff, and bulkheads (isolation between components)
- Real-time drift, fidelity, and calibration monitoring
- Human-in-the-loop for high-impact decisions
- Blameless post-incident reviews and near-miss tracking
- Versioned configs, data lineage, and audit logs
- Buffers: schedule, capacity, inventory, and error budgets
- Regular chaos/gameday exercises

Bottom line: A resilient system doesn't promise perfection; it expects surprises and is built to absorb them, adjust quickly, and come back stronger—protecting people, operations, and trust over the long run.

Enhance Interpretability

Understanding why or how AI or quantum systems behave the way they do, particularly in chaotic contexts, is crucial. Enhancing interpretability involves using tools and methods that help humans grasp how these systems arrive at their decisions. Techniques such as adversarial testing (systematically probing for vulnerabilities), quantum state analysis (careful evaluation of quantum behaviors), and sensitivity analysis (exploring how small changes affect outcomes) provide critical insights into complex behaviors (Lundberg & Lee, 2017; Ribeiro, Singh, & Guestrin, 2016; Nielsen & Chuang, 2010). By illuminating the inner workings of these intricate technologies, we can better anticipate, prevent, or mitigate unpredictable responses.

Promote Model Diversity

Another effective way to manage complexity is through diversity, relying on multiple different types of models rather than a single, potentially brittle solution. For instance, using ensemble modeling, which combines multiple models, can significantly reduce the likelihood that one model's errors or chaotic behaviors propagate unchecked (Dietterich, 2000). Similarly, blending classical and quantum computing methods into hybrid architectures can balance the stability of classical computing with the power of quantum approaches, smoothing out unpredictability and providing more stable and reliable outcomes (McClean et al., 2016; Preskill, 2018).

Implement Iterative Oversight

Finally, as these computational systems continually evolve, governance and oversight practices must keep pace. Rather than relying on fixed rules or static oversight mechanisms, iterative oversight frameworks allow ethical standards and risk management processes to evolve continuously, guided by real-world experiences and changing data (Floridi & Cowls, 2019; Cohen et al., 2024). Such dynamic, ethics-driven oversight ensures responsible adaptation as technologies change, proactively addressing emerging risks, societal concerns, and ethical dilemmas before they escalate.

By integrating these principles, resilience, interpretability, diversity, and iterative oversight, organizations can better navigate the inherent unpredictability and complexity of modern computational systems. This approach not only mitigates risks but also fosters greater confidence, trust, and accountability in deploying cutting-edge AI and quantum technologies in real-world contexts.

Conclusion

More than a century ago, Henri Poincaré laid down profound insights that forever changed our understanding of complexity through his groundbreaking work in chaos theory. Although he couldn't have imagined today's advanced computational systems, his ideas continue to resonate deeply, offering us valuable lessons for managing the complex and often unpredictable behaviors of contemporary AI and quantum technologies (Poincaré, 1890; Gleick, 1987).

Poincaré emphasized that even systems governed by clear, deterministic rules could behave in ways that were unpredictable and sensitive to the smallest initial differences, a concept famously referred to as the "butterfly effect" (Lorenz, 1963; Gleick, 1987). Today, this insight is extraordinarily relevant when working with modern computational tools, such as deep learning models, generative AI, machine learning frameworks, and quantum computing platforms, all of which exhibit behaviors that reflect these chaotic characteristics.

Understanding and embracing chaos theory equips us to build more resilient computational systems. Rather than trying to eliminate all uncertainty, an impossible task, we focus instead on designing flexible systems that can gracefully handle unexpected outcomes and swiftly adapt to new circumstances (Hollnagel et al., 2007; Taleb, 2012). Such resilience helps ensure that these technologies remain dependable even amidst uncertainty.

Chaos theory also underscores the critical importance of interpretability. Since slight variations can significantly alter outcomes, it's essential to understand precisely how and why computational systems make decisions. By adopting interpretability techniques such as SHAP, LIME, and sensitivity analysis, we gain clarity about the decision-making processes within complex AI models, allowing us to spot emerging risks or unintended biases before they escalate into larger problems (Lundberg & Lee, 2017; Ribeiro, Singh, & Guestrin, 2016).

To put those techniques to work, day to day, build a live interpretability dashboard that turns SHAP, LIME, and sensitivity analysis into continuous signals people can act on. The dashboard should surface top shifting features (SHAP) by cohort and over time, show variance bands around attributions, and embed case level LIME spot checks for any flagged decisions alongside sensitivity sliders that let users nudge inputs and watch prediction deltas in real time. Include calibration curves, PPV/NPV and fairness slices by subgroup, plus data drift indicators that warn when the model is operating outside its training envelope. Every tile should have thresholds and alerts that route to a named risk owner with options to pause, canary, or roll back and to trigger targeted retraining; explanations and actions are logged for audit. Offer layered views: plain language drivers and recourse for frontline staff, distribution plots and confidence intervals for engineers, and trend summaries with exception counts for leaders. In short, the dashboard closes the loop making chaos aware analysis visible, explainable, and interruptible before small variations snowball into harm (Lundberg & Lee, 2017; Ribeiro, Singh, & Guestrin, 2016).

Moreover, governance of AI and quantum technologies greatly benefits from applying chaos-informed principles. Acknowledging that these systems operate in inherently uncertain and dynamic contexts highlights the importance of adaptive oversight. Instead of static policies, dynamic governance frameworks that evolve iteratively and flexibly in response to real-time feedback enable effective regulation of emerging complexities (Floridi & Cowls, 2019; Cohen et al., 2024).

As AI and quantum technologies continue to rapidly advance, applying these insights from chaos theory is not just valuable, it is increasingly essential. By thoughtfully integrating lessons from pioneers like Poincaré, we position ourselves better to harness the extraordinary potential of these powerful technologies while responsibly navigating their inherent unpredictability and complexity (Preskill, 2018; Mitchell, 2019).

In short, by appreciating the wisdom embedded in chaos theory, we equip ourselves to build more robust, transparent, and ethically sound technologies that serve human interests, rather than being overwhelmed by uncertainty and complexity.

Chapter 2: From Planck to Lorenz – Quantum Foundations and Chaotic Complexity

Abstract

Edward N. Lorenz fundamentally transformed the way we understand complexity, shifting the scientific community's perspective away from predictability and toward a deeper appreciation of uncertainty and the surprising ways nature behaves. In the early 1960s, Lorenz uncovered a profound phenomenon now famously known as the "butterfly effect," illustrating that even tiny, seemingly insignificant changes at the outset of a system can lead to dramatically different and unforeseen outcomes over time (Lorenz, 1963; Gleick, 1987). This concept shattered the long-held classical deterministic belief that systems governed by precise laws would behave predictably, opening our eyes to the inherent unpredictability embedded within complex systems.

Lorenz's groundbreaking work vividly illustrates that deterministic rules that are clear, fixed, and seemingly straightforward could nonetheless produce behaviors rich in complexity, unpredictability, and subtle patterns of chaos. This discovery challenged and enriched earlier probabilistic frameworks established by quantum mechanics pioneers like Max Planck, who described a universe characterized fundamentally by uncertainty and probability at microscopic scales (Prigogine & Stengers, 1984). Lorenz's findings demonstrated that such unpredictability could also emerge in everyday phenomena and larger-scale natural processes, revealing that the delicate balance between order and chaos is pervasive, extending far beyond quantum realms into classical, macroscopic contexts.

By emphasizing sensitive dependence on initial conditions, Lorenz's insights provided an essential conceptual bridge connecting classical chaos theory and modern computational paradigms such as quantum computing. Just as quantum computing harnesses principles of uncertainty, superposition, and entanglement, Lorenz's chaos theory illuminates how sensitive systems require careful handling of initial conditions and minor disturbances, which can drastically alter the system's behavior (Nielsen & Chuang, 2010; Preskill, 2018).

Today, Lorenz's legacy resonates strongly within contemporary computational intelligence, particularly in advanced artificial intelligence and machine learning fields. Neural networks, generative AI models, and quantum algorithms frequently exhibit behaviors reminiscent of Lorenz's chaotic systems displaying sensitivity to initial conditions, unpredictability in their outcomes, and emergent complexity that defies simple interpretation (Goodfellow, Bengio, & Courville, 2016; Mitchell, 2019). Lorenz's contributions have not only expanded our understanding of the natural world but also equipped us with valuable insights for navigating, harnessing, and responsibly managing the complexities and uncertainties inherent in modern computational technologies.

In essence, Edward Lorenz's revolutionary insights have enduringly shaped complexity theory, providing us with a richer, more nuanced appreciation of nature's inherent unpredictability. By embracing his ideas, contemporary researchers and practitioners continue to uncover innovative approaches to computational intelligence, weaving Lorenz's pioneering legacy into the fabric of modern technological advancement.

Lorenz and the Butterfly Effect

Edward Lorenz is most famously remembered for introducing the captivating concept known as the "butterfly effect," a vivid metaphor illustrating the remarkable sensitivity of complex systems to tiny differences in their initial conditions. This powerful idea emerged from Lorenz's pioneering attempts to mathematically model atmospheric convection. The movement of air masses and the intricate patterns they create using simplified but profound nonlinear differential equations. Lorenz demonstrated that even microscopic changes at the very start of these systems, such as rounding off a decimal point or slightly altering initial data, could dramatically alter long-term outcomes, giving rise to entirely different weather patterns (Lorenz, 1963; Gleick, 1987).

To humanize this idea, Lorenz poetically suggested that something as seemingly insignificant as the flap of a butterfly's wings in Brazil could eventually trigger a tornado thousands of miles away, weeks later, in Texas. Though metaphorical, this image beautifully captures how sensitive, interconnected, and unpredictable complex systems can be, highlighting the dramatic and unforeseen ways that tiny influences propagate through interconnected networks (Lorenz, 1963; Gleick, 1987).

To visualize this intriguing phenomenon, Lorenz introduced what is now known as the "Lorenz attractor," a striking graphical representation of these chaotic dynamics. The attractor reveals trajectories in an abstract mathematical space called "state space," where, despite being governed by deterministic equations, the paths never precisely repeat and appear unpredictably random. Nevertheless, these trajectories exhibit stunningly intricate and aesthetically fascinating fractal patterns, symbolizing the hidden order within apparent chaos, a cornerstone of complexity theory (Frahm, 2025).

The following figure illustrates phase-space trajectories, contrasting predictable periodic trajectories with chaotic trajectories sensitive to initial conditions.

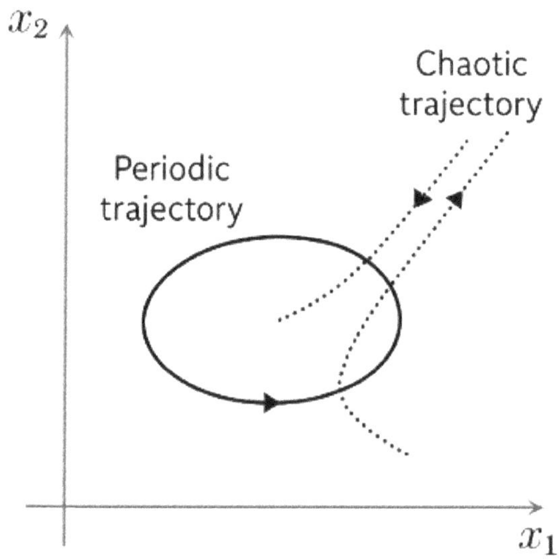

Figure 2.1. *Phase-space trajectories in chaos theory. Author's illustration (2025).*

Note. This figure presents a phase-space diagram contrasting predictable periodic trajectories with chaotic trajectories sensitive to initial conditions. Inspired by Poincaré's and Lorenz's foundational work, it visualizes how even small differences in starting conditions can lead to dramatically divergent outcomes. This representation provides an intuitive visual anchor for chaos theory's application in AI and quantum simulations.

Lorenz's groundbreaking insights extend far beyond meteorology, echoing powerfully across a multitude of disciplines, including ecology, economics, sociology, and even psychology and organizational behavior. In ecology, for example, his principles help clarify how slight changes in initial conditions can radically shift population dynamics or ecosystem stability. In economics, Lorenz's ideas have provided a framework for understanding unpredictable market fluctuations and systemic financial risks. Even within human behavior studies, his concepts illuminate how minor initial differences in decision-making or perception can lead to profoundly divergent social outcomes (Gleick, 1987; Kauffman, 1993).

This widespread applicability highlights a universal truth revealed by Lorenz—that complexity and spontaneous order can naturally emerge without direct instruction, centralized control, or deliberate intention. It underscores the profound interconnectedness within our world, reinforcing the importance of embracing uncertainty and complexity rather than seeking to eliminate it entirely (Prigogine & Stengers, 1984; Mitchell, 2009).

Lorenz's visionary work continues to enrich our understanding of complexity, inspiring contemporary approaches in machine learning, artificial intelligence, and quantum computing. His elegant yet profound concepts challenge us to appreciate how small beginnings can lead to extraordinary consequences, guiding us toward more insightful and adaptive ways of understanding and interacting with the intricate systems around us.

Figure 2.1 below presents the Lorenz attractor, a fascinating and visually compelling representation of chaotic dynamics. At first glance, the pathways traced in this three-dimensional state space seem unpredictable, weaving intricate loops and spirals without ever repeating the same path twice. Yet, upon closer inspection, a striking fractal pattern emerges—an elegant, repeating structure hidden within apparent randomness (Lorenz, 1963; Gleick, 1987).

This visual metaphor vividly captures key ideas in chaos theory and complexity science, beautifully illustrating Michael Frahm's insights into how simple deterministic equations can yield unexpectedly intricate behaviors (Frahm, 2025). Frahm emphasizes the subtle interplay between predictability and surprise, plus order and chaos showing how deep, structured complexity can spontaneously emerge from straightforward yet highly sensitive starting conditions. The Lorenz attractor thus serves as a powerful example of Frahm's broader narrative about complexity, making clear how even systems guided by precise mathematical rules can produce rich, beautifully complex outcomes that defy simple prediction (Frahm, 2025).

The following figure illustrates the Lorenz attractor, a fractal structure in state space, which demonstrates how trajectories that appear random can reveal distinct and repeating patterns, a hallmark of complexity science.

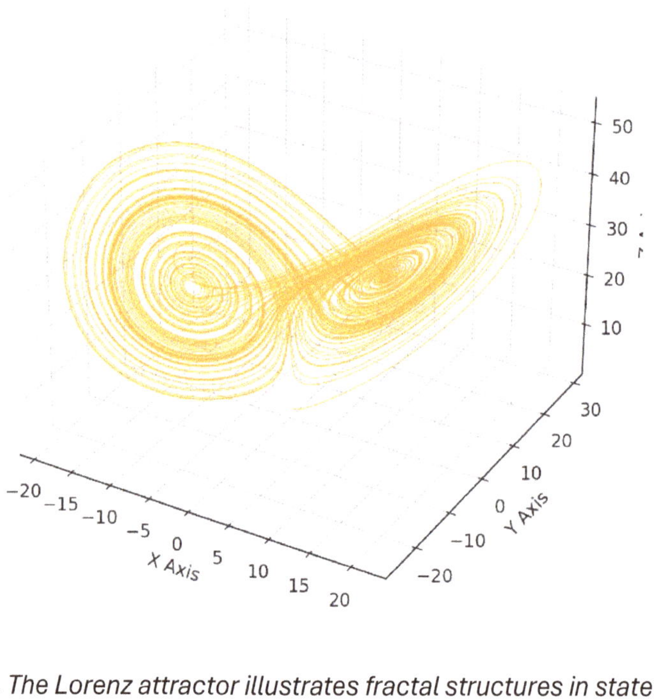

Figure 2.2. *The Lorenz attractor illustrates fractal structures in state space, where self-similar patterns emerge at multiple scales. These repeating dynamics can be seen in coastlines and neural networks, where oversight challenges recur both locally and system-wide, a defining feature of complexity science. Author's illustration (Frahm, 2025).*

Note. This visualization of the Lorenz attractor highlights the interplay between apparent randomness and underlying order in chaotic systems. The fractal structure serves as a visual anchor for understanding how complexity science bridges chaos theory with modern applications in AI and quantum simulations.

Chaos, Entropy, and Complexity

Edward Lorenz's profound insights into chaos theory offer a remarkable complement to the foundational thermodynamic concepts first introduced by Max Planck. In the early 20th century, Planck revolutionized our understanding of physics by introducing ideas of entropy and quantization, paving the way toward a probabilistic view of the universe, especially at the microscopic level. Planck's insights revealed a universe inherently uncertain, characterized by probabilities rather than precise certainties, a stark departure from classical determinism (Prigogine & Stengers, 1984; Nielsen & Chuang, 2010).

Entropy is nature's way of tracking disorder or randomness within a system; an idea rooted in thermodynamics. Think of it like your desk: even if you tidy it up perfectly, over time, papers, books, and notes naturally scatter again, making it messy. Similarly, entropy measures how energy naturally spreads out and becomes less organized. In isolated systems, entropy tends to increase, meaning things naturally drift toward greater chaos or disorder over time, unless energy is actively used to maintain order (Prigogine & Stengers, 1984).

Quantization, an idea first introduced by physicist Max Planck, suggests that energy doesn't flow smoothly or continuously, like water from a faucet, but instead moves in small, distinct, indivisible "packets," known as quanta. Imagine climbing stairs rather than walking up a smooth ramp; each step represents a specific amount of energy, and you can't stop halfway between steps. This simple yet profound insight became a cornerstone of quantum mechanics, changing our understanding of the microscopic world by revealing how atoms and particles exchange energy in precise, fixed amounts rather than in a smooth, continuous manner (Nielsen & Chuang, 2010).

Lorenz extended these groundbreaking ideas into new domains by demonstrating that unpredictability isn't confined solely to microscopic scales but permeates even seemingly predictable, deterministic systems at macroscopic levels, such as weather patterns and atmospheric conditions. Lorenz showed that even models built on fixed rules could spiral into unpredictability. This insight—often captured in the 'butterfly effect'—mirrors governance systems where minor oversights or delays cascade into disruptive project outcomes (Lorenz, 1963; Gleick, 1987).

What makes Lorenz's insights particularly fascinating is the way they expand our understanding of entropy, which is the measure of disorder in a system. While Planck highlighted entropy's universal tendency to increase within isolated systems, Lorenz introduced a nuanced perspective, revealing how localized pockets of order and complexity could spontaneously form amidst broader contexts of rising entropy. He showed how complexity and structure naturally emerge from the interplay between order and chaos, a dynamic equilibrium where localized decreases in entropy also known as negentropy, can occur by exporting disorder into surrounding environments (Prigogine & Stengers, 1984; Frahm, 2025).

This delicate dance between order and chaos, between entropy and negentropy, finds echoes throughout the natural world. It is vividly illustrated in ecosystems, where life flourishes and complexity emerge by continuously exchanging energy and matter with the environment, effectively "exporting" entropy. Biological evolution similarly reflects these principles, continually crafting intricate structures and increasingly complex life forms out of simpler components. Even economic and social systems exhibit this phenomenon, organizing themselves into structured patterns and institutions amidst broader societal fluctuations and uncertainties (Kauffman, 1993; Mitchell, 2009).

"Entropy" means messiness or disorder. In the real world, small areas of order can appear and grow, but only by using energy and pushing mess/heat somewhere else. That local order is sometimes called negentropy.

Basic examples

- **Refrigerator:**

Order here: Inside gets cold and tidy.

Mess moved out: The coils on the back heat your kitchen.

- **Snowflake forming:**

Order here: Water vapor arranges into a beautiful crystal.

Mess moved out: Heat is released into the surrounding air.

- **Soup on the stove:**

Order here: Rolling patterns appear as the soup circulates.

Mess moved out: The stove dumps heat into the room.

- **Hurricane:**

Order here: A well organized spinning storm.

Mess moved out: It burns through warm ocean energy and spreads heat and moisture into the atmosphere.

- **Your body:**

Order here: Cells stay organized and working.

Mess moved out: You give off heat and waste (CO_2, etc.) from the food you eat.

- **Forest or coral reef:**

Order here: Many species fit together in a complex, stable web.

Mess moved out: Sunlight is used up and turned into heat and waste products that leave the system.

- **City:**

Order here: Roads, buildings, schedules, and services line up into a working pattern.

Mess moved out: High energy use, heat, trash, and emissions flow to the wider environment.

Takeaway

Local order doesn't break the rules of entropy; it works with them: you get pockets of structure by spending energy and exporting disorder. When the energy flow stops, the order fades.

Lorenz's and Planck's complementary insights thus present a unified, coherent framework for understanding complexity in both microscopic and macroscopic realms. Their combined legacy has profoundly influenced complexity theory, quantum computing, artificial intelligence, and machine learning, fields where uncertainty, sensitivity to initial conditions, and emergent complexity play critical roles (Nielsen & Chuang, 2010; Preskill, 2018).

The interplay between Lorenz's chaos theory and Planck's thermodynamics provides a deeply humanized, integrated narrative about how our universe operates. Embracing their wisdom enables us to better navigate, harness, and responsibly manage the profound complexity and uncertainty that characterize modern computational technologies.

Bridging Chaos Theory and Quantum Computing

The connection between Edward Lorenz's chaos theory and the modern field of quantum computing offers a uniquely insightful perspective into the complexity and unpredictability at the core of nature. Quantum computing, a groundbreaking approach to computation, leverages the inherently probabilistic and uncertain nature of quantum mechanics, concepts initially introduced by pioneering physicists like Max Planck, Werner Heisenberg, and Erwin Schrödinger. In principle, quantum computations operate at the microscopic level, where processes are ideally reversible and generate minimal entropy or disorder. Ideally, quantum systems can evolve both forward and backward without information loss, yielding extraordinary computational efficiency (Nielsen & Chuang, 2010).

The following figure illustrates how chaos theory and quantum computing can be bridged through shared principles, highlighting their conceptual alignment.

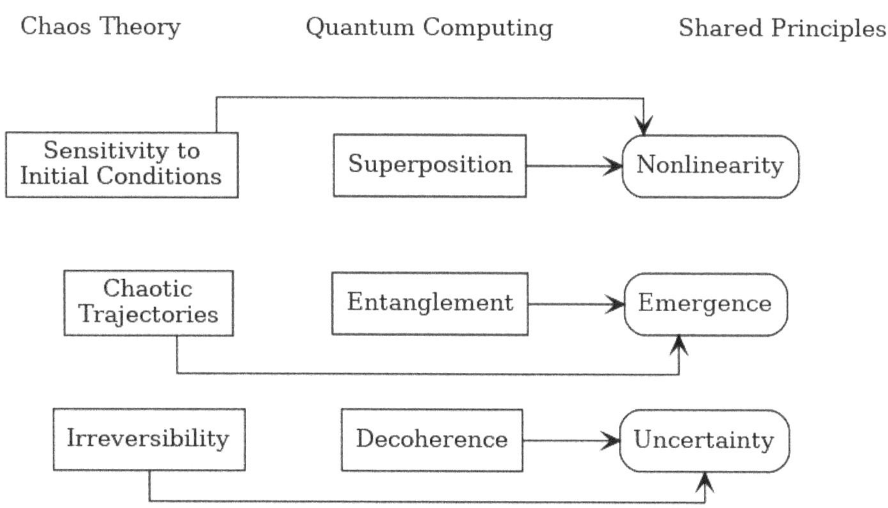

Figure 2.3. *Bridging chaos theory and quantum computing through shared principles. Author's illustration (2025).*

Note. The parallel layout aligns each concept row:

Chaos Theory (left): Sensitivity to initial conditions → Chaotic trajectories → Irreversibility

Quantum Computing (center): Superposition → Entanglement → Decoherence

Arrows from both sides into the center emphasize how these domains meet at shared principles that explain complex, unpredictable behavior across scales.

Shared Principles (right): Nonlinearity • Emergence • Uncertainty

Yet, when these systems are translated from theory into practice, a far more nuanced picture emerges. Real-world quantum computing faces significant hurdles due to quantum measurement, decoherence, and the complex requirements of error correction (Preskill, 2018). These challenges introduce considerable complexity and uncertainty, much like the chaotic behaviors famously described by Lorenz. Quantum measurement alone can disrupt the delicate quantum states, causing uncertainty and unpredictability. Decoherence, the loss of quantum coherence as quantum states interact uncontrollably with their surroundings, echoes Lorenz's insight into how small disturbances can dramatically alter the outcome of seemingly deterministic systems.

In this way, quantum computing sits at the fascinating crossroads between the microscopic realm of ideal quantum mechanics, characterized by reversibility and minimal entropy, and the macroscopic reality where irreversibility, unpredictability, and complexity dominate. Just as Lorenz illustrated how deterministic systems (such as weather patterns) could become unpredictably chaotic due to sensitivity to initial conditions, quantum computing reveals how the idealized theoretical control of quantum states is challenged by inevitable interactions with the environment, making practical quantum outcomes surprisingly difficult to predict and control (Lorenz, 1963; Gleick, 1987).

To summarize, quantum computing vividly embodies Lorenz's foundational insights, highlighting the delicate balance between microscopic order and macroscopic chaos. This interplay helps researchers appreciate the importance of robust error-correcting strategies, interpretability frameworks, and adaptive oversight mechanisms essential for reliably harnessing quantum technology's enormous potential while responsibly managing its inherent complexity and uncertainty (Preskill, 2018; Frahm, 2025).

Diagram 2.4 below depicts the following:

Blue Arrow: Microscopic Reversibility (Ideal Quantum Computing)

The blue arrow symbolizes the idealized vision of quantum computing—an elegant theoretical realm where everything operates perfectly, without interference or loss. Imagine a perfectly choreographed dance, guided smoothly and precisely by Schrödinger's equation, a fundamental rule in quantum mechanics describing how quantum states evolve over time (Nielsen & Chuang, 2010). Within this theoretical scenario, quantum processes unfold effortlessly in both forward and reverse directions, a property known as microscopic reversibility.

In such an ideal quantum world, information flows seamlessly, neither lost nor spontaneously created, maintaining a perfect balance. Entropy, the measure of disorder, remains minimal or even effectively absent, reflecting an optimal state of orderliness and coherence. This scenario represents the pinnacle of quantum computing, where quantum states are preserved in a pure and stable form, untouched by disturbances or noise, allowing precise manipulation for reliable and extraordinarily efficient computations (Preskill, 2018).

However, while this elegant vision captures the foundational principles of quantum mechanics, achieving it, in reality, is tremendously challenging. The blue arrow thus beautifully symbolizes both the promise and the aspiration of quantum computing, serving as a guiding vision for researchers striving toward harnessing quantum phenomena to revolutionize computing technology (Nielsen & Chuang, 2010; Frahm, 2025).

Red Arrow: Quantum Computing Challenges (Measurement, Decoherence, Error Correction)

The red arrow vividly represents the reality-check that quantum computing faces when moving from theoretical elegance into the messy complexities of real-world practice. While quantum mechanics promises astonishing computational potential, it is like holding a drone in a steady hover amid gusts, constant small corrections are required to avoid drift and crash (Preskill, 2018).

In actual operation, quantum systems are exceedingly fragile, continually influenced and disrupted by their surroundings. Quantum measurement is a double edged sword: it's essential to get an answer, but it collapses delicate states. It's like trying to touch a soap bubble to prove it's their contact gives you evidence, but it also pops the bubble, leaving only a definite remnant where a shimmering film once existed. The readout yields one outcome, ending the subtle superposition and introducing irreversibility and uncertainty (Nielsen & Chuang, 2010).

Another major practical hurdle is decoherence, the process by which everyday disturbances nudge a quantum system out of its finely tuned state. It's like taking a long exposure photo with slight hand shake: the clean lines blur into streaks. That blur is the loss of coherence that undermines dependable quantum computation (Zurek, 2003; Preskill, 2018).

Error correction methods, though vital for maintaining the stability and accuracy of quantum computations, add further layers of complexity. To keep quantum states robust and usable, error correction involves continuously detecting and correcting disturbances. Yet, each correction step inherently introduces additional complexity, entropy, and opportunities for new errors, resembling a constantly escalating tug-of-war between precision and disturbance (Preskill, 2018; Terhal, 2015).

Collectively, these real-world challenges significantly impact quantum computing performance, transforming elegant theoretical predictions into highly complex practical tasks. Overcoming these hurdles is critical, requiring innovative strategies, adaptive governance, and continuous improvement. Embracing this complexity is essential for realizing the true potential of quantum computing, ensuring this powerful technology develops responsibly, transparently, and sustainably (Frahm, 2025; Preskill, 2018).

Green Arrow: Macroscopic Irreversibility (Lorenz's Chaotic Systems)

The green arrow symbolizes the concept of macroscopic irreversibility capturing the essence of unpredictability that characterizes Edward Lorenz's groundbreaking contributions to chaos theory. Lorenz famously revealed how seemingly predictable and deterministic systems, like weather patterns, could behave in ways that are astonishingly complex and unpredictable due to their extreme sensitivity to tiny differences in initial conditions (Lorenz, 1963; Gleick, 1987).

To put it in perspective, consider the now-famous analogy known as the "butterfly effect": something as minor and seemingly insignificant as the flutter of a butterfly's wings could eventually set off a chain of events, causing a dramatic shift in weather patterns thousands of miles away. Lorenz's insights vividly illustrate how small variations or disturbances in a system's starting conditions can, over time, evolve unpredictably into vastly different outcomes, creating complexity and uncertainty at large scales (Lorenz, 1963; Gleick, 1987).

This macroscopic irreversibility, where actions and outcomes cannot simply be reversed or precisely controlled, mirrors the complexities encountered in quantum computing. While quantum systems, at a microscopic level, ideally permit reversibility, the practical reality at larger scales or longer times becomes fraught with unpredictability and instability. Just as tiny differences in initial conditions produce significant changes in Lorenz's chaotic systems, subtle quantum disturbances, decoherence, and interactions with the environment profoundly affect quantum computations, rendering them highly unpredictable and difficult to manage in real-world scenarios (Preskill, 2018; Nielsen & Chuang, 2010).

Thus, the green arrow beautifully encapsulates a key idea from Lorenz's chaos theory: that complexity, uncertainty, and irreversibility inevitably emerge as systems scale up and interact with their surroundings, whether in weather forecasting, ecosystems, financial markets, or quantum computing. By acknowledging and embracing this fundamental unpredictability, researchers and technologists can better design resilient systems and adaptive strategies to effectively manage complexity, rather than attempting to eliminate it entirely (Frahm, 2025; Prigogine & Stengers, 1984).

Embracing Lorenz's insight means designing for uncertainty rather than denying it. In practice, that looks like modular, loosely coupled architectures with buffers, redundancy, and reversible changes; live dashboards that watch volatility, drift, coupling, and interpretability signals with named owners and automated pause/canary/rollback actions; graceful degradation and fallback modes when stress rises; and a tight learn loop—blameless reviews and near miss tracking—to update guardrails continuously. Across weather systems, ecosystems, markets, quantum hardware, and AI, these habits keep small disturbances small, protect against irreversible moves, and let structure re form after shocks (Frahm, 2025; Prigogine & Stengers, 1984).

Purple Arrow: Entropy Increase (Overall Thermodynamic Trend)

The purple arrow symbolizes one of the most profound and universal truths in physics, the inevitable drift toward greater disorder or entropy, as articulated by the second law of thermodynamics. To humanize this concept, imagine leaving your garden untended; over time, weeds grow, flowers wilt, and structures slowly deteriorate, naturally shifting toward greater disorder. Similarly, in the world of physics, entropy describes how systems spontaneously evolve toward increasing levels of chaos and disorganization (Prigogine & Stengers, 1984; Gleick, 1987).

In quantum computing and chaotic systems alike, despite theoretical possibilities of perfect order and reversibility at microscopic scales, the realities of everyday interactions such as measurement processes, decoherence, and environmental disturbances unavoidably push systems toward higher entropy states. Measurement processes, for instance, disrupt quantum states, introducing irreversibility. Decoherence, where quantum systems lose their coherence by interacting uncontrollably with their environment, further accelerates the transition toward disorder. This continual interaction with the environment ensures that perfect isolation and control remain elusive, increasing entropy over time (Nielsen & Chuang, 2010; Zurek, 2003).

The purple arrow thus serves as a powerful reminder of the practical challenges facing quantum and complex systems. It underscores the idea that no real-world system, whether it's an advanced quantum computer, an ecological system, or a weather pattern can fully escape entropy’s persistent increase. Recognizing this unavoidable reality, scientists and technologists are compelled to design resilient systems and strategies that manage complexity, mitigate entropy generation, and gracefully navigate the natural drift toward disorder (Preskill, 2018; Frahm, 2025).

By highlighting this fundamental principle, the purple arrow connects theoretical physics to practical experiences, offering a deeply human and intuitive way to grasp the universal inevitability of increasing entropy. It encourages researchers and practitioners alike to embrace uncertainty, complexity, and the continuous challenge of sustaining order amidst the ever-present pull toward disorder and chaos (Prigogine & Stengers, 1984; Gleick, 1987).

The following figure provides a revised visualization of the relationship between quantum systems, chaotic macroscopic behavior, and local order in open systems. It clarifies how reversibility, irreversibility, and entropy interact across scales.

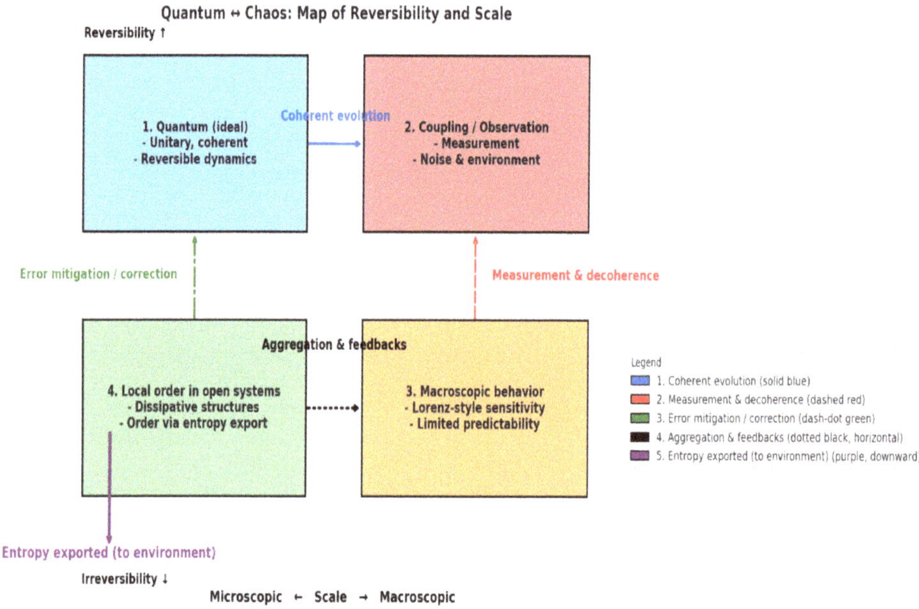

Figure 2.4. *Quantum ↔ Chaos: Map of reversibility and scale. Author's illustration (2025).*

Note. This diagram links ideal quantum evolution (unitary, reversible) to macroscopic irreversibility through measurement and environmental coupling (decoherence). It also shows how local order in open systems can persist by exporting entropy. Arrows indicate key processes: coherent evolution (blue), measurement and decoherence (red), error mitigation and correction (green), aggregation and feedback (orange), and entropy export (purple). Concepts draw on Nielsen & Chuang (2010), Lorenz (1963), Prigogine & Stengers (1984), and Preskill (2018).

Conceptual Synergy and Relevance to Complexity

Edward Lorenz's insights into chaos theory offer profound lessons about the subtle interplay between order and chaos, fundamentally reshaping how we perceive complexity. Lorenz revealed that even systems governed by simple and clear rules such as weather patterns can unexpectedly produce intricate, seemingly random behaviors, largely because they're extremely sensitive to initial conditions (Lorenz, 1963; Gleick, 1987). Like Max Planck before him, Lorenz challenged the long-held classical belief that nature was fully predictable and deterministic, suggesting instead that embracing uncertainty and probability is essential for truly understanding complex phenomena.

Lorenz's ideas have humanized our scientific perspective by illustrating how structured complexity can spontaneously emerge from seemingly random processes. Consider how clouds, initially forming from seemingly random distributions of water vapor, self-organize into structured storms. This balance between randomness and order mirrors Planck's insights into quantum mechanics, where uncertainty and probability lie at the very core of physical reality at microscopic levels (Prigogine & Stengers, 1984; Nielsen & Chuang, 2010).

The intersection of Lorenz's chaos theory and Planck's quantum insights holds significant implications for contemporary computational methods, particularly in machine learning and generative artificial intelligence. Modern AI systems, much like natural ecosystems, need to manage and even harness chaotic behaviors rather than simply avoiding or suppressing them. Predictive models, for instance, are inherently challenged by uncertainty and subtle changes in input conditions, exactly the kind of complexity described by Lorenz. By embracing chaos theory's principles, AI practitioners can design more resilient, adaptive, and robust algorithms capable of thriving in real-world conditions where unpredictability and noise are inevitable (Frahm, 2025; Mitchell, 2019).

In short, Lorenz's pioneering work encourages us to shift away from rigid determinism and toward a deeper appreciation of probabilistic, systemic thinking. This perspective empowers us not only to better understand the natural world but also build computational systems like deep neural networks and generative AI that gracefully handle complexity, uncertainty, and unpredictability, transforming challenges into opportunities for innovation and discovery (Frahm, 2025; Mitchell, 2019).

Philosophical Convergence

Both Edward Lorenz and Max Planck significantly reshaped how we understand the world around us, leading a profound philosophical shift from a classical, linear, and deterministic view—one where every outcome could, in principle, be precisely predicted to a perspective that embraces uncertainty, complexity, and nonlinear probabilistic thinking. Lorenz's contributions to chaos theory helped us see that seemingly predictable systems, such as weather or ecological networks, can display striking unpredictability and complexity due to tiny initial differences, famously depicted through the butterfly effect (Lorenz, 1963; Gleick, 1987).

Similarly, Max Planck's revolutionary ideas in quantum mechanics unveiled the probabilistic nature of reality at microscopic scales, demonstrating that the behavior of particles such as electrons or photons cannot be predicted with absolute certainty, but rather can only be understood in terms of probabilities and tendencies (Nielsen & Chuang, 2010; Prigogine & Stengers, 1984). Together, Lorenz's and Planck's theories challenged traditional linear determinism, inspiring scientists and philosophers to rethink how complexity emerges, evolves, and behaves in real-world contexts.

By humanizing these theoretical insights, we can think of Lorenz and Planck as guiding us toward humility and adaptability. Rather than insisting on complete control and perfect predictability, their combined legacy encourages us to accept that uncertainty and complexity are inherent aspects of nature. This probabilistic perspective allows for richer, more nuanced understandings of complex phenomena such as climate change, biological evolution, economic fluctuations, and social dynamics (Mitchell, 2009; Frahm, 2025).

In contemporary fields like artificial intelligence, quantum computing, and systems biology, the complementary insights from Lorenz and Planck have proven essential. By adopting nonlinear and probabilistic approaches, scientists and engineers have become better equipped to model, predict, and manage inherently uncertain environments. Lorenz's chaotic systems help us understand the limits of prediction, while Planck's quantum concepts underline the necessity of embracing uncertainty as a fundamental feature of reality (Preskill, 2018; Nielsen & Chuang, 2010).

In essence, the philosophical convergence of Lorenz's and Planck's ideas provides a deep human lesson in humility, resilience, and adaptability, one that empowers us to build systems capable of gracefully navigating uncertainty rather than being constrained by it.

Conclusion

Edward N. Lorenz's pioneering contributions to chaos theory profoundly enrich our understanding of the subtle and intricate dynamics within complex systems. Rather than offering simple solutions or straightforward predictability, Lorenz illuminated how complexity often arises spontaneously, bridging the delicate boundary between determinism, where outcomes appear certain, and randomness, where outcomes defy precise forecasting. His groundbreaking insights revealed that even the smallest changes in initial conditions can drastically shift outcomes, illustrating how predictability and unpredictability are deeply intertwined which is an idea elegantly encapsulated in the now-famous "butterfly effect" (Lorenz, 1963; Gleick, 1987).

Lorenz's insights resonate powerfully with and extend the foundational principles introduced decades earlier by physicist Max Planck, who first recognized the fundamentally probabilistic and uncertain nature of physical processes at microscopic scales (Prigogine & Stengers, 1984; Nielsen & Chuang, 2010). Together, Lorenz and Planck guide us toward a more nuanced and realistic view of the natural world, one that acknowledges uncertainty and complexity not as problems to avoid, but as essential characteristics to embrace and leverage.

Today, as quantum computing rapidly advances, Lorenz's theoretical insights have become increasingly valuable, offering vital conceptual tools to navigate the intricate interplay between order and chaos. In practical quantum computing, challenges such as decoherence, measurement, and environmental disturbances continuously highlight the real-world complexity that Lorenz described so vividly (Preskill, 2018; Nielsen & Chuang, 2010). By applying Lorenz's concepts, researchers and technologists can better understand, manage, and even harness these complexities to develop more robust quantum algorithms and adaptive computational strategies.

Moreover, Lorenz's legacy informs advanced computational methodologies in artificial intelligence and machine learning, where managing uncertainty and complexity is essential for successful performance. His work inspires strategies that are resilient, flexible, and capable of gracefully adapting to the inevitable unpredictability encountered in real-world environments (Mitchell, 2019; Frahm, 2025).

Thus, Edward Lorenz's profound contributions not only deepen our philosophical understanding of complexity, they also fundamentally enhance our practical ability to operate effectively within complex and chaotic environments. By appreciating and embracing both the orderly and chaotic dimensions of reality, we become better equipped to harness complexity's full potential, transforming apparent unpredictability into opportunities for innovation, discovery, and advanced computational intelligence.

Chapter 3: Holland and Kauffman – Genetic Algorithms, Adaptive Systems, and the Emergence of Self-Organization in Complexity

Abstract

Chapter Three continues our exploration into the fascinating world of complexity, spotlighting two influential thinkers whose ideas have greatly enriched our understanding of how complex systems adapt, evolve, and spontaneously create order out of chaos, John Holland and Stuart Kauffman.

Drawing upon the groundbreaking concepts introduced earlier by Henri Poincaré in chaos theory, and Edward Lorenz's insights into the unpredictability caused by tiny initial changes, John Holland introduced genetic algorithms which is a computational approach inspired by natural evolution. Holland's genetic algorithms demonstrate beautifully how complexity can arise spontaneously from simple rules applied repeatedly. Just as nature uses processes like selection, mutation, and adaptation to shape life, genetic algorithms evolve complex and sophisticated solutions through similar iterative cycles. These principles not only offer powerful insights into natural evolution but also closely parallel how today's generative artificial intelligence systems operate, continuously adapting and learning.

In parallel, Stuart Kauffman brings another perspective, emphasizing the power of self-organization, the natural tendency for systems to create structure without any central control or explicit instructions. Kauffman's influential NK landscape model offers a compelling way to visualize how complex systems adapt, explore solutions, and find balance between chaos and order. This model is particularly insightful when considering how deep neural networks learn or how quantum computing systems evolve, continually exploring new possibilities and adjusting to dynamic conditions.

Together, Holland and Kauffman provide us with valuable conceptual tools that deepen our ability to understand, manage, and responsibly guide complex technologies. Their combined insights offer practical wisdom for navigating today's rapidly changing landscape, where artificial intelligence and quantum computing constantly blur the lines between predictability and surprise.

By weaving these visionary ideas into the broader story of complexity, Chapter Three enriches our philosophical and practical understanding, emphasizing the importance of thinking adaptively and probabilistically. As we step deeper into the age of AI and quantum computing, this adaptive mindset becomes increasingly crucial for responsibly harnessing and ethically guiding the powerful, dynamic systems shaping our future.

John Holland

Introduction to John Holland and Genetic Algorithms

Biography and academic contributions

John Henry Holland (1929–2015) was not only a pioneering scientist but also a remarkable thinker who reshaped our understanding of complexity and adaptation in computational systems. Born in Fort Wayne, Indiana, Holland demonstrated an exceptional interdisciplinary approach throughout his career, effortlessly weaving together insights from psychology, mathematics, computer science, and engineering. This interdisciplinary talent defined his academic journey and allowed him to make groundbreaking contributions to our understanding of complex adaptive systems (Mitchell, 2009).

After receiving his Ph.D. in Communication Sciences from the University of Michigan in 1959, Holland became a prominent figure at the university, eventually serving as a professor in psychology, electrical engineering, and computer science. His work at Michigan's Center for the Study of Complex Systems provided a nurturing environment that encouraged innovation and interdisciplinary collaboration, laying the groundwork for revolutionary ideas in adaptive systems and computational evolution (Mitchell, 2009).

Foundational Theory of Genetic Algorithms

Holland's most enduring and transformative contribution is the development of genetic algorithms (GAs), computational models inspired by biological evolution. Genetic algorithms apply evolutionary principles such as natural selection, mutation, and crossover to iteratively refine and improve solutions to complex computational challenges. His seminal work, "Adaptation in Natural and Artificial Systems," offered a robust theoretical foundation and practical methodology for applying these evolutionary principles to computational problem-solving (Holland, 1975).

Central to Holland's genetic algorithms is the concept of representation, where complex problems are encoded into simplified forms known as chromosomes. Each chromosome represents a potential solution, simplifying complex real-world issues into manageable computational forms. This encoding approach is a profound reflection of how nature simplifies genetic information, facilitating efficient adaptation and evolutionary progress (Goldberg, 1989; Holland, 1975).

Selection is another critical element in genetic algorithms, emulating nature's mechanism of "survival of the fittest." Solutions are evaluated based on their performance or fitness, and the most effective ones are selected to pass their characteristics to subsequent generations. Through iterative selection, genetic algorithms systematically improve solutions, much like how evolution gradually refines species through generations (Mitchell, 2009; Goldberg, 1989).

Why Genetic Algorithms Matter in Complexity and Adaptation

Genetic algorithms, a foundational innovation introduced by complexity theorist John Holland, represent a powerful computational approach inspired directly by the principles of biological evolution. The central idea behind genetic algorithms is the process of gradual improvement, selecting, combining, and modifying candidate solutions iteratively until optimal or sufficiently effective solutions emerge. This diagram clearly outlines the key stages of a genetic algorithm, providing readers with a practical understanding of each step.

The following figure illustrates the evolutionary process of genetic algorithms, demonstrating how candidate solutions are initialized, evaluated, selected, and refined through genetic operators and iterative feedback loops. This visualization highlights the adaptive nature of optimization as solutions evolve toward convergence.

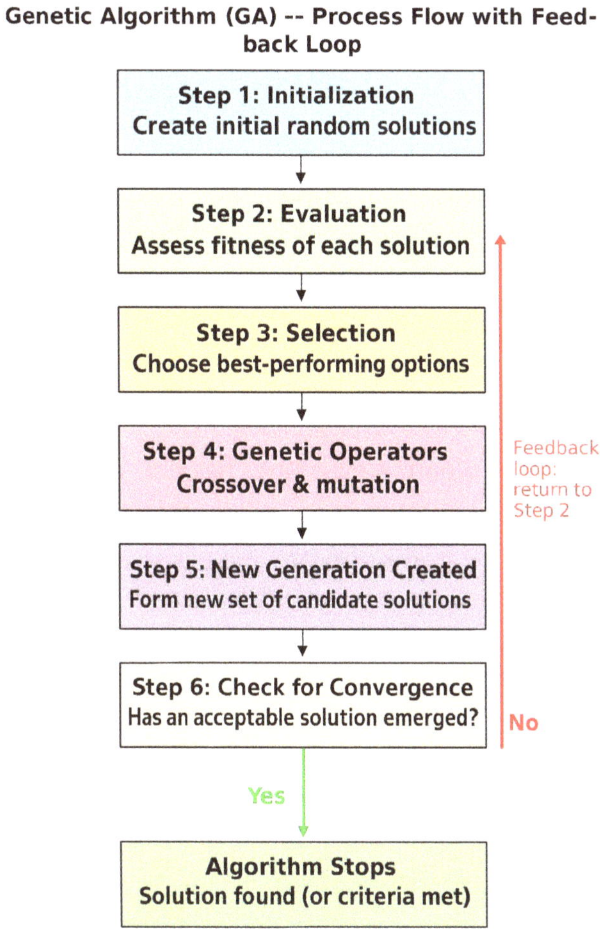

Figure 3.1. *The evolutionary process of genetic algorithms—From initial solutions to adaptive optimization. Author's illustration (2025).*

Note. The diagram depicts the step-by-step flow of a genetic algorithm (GA). Beginning with the initialization of candidate solutions, each cycle evaluates solution fitness, selects high-performing candidates, and applies genetic operators (crossover and mutation) to generate new solutions. A feedback loop checks for convergence, repeating until an optimal or acceptable solution is achieved. This process models adaptive evolution, emphasizing the iterative refinement that drives optimization in both natural and computational systems.

Step-by-Step Explanation of Figure 3.1:

Step 1: Initialization

The genetic algorithm begins with an initial group of randomly generated candidate solutions. These initial solutions serve as the foundation or starting population from which future solutions evolve. The diversity introduced at this stage is crucial, enabling the algorithm to explore a wide range of possibilities.

Step 2: Evaluation

Each candidate solution is evaluated against specific criteria (the "fitness function") that measures how effectively it solves the given problem. Solutions that perform better receive higher fitness scores, guiding the algorithm toward promising pathways.

Step 3: Selection

Solutions with higher fitness scores are selected to move forward into subsequent steps. By prioritizing solutions that demonstrate superior performance, the algorithm progressively favors those characteristics and strategies most likely to produce effective outcomes.

Step 4: Genetic Operators (Crossover and Mutation)

This critical phase uses two main methods:

Crossover (Recombination): This step involves combining parts from selected solutions to form new ones, allowing the algorithm to explore combinations that may outperform original solutions. It resembles biological reproduction, where offspring inherit characteristics from parents.

Mutation (Variation): Here, the algorithm introduces minor, random changes into solutions. Mutation ensures continuous exploration of the solution space and helps prevent the population from stagnating at suboptimal solutions.

Step 5: New Generation Created

Following crossover and mutation, a new set ("generation") of candidate solutions emerges, composed of selected solutions, newly combined solutions, and mutated variations. This new generation represents refined solutions that ideally move closer toward optimal outcomes.

Step 6: Check for Convergence (close the loop)

At each generation the algorithm runs a feedback loop: it measures how well the current population is doing, compares those signals to pre set convergence criteria, and then acts by either stopping or adjusting how the next generation is created. If the criteria are met, the process ends, and the best solution is returned. If not, the loop feeds back into the workflow—returning to Step 2 (Evaluation) with updated parameters, penalties, or sampling so the algorithm can learn from what just happened and refine the next round.

What to check at Step 6 (the signals)

> **Improvement**: Has the best/median fitness improved beyond a small threshold (e.g., < 0.1% change over the last k generations = plateau)?
>
> **Stability**: Are scores oscillating (up down) rather than trending? Use a moving average or Exponentially Weighted Moving Average (EWMA) to smooth noise.

Diversity: Is the population becoming too similar (e.g., genotype/phenotype diversity below a floor)? Low diversity = risk of premature convergence.

Constraint satisfaction: Are violations (budget, deadlines, safety limits) trending down? If not, treat it as non converged.

Generalization/robustness: Do top solutions hold up on a validation set, slight noise, or scenario stress tests?

Budget/latency: Have we hit a hard cap (max generations, time, energy/cost)? This is a practical stop even if the optimum isn't proven.

If "No," how the loop learns before returning to Step 2

Rather than simply retrying, use the feedback to adapt the search:

Tune operators: Increase mutation or decrease selection pressure to escape a local optimum; or do the reverse if search is too random.

Inject diversity: Add random immigrants, shuffle sub populations, or use an island model to re seed exploration.

Adaptive penalties: Strengthen constraint penalties that remain violated; relax ones already satisfied to refocus search effort.

Resample & reweight fitness: Update evaluation data (new scenarios, adversarial cases) so Step 2 doesn't reward brittle solutions.

Elitism & restarts: Keep a small elite set, but trigger a soft restart if progress stalls for p generations.

Population sizing: Grow the population when exploration is needed; shrink it to speed exploitation once a promising region is found.

Hyper parameter schedules: Apply annealing/cooling schedules to mutation rates, crossover probabilities, or selection temperature.

Positive vs. negative feedback (why the loop works)

Positive feedback accelerates promising directions (good solutions reproduce more).

Negative feedback prevents lock in and collapse (diversity floors, penalty increases, caps on clones).

A healthy loop balances both, so progress continues without getting trapped.

Multi objective note (if optimizing several goals)

When there are multiple objectives (e.g., cost, time, risk), Step 6 checks Pareto front quality (Pareto front (aka Pareto frontier) = the set of best trade offs in a multi objective problem.). "Converged" means the Pareto front stops improving meaningfully; "No" means the loop returns to Step 2 with tweaks that improve coverage or dominance.

Good governance for the loop

Thresholds with owners: Pre define the exact convergence tests (plateau ε, patience k, diversity floor, max budget) and who can change them.

Explainability: Log which signals triggered "No," which adaptations were applied, and why.

Safety checks: Before declaring "Yes," verify on hold out data and run a quick stress test; for high stakes use, require a human sign off.

One line condition you can use

Stop if improvement < ε for k generations and diversity ≥ floor and constraints satisfied; else adapt parameters and return to Step 2.

This makes Step 6 the control room of the algorithm: measure → compare → intervene → verify → document—so each "No" isn't a setback but an informed adjustment that drives the next generation forward.

Classifier Systems and Adaptive Agents

Extending beyond genetic algorithms, Holland introduced classifier systems, which merge genetic algorithms with reinforcement learning principles. Classifier systems utilize simple, rule-based structures enabling artificial agents to learn effectively from their environment. These adaptive agents refine their behaviors continuously through interactions, mirroring how living organisms adaptively respond to their surroundings. This innovation provides a practical, evolutionary-inspired framework for creating adaptive and intelligent computational systems (Holland, Holyoak, Nisbett, & Thagard, 1986).

Classifier systems exemplify Holland's vision of computational adaptation, demonstrating how simple iterative processes can produce highly sophisticated behaviors. This iterative learning and adaptation reflect a humanistic appreciation for continuous improvement and responsiveness, emphasizing adaptability and resilience in complex environments (Holland, 1992).

Complex Adaptive Systems

Holland significantly expanded our theoretical understanding of complex adaptive systems (CAS), highlighting how complexity and sophisticated behaviors naturally emerge from simple interactions.

According to Holland, complex adaptive systems are decentralized, composed of numerous simple components that interact without central control, yet spontaneously generate complex, organized patterns of behavior. This insight has fundamentally reshaped our understanding of complexity in ecosystems, economics, social systems, and computational intelligence (Holland, 1992).

Holland's conceptualization of complex adaptive systems aligns closely with chaos theory principles previously discussed, especially the spontaneous emergence of order from apparent randomness. This intersection provides profound philosophical and practical insights, deepening our understanding of how adaptive systems evolve complexity naturally and dynamically (Lorenz, 1963; Kauffman, 1993).

Genetic algorithms are widely applied in real-world domains where adaptation and optimization are essential. The following figure highlights three representative areas, logistics, finance, and robotics, demonstrating their versatility in addressing complex challenges.

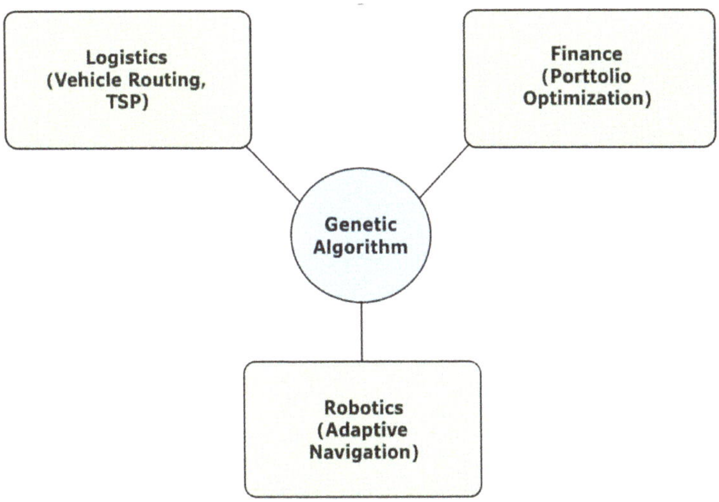

Figure 3.2. *Applications of genetic algorithms in real-world systems. Adapted from Holland (1992), Goldberg (1989), Potvin (2009), and Mitchell (2009).*

Note. This diagram highlights three diverse application areas of genetic algorithms: logistics (e.g., solving the vehicle routing and traveling salesman problems), finance (portfolio optimization under dynamic market conditions), and robotics (adaptive navigation and decision-making in complex environments). These domains illustrate the versatility of GAs in addressing complexity through adaptive computation.

Applications to Real-World Problems

Genetic algorithms have seen widespread application across diverse real-world scenarios, demonstrating their versatility and robustness. In logistics optimization, genetic algorithms effectively solve complex routing and scheduling challenges, significantly reducing transportation costs and enhancing operational efficiency. Problems such as the Vehicle Routing Problem (VRP) and the Traveling Salesman Problem (TSP) have been greatly advanced through genetic algorithms, leading to meaningful improvements in real-world logistics systems (Goldberg, 1989; Potvin, 2009).

In the realm of economics, genetic algorithms have transformed financial modeling and portfolio optimization. These algorithms dynamically balance risk and reward, continually refining investment strategies in response to changing market conditions. This adaptability has empowered financial analysts to make informed, responsive decisions, effectively navigating the complexity and volatility of financial markets (Holland, 1992; Mitchell, 2009).

Evolutionary robotics is another significant area impacted by genetic algorithms. Robots leveraging these algorithms autonomously develop robust adaptive behaviors for navigating complex environments. From autonomous vehicles to planetary rovers, genetic algorithms enable robots to continuously evolve their decision-making capabilities, adapting effectively to unpredictable circumstances. This evolutionary process mirrors biological adaptation, emphasizing the profound potential of genetic algorithms in enhancing robotic autonomy and intelligence (Holland, 1992; Goldberg, 1989).

Ethical and Governance Considerations

Despite their remarkable potential, the autonomous and adaptive nature of genetic algorithms introduces significant ethical and governance challenges. Issues such as transparency, accountability, and unintended biases become critical as these algorithms autonomously evolve. The complexity and adaptability inherent in genetic algorithms necessitate robust governance structures capable of continuous oversight and dynamic risk management (Floridi & Cowls, 2019; O'Neil, 2016).

Transparency and interpretability pose particularly challenging governance issues. Genetic algorithms often operate as "black boxes," making their decision-making processes difficult to interpret clearly. This opacity complicates efforts to ensure fairness, accountability, and ethical alignment. Robust interpretability tools and transparent reporting processes thus become essential to responsible governance of these adaptive systems (Rudin, 2019; Ribeiro, Singh, & Guestrin, 2016).

Governance frameworks must also clearly define accountability and responsibility, addressing the complexity of autonomous decision-making. Establishing transparent, adaptive governance processes is essential to ensure alignment with societal values, mitigating risks, and proactively addressing ethical concerns as they emerge (Cohen, Kolt, Bengio, Hadfield, & Russell, 2024; Wallach & Marchant, 2018).

Synthesis and Conclusion

John Holland's visionary contributions through genetic algorithms significantly advanced our understanding of complex adaptive systems, offering powerful tools for addressing real-world challenges across multiple domains. By bridging the foundational insights of earlier thinkers like Henri Poincaré and Edward Lorenz, Holland emphasized the dynamic interplay between simplicity, complexity, and adaptability. His humanistic vision invites us to embrace complexity, highlighting our innate capacity for creativity, exploration, and continuous improvement (Frahm, 2025; Mitchell, 2009).

Holland's legacy continues to inspire researchers and practitioners alike, fostering innovative approaches to complexity and adaptation. As genetic algorithms become increasingly embedded within our technological landscape, their responsible governance and ethical alignment with human values become paramount, ensuring these powerful tools benefit humanity and reflect our collective ethical commitments.

Stuart Kauffman and Self-Organization

Biography and Contributions to Complexity Theory

Stuart Kauffman, born on September 28, 1939, is a prominent theoretical biologist and complexity scientist renowned for his pioneering contributions to understanding self-organization in biological and complex systems. Kauffman's interdisciplinary approach has enabled him to profoundly reshape scientific thinking around complexity and evolution. His remarkable ability to weave together insights from biology, physics, mathematics, and philosophy has deeply enriched our understanding of how complexity and order spontaneously emerge within systems without centralized control (Kauffman, 1993).

Kauffman's seminal work, "The Origins of Order," introduced revolutionary ideas about how complex structures and patterns can arise spontaneously from simple interactions. His groundbreaking insights challenge traditional evolutionary biology views, highlighting the natural tendency of systems to self-organize and generate order from seemingly chaotic conditions. His theories significantly contribute to broader complexity science, demonstrating how simplicity and interaction can yield highly intricate and sophisticated systems (Kauffman, 1993).

Principles of Self-Organization

Central to Kauffman's theories are three critical concepts: spontaneous order, autocatalytic sets, and attractors. These ideas collectively explain how complexity naturally arises without explicit guidance or central coordination. Spontaneous order refers to the emergence of organized structures or patterns from the interactions of simpler components, much like how birds spontaneously form flocks without external direction (Kauffman, 1993).

Autocatalytic sets, another cornerstone of Kauffman's theory, describe how groups of molecules or elements can catalyze each other's formation and growth, sustaining and reinforcing the emergence of complexity within systems. These self-sustaining interactions provide a powerful metaphor for understanding evolutionary dynamics and the emergence of complex adaptive systems (Kauffman, 1993).

Attractors further enrich this understanding, representing states toward which complex systems naturally evolve. Attractors illustrate how systems, despite their inherent unpredictability, tend toward specific patterns or behaviors, much like water inevitably flowing toward the lowest point. Kauffman's insights into attractors help clarify how complexity and order spontaneously emerge and stabilize within systems characterized by chaotic unpredictability (Kauffman, 1993).

Kauffman's principles closely resonate with Lorenz's chaos theory, particularly regarding the sensitive dependence on initial conditions and emergent complexity. While Lorenz emphasizes how small initial changes can lead to unpredictably divergent outcomes, Kauffman highlights how these same chaotic processes can spontaneously yield structured order. Together, their insights provide a rich, integrated understanding of complexity, emphasizing the complementary nature of chaos and order within adaptive systems (Lorenz, 1963; Kauffman, 1993).

Kauffman's NK Model and Its Relevance to AI

Stuart Kauffman's NK model provides an influential conceptual framework for understanding adaptation and optimization within complex adaptive systems. In this model, "N" represents the number of system components, while "K" signifies their interactions or interdependencies. The NK landscape vividly illustrates how complex systems evolve through adaptive walks, searching for optimal states or solutions. These landscapes represent various states of system fitness, with higher points indicating better adaptation or solutions (Kauffman, 1993).

This concept is strikingly analogous to training landscapes encountered in deep neural networks and quantum computational systems. Just as neural networks seek optimal configurations by navigating a complex fitness landscape filled with high points of advantage and low points of constraint that organizations must navigate when making trade-offs., quantum systems also explore state spaces shaped by quantum interactions and superpositions. Kauffman's NK model thus provides valuable insights into how these systems adaptively explore potential solutions and manage inherent complexity and uncertainty (Goodfellow, Bengio, & Courville, 2016; Nielsen & Chuang, 2010).

The NK model's relevance extends to practical optimization challenges faced in artificial intelligence, where finding effective solutions often involves balancing exploration and exploitation. By illustrating how complex adaptive systems navigate rugged landscapes,

Kauffman's model helps clarify strategies for managing complexity and achieving robust solutions within AI-driven computational models (Kauffman, 1993).

In practical terms, N represents the number of decision variables in a model, while K captures how strongly each variable's payoff depends on K others (i.e., the degree of cross dependence or "epistasis"). As K rises, the landscape becomes rugged, full of local peaks separated by steep drops, so greedy moves (e.g., simple hill climbing or plain gradient steps) stall quickly. The NK lens suggests two complementary tactics in AI: (1) adapt the search to ruggedness by using population based methods (genetic algorithms, evolution strategies), simulated annealing (Annealing = gradually cooling a system so it settles into a stable, low energy state). or tempered sampling, random restarts, island models, and diversity maintenance/novelty search to keep exploring; and (2) reshape the landscape to lower the effective K—modular architectures, sparsity and regularization to reduce spurious interactions, problem decomposition, curriculum learning, and constraint handling that smooths cliffs. Step to step feedback loops then monitor improvement, diversity, and constraint violations; when progress plateaus or the population collapses around a narrow peak, the loop increases exploration (e.g., higher mutation, broader sampling) or changes decomposition to re open pathways. Read this way, the NK model is not just a metaphor but a design guide for choosing search operators, setting schedules, and structuring models so that robust solutions emerge despite rugged, high dependency objective surfaces (Kauffman, 1993).

Kauffman's NK model provides a powerful framework for understanding the complexity of evolutionary search processes. As the degree of interdependence among genetic components (K) increases, fitness landscapes become more rugged, producing multiple local optima. These rugged landscapes illustrate the difficulty of adaptive systems in achieving global optimization. Figure 3.3 visualizes this concept, showing how genetic algorithms perform adaptive walks across landscapes of varying complexity.

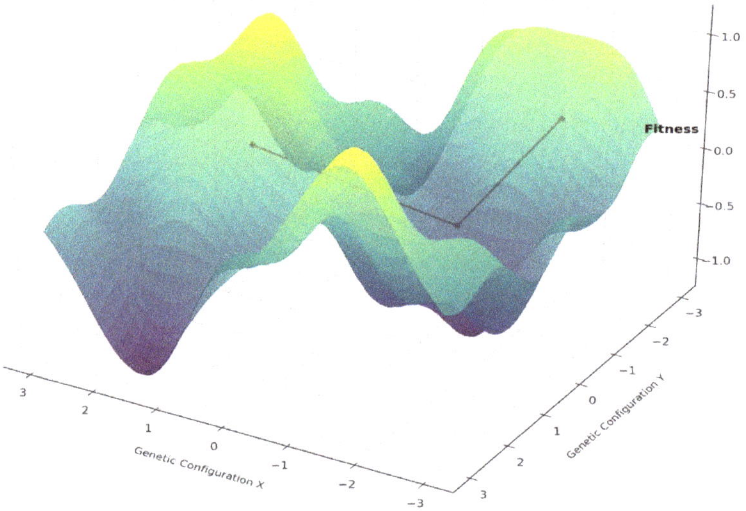

Figure 3.3. *NK fitness landscape illustrating adaptive walks toward local and global optima. Adapted from Kauffman (1993).*

Note. This figure depicts Kauffman's NK model, where fitness values are represented as a rugged three-dimensional landscape. Peaks signify local optima, while valleys represent low-fitness regions. Genetic algorithms explore such landscapes through adaptive walks, gradually climbing to higher peaks but often becoming trapped in local maxima rather than reaching the global optimum. The visualization underscores the inherent trade-offs in evolutionary computation, balancing exploration of new regions with exploitation of known solutions.

Emergent Complexity in Neural Networks and Generative AI

The principles of self-organization outlined by Kauffman also provide profound insights into emergent complexity observed in neural networks and generative artificial intelligence systems. Neural networks, through iterative learning and adaptation processes, spontaneously generate complex patterns and behaviors not explicitly programmed into them. These emergent behaviors reflect how simple rules and interactions can yield sophisticated outcomes, closely aligning with Kauffman's theories of self-organization and spontaneous order (Mitchell, 2019; Goodfellow, Bengio, & Courville, 2016).

For instance, generative AI models demonstrate spontaneous creativity by transforming simple input prompts into novel, often unexpected outputs. These outputs exhibit complexity and creativity arising naturally from the model's underlying probabilistic and nonlinear interactions. This emergent complexity exemplifies Kauffman's self-organizing principles, highlighting how sophisticated structures and behaviors spontaneously develop without explicit instructions or centralized control (Goodfellow, Bengio, & Courville, 2016).

Philosophical Implications

Beyond their scientific value, Kauffman's insights hold profound philosophical implications, particularly regarding the nature of life and the spontaneous emergence of order. His ideas challenge traditional deterministic and reductionist perspectives, proposing instead that life and complexity naturally arise from simple rules and interactions. This philosophical viewpoint encourages a deeper appreciation of how uncertainty, complexity, and adaptability are intrinsic and valuable features of natural and computational systems alike (Kauffman, 1993).

Reflecting on artificial intelligence and quantum computing, Kauffman's philosophy underscores the importance of embracing complexity and self-organization as natural phenomena. Rather than attempting to rigidly control or eliminate uncertainty, his insights invite us to embrace adaptive, flexible approaches that respect and leverage complexity's inherent spontaneity and potential. This philosophical stance encourages humanistic values of resilience, adaptability, and creative exploration, guiding how we responsibly develop and govern complex technologies (Frahm, 2025; Mitchell, 2019).

Synthesis and Reflection

Connecting Holland and Kauffman to Poincaré and Lorenz

Reflecting upon the visionary contributions of John Holland and Stuart Kauffman in the broader context of complexity theory, it becomes evident how their groundbreaking work extends and enriches the foundational concepts established by earlier visionaries such as Henri Poincaré and Edward Lorenz. The intellectual journey from Poincaré's insights on chaotic dynamics and sensitivity to initial conditions, through Lorenz's exploration of unpredictability and macroscopic irreversibility, naturally culminates in Holland's and Kauffman's sophisticated explorations of genetic algorithms and self-organization (Lorenz, 1963; Kauffman, 1993; Holland, 1992).

Poincaré and Lorenz provide foundational ideas on chaos and unpredictability, fundamentally reshaping how we perceive deterministic yet complex systems. They showed us that even simple systems could behave unpredictably due to small variations at their starting points. Building upon these insights, Holland demonstrated how similar principles of initial condition sensitivity and adaptive complexity could be computationally harnessed to create innovative solutions through genetic algorithms. Holland's algorithms echoed nature's evolutionary processes, illustrating vividly how structured complexity spontaneously emerges through iterative adaptation (Holland, 1992; Lorenz, 1963).

Kauffman further extended these insights, emphasizing self-organization and spontaneous order emerging from seemingly chaotic interactions. His NK landscape model provided a practical framework for visualizing how complexity arises and evolves within adaptive systems, bridging the unpredictability emphasized by Lorenz and the structured adaptive behaviors showcased by Holland. Kauffman's work highlights that complexity and order do not require centralized control but rather naturally emerge from simple rules and interactions, complementing and extending the principles established by Poincaré, Lorenz, and Holland (Kauffman, 1993; Holland, 1992).

Conclusion

As we delve deeper into the age of artificial intelligence and quantum computing, understanding and integrating these insights from complexity theory become crucial for responsible governance and ethical stewardship of advanced technologies. Holland's genetic algorithms and Kauffman's self-organizing principles offer essential conceptual tools for managing complex adaptive systems, emphasizing adaptability, resilience, and continuous learning.

Moving forward, these principles highlight the need for adaptive governance frameworks capable of dynamically responding to emerging complexities. Rather than adhering strictly to static rules, governance processes should evolve iteratively, mirroring the adaptive and evolutionary principles intrinsic to genetic algorithms and self-organizing systems. This approach ensures that governance frameworks remain effective, responsive, and ethically aligned, continuously adapting to new challenges as they emerge (Floridi & Cowls, 2019; Cohen, Kolt, Bengio, Hadfield, & Russell, 2024).

Embracing the philosophical and practical lessons from Poincaré, Lorenz, Holland, and Kauffman equip us with the wisdom and adaptability necessary for navigating and harnessing complexity responsibly. As we continue this intellectual journey, future chapters will further explore contributions from other transformative thinkers such as Gregory Bateson, whose work on feedback loops enriches our understanding of system interactions; Ilya Prigogine, whose insights into dissipative structures inform the dynamics of evolving complexity; Murray Gell-Mann, who advanced our comprehension of complex adaptive systems; and Claude Shannon, whose foundational ideas on information entropy illuminate the intricate balance between order and uncertainty. Their combined legacies further expand and enrich our ability to navigate and manage complexity, reinforcing the deeply interconnected progression of thought that underlies contemporary innovations in artificial intelligence and quantum computing.

By respecting the delicate interplay between order and chaos, predictability and unpredictability, we enhance our capacity for innovation and ethical stewardship in an increasingly complex technological landscape. This humanistic vision underscores our innate potential for creativity, resilience, and continuous adaptation, ensuring we leverage complexity thoughtfully and responsibly as we forge our collective future.

Chapter 4: Bateson and Prigogine – Systems Thinking, Dissipative Structures, and Complexity at the Edge of Chaos

Introduction

Building upon our earlier journey through the transformative ideas of Poincaré, Lorenz, Holland, and Kauffman, Chapter 4 delves deeper into the fabric of complexity by exploring the ground-breaking contributions of Gregory Bateson and Ilya Prigogine. Each of these visionary thinkers uniquely enriches our understanding by illuminating how complex systems ranging from ecological environments to advanced computational frameworks can spontaneously generate intricate patterns, behaviors, and structures from seemingly simple interactions.

Bateson introduces us to systemic thinking and the profound impact of feedback loops, providing essential insight into the intricate interdependencies that shape our increasingly interconnected world. Prigogine, on the other hand, guides us through the fascinating world of dissipative structures and irreversibility, offering a nuanced understanding of how order and complexity naturally emerge even as systems continuously exchange energy with their environments.

A dissipative structure, in the simplest terms, can be thought of as a remarkable example of nature's creativity. It describes how complex patterns, shapes, or systems spontaneously emerge and maintain their structure through constant exchanges of energy and materials with their surroundings. Unlike a machine running in isolation, dissipative structures thrive precisely because they are open and continuously interacting with their environment. Imagine something like a hurricane or a whirlpool, continuously drawing energy from its environment to sustain its distinctive form. Through ongoing energy exchanges, these systems self-organize into coherent patterns, balancing chaos and order, unpredictability and stability. Introduced by Nobel laureate Ilya Prigogine, dissipative structures remind us that complexity and creativity naturally flourish amidst continual change, underscoring the deep interconnectedness between systems and their environments, and inspiring us to embrace adaptability and resilience in our own lives and communities.

Together, Bateson and Prigogine empower us with the conceptual clarity to navigate the complexities of artificial intelligence, quantum computing, and dynamic governance frameworks. Their work inspires us not only to appreciate complexity's inherent dynamism and interconnectedness but also to approach technological and ecological challenges with humility, adaptability, and ethical responsibility. By integrating these philosophical and practical insights, we deepen our capacity to manage, innovate, and thoughtfully steward advanced technologies that align with our collective well-being and sustainable future.

Gregory Bateson: Systemic Thinking and Feedback Loops

Biography and Academic Contributions

Gregory Bateson (1904–1980) was a visionary intellectual whose multidisciplinary insights have deeply influenced our comprehension of complexity, communication, and adaptive systems. Born in Grantchester, England, Bateson's academic path was uniquely rich, traversing disciplines from anthropology to cybernetics, biology, psychology, and philosophy.

His early anthropological work, particularly his studies among the Latmul people of New Guinea, greatly influenced his ideas about human communication and systemic interactions, leading to groundbreaking contributions in systems theory and complexity science (Bateson, 1972; Harries-Jones, 1995).

In his seminal book Steps to an Ecology of Mind (1972), Bateson articulated his groundbreaking ideas, fundamentally shifting our understanding of human cognition, communication, and complex system interactions. This collection of essays profoundly influenced multiple fields, including psychology, ecology, artificial intelligence, and organizational studies, highlighting his conviction that systems cannot be adequately understood by examining their parts in isolation. Instead, Bateson argued, understanding arises from recognizing how elements dynamically interrelate and communicate within holistic systems (Bateson, 1972).

Key Principles: Feedback Loops and Communication

Gregory Bateson showed that complex systems stay stable not by standing still, but by using feedback loops, taking in the results of their own actions, adjusting, and evolving. Bateson skillfully distinguished two essential types: positive feedback loops, which amplify initial changes within systems driving transformative growth, and negative feedback loops, which moderate and stabilize systems by minimizing fluctuations. Imagine an orchestra responding sensitively to each musician's cues, where feedback loops act as the conductor of an orchestra, subtly guiding each instrument's volume and pace. Positive loops can dramatically amplify melodies, leading to crescendos, while negative loops ensure the orchestra stays harmoniously balanced, correcting deviations swiftly to maintain coherence. Bateson believed that communication and information flow within systems serve as essential conduits of these feedback loops, shaping system behavior and evolution, allowing systems to self-organize and adapt meaningfully to their environments (Bateson, 1972).

Bateson further emphasized that these feedback loops are inherently driven and moderated by the flow of information and effective communication within and across systems. Communication, in his view, was not merely the exchange of information but a foundational and shaping force that defines systemic interactions and evolutionary trajectories. Bateson argued that all living and non-living systems rely fundamentally on communication processes to remain cohesive and adaptive, continually responding and adjusting their structures and behaviors based on informational feedback. This profound insight underscores communication's crucial role in maintaining system integrity and adaptability, revealing how deeply interconnected and interdependent complex systems truly are (Bateson, 1972).

Gregory Bateson conceptualized learning in complex systems as a multi-level recursive process. At the most basic level, systems engage in single-loop learning, adjusting actions in response to feedback from the environment. Beyond this, double-loop learning involves reflecting on and modifying the underlying assumptions that guide those actions. A third level, often called triple-loop learning, challenges the deeper epistemological frameworks through which systems interpret reality. Figure 4.1 illustrates these nested and dynamic feedback processes, emphasizing how governance adapts not only operationally but also reflectively and philosophically.

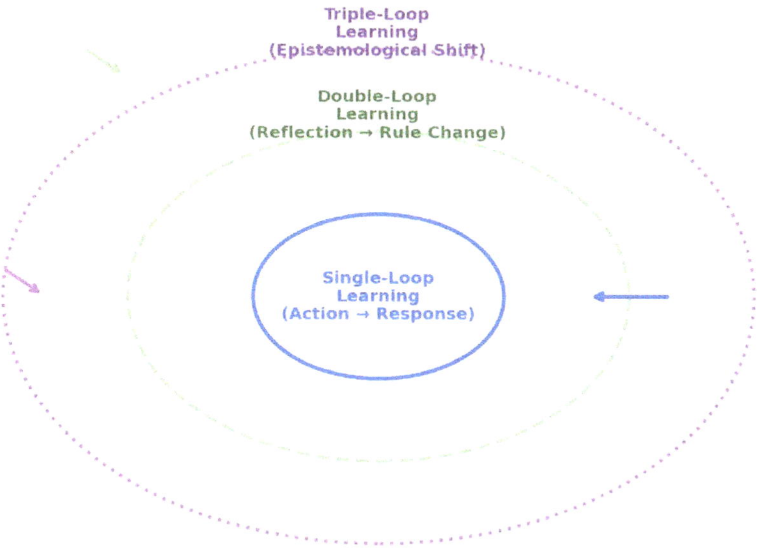

Figure 4.1. *Recursive levels of learning: single-loop, double-loop, and triple-loop feedback. Adapted from Bateson (2000/1972).*

Note. This figure illustrates Bateson's layered model of learning. Single-loop feedback focuses on correcting errors within existing rules; double-loop feedback questions and revises the governing rules themselves; triple-loop feedback interrogates the very frameworks of meaning and epistemology. In governance, these layers correspond to operational adjustments, policy or structural reforms, and paradigm shifts in how problems and solutions are understood.

Practical Application of Bateson's Concepts

The concepts introduced by Bateson are remarkably pertinent in modern technological contexts, especially within artificial intelligence and machine learning systems. Consider the operation of algorithmic recommendation platforms, which rely heavily on positive and negative feedback loops. Positive loops amplify content aligned closely with user preferences, creating a tailored and engaging user experience. In contrast, negative feedback loops manage and mitigate unwanted outcomes, such as misinformation or bias amplification. By understanding and managing these dynamic interactions, technologists and policymakers can ensure more ethically sound, transparent, and adaptive technological platforms, thereby addressing crucial societal concerns surrounding algorithmic fairness and systemic bias (Floridi & Cowls, 2019). For instance, smart city technologies utilize feedback loops extensively, adjusting urban traffic and energy usage dynamically in response to real-time data, ensuring optimal efficiency and sustainability.

Examples include adaptive traffic signals that lengthen or shorten phases to dissipate queues; bus headway control that holds vehicles to prevent bunching; dynamic congestion pricing that raises tolls as flow nears capacity; smart parking that adjusts prices and guidance from sensor data to spread demand; demand response energy/district heating that trims load during peaks; and air quality–triggered speed limits or low emission zones that activate when pollution spikes.

Moreover, Bateson's systemic insights address key technological challenges such as algorithmic transparency and systemic bias. By understanding how feedback loops amplify or mitigate specific behaviors, developers and regulators can better navigate complex ethical landscapes. For instance, awareness of feedback loops has become critical in managing algorithm-driven polarization on social media platforms, where unchecked amplification can lead to echo chambers and misinformation. Because many recommendation engines operate as "black boxes," their opaque ranking and amplification logic can hide these feedback loops, making it harder for users and regulators to detect, audit, and correct echo chambers and misinformation. Consequently, Bateson's insights provide invaluable guidance in designing adaptive governance frameworks, promoting systemic awareness, and ensuring technological deployments remain ethically sound, balanced, and reflective of diverse societal values (Floridi & Cowls, 2019).

Philosophical Implications

Bateson's philosophical contributions offer a profound shift from traditional linear thinking to recognizing profound interconnectedness and interdependency. He prompts us to see beyond isolated components to the intricate web of relationships underpinning all complex systems, be they ecological, technological, or social. This holistic approach fosters a deeper ethical responsibility, urging us to carefully consider the ecological and societal implications of technological innovations. By championing interconnectedness, Bateson's philosophy promotes greater ecological sensitivity and ethical mindfulness, encouraging responsible, adaptive stewardship of technology and nature for collective human and ecological wellbeing (Bateson, 1972).

This philosophical perspective significantly reshapes our ethical responsibilities, advocating for ecological sensitivity and responsible technological stewardship. Bateson's emphasis on interconnectedness reminds us of our inherent role within broader ecological and technological networks, highlighting our shared responsibilities towards sustainable development and harmonious coexistence. His holistic approach encourages humility, adaptive thinking, and a deep appreciation for the complexities and uncertainties inherent within natural and artificial systems alike, guiding us to engage with technology in ethically responsible and ecologically conscious ways (Bateson, 1972).

Ilya Prigogine: Dissipative Structures and Irreversibility

Biography and Academic Contributions

Ilya Prigogine (1917–2003) stands as a pioneering figure whose profound insights significantly transformed scientific understanding of complexity, entropy, and self-organization. Born in Moscow and later based in Belgium at the Free University of Brussels, Prigogine cultivated a highly interdisciplinary career bridging chemistry, physics, and philosophy. His groundbreaking concept of dissipative structures earned him the Nobel Prize in Chemistry in 1977, reflecting the transformative impact of his work on traditional thermodynamics and complexity science. Prigogine demonstrated how order and complexity spontaneously emerge within dynamic, non-equilibrium systems, fundamentally shifting our scientific and philosophical paradigms toward appreciating complexity as inherent and creatively emergent (Prigogine & Stengers, 1984).

Throughout his extensive career, Prigogine extensively explored the thermodynamics of non-equilibrium systems that continuously exchange energy and matter with their environments, operating far from a state of balance. His groundbreaking research culminated in the concept of "dissipative structures," a term he coined to describe complex, organized states emerging spontaneously within chaotic environments. Dissipative structures are characterized by their inherent irreversibility and ongoing energy exchange, challenging classical scientific paradigms that typically focused on equilibrium and reversibility (Prigogine & Stengers, 1984).

Awarded the Nobel Prize in Chemistry in 1977, Prigogine's seminal contributions significantly reshaped scientific thought across multiple fields, including ecology, economics, biology, and artificial intelligence. His most influential publication, Order Out of Chaos: Man's New Dialogue with Nature (co-authored with Isabelle Stengers, 1984), eloquently presented these groundbreaking ideas to both academic and general audiences. This work emphasized that far-from-equilibrium systems naturally evolve into organized and coherent patterns, fundamentally shifting our scientific approach toward appreciating complexity and unpredictability as inherent aspects of reality (Prigogine & Stengers, 1984).

Prigogine's revolutionary ideas offered fresh insights into understanding natural processes, ecological systems, biological evolution, and the dynamics of human societies. His theories on entropy, irreversibility, and self-organization have deeply influenced how we conceptualize sustainability, resilience, and adaptation within complex systems. By embracing Prigogine's principles, contemporary scientists and philosophers can better appreciate the spontaneous creativity and adaptability inherent in complex systems, including those emerging within modern computational frameworks like quantum computing and artificial intelligence (Nielsen & Chuang, 2010; Preskill, 2018).

Prigogine's interdisciplinary perspective emphasized the philosophical importance of unpredictability and irreversible processes, inspiring a broader cultural shift from deterministic to probabilistic thinking. His profound philosophical contributions encourage a humanistic appreciation of complexity, adaptability, and resilience, highlighting the necessity of ethical and responsible stewardship in technology and ecology alike. Prigogine's enduring legacy not only enhances scientific knowledge but also promotes deeper awareness, ecological sensitivity, and ethical engagement with complex systems in an interconnected world.

Fundamental Concepts: Dissipative Structures and Non-equilibrium Systems

At the core of Prigogine's innovative scientific legacy lies the concept of dissipative structures—complex, self-organizing patterns emerging spontaneously in open systems actively exchanging energy and materials with their environments. Unlike static equilibrium systems, dissipative structures thrive precisely because of their ongoing interactions with their surroundings, much like a thriving ecosystem continuously reshaping itself through energy exchange and adaptation. This continuous dynamic interaction highlights entropy and irreversibility as constructive rather than destructive forces, emphasizing that systems spontaneously evolve complexity and stability amidst chaos. Prigogine's insights broaden our comprehension of how sophisticated patterns, structures, and behaviors naturally emerge from simple, dynamic interactions, enhancing our understanding across disciplines such as ecology, biology, and artificial intelligence (Prigogine & Stengers, 1984).

In introducing the idea of dissipative structures, Prigogine fundamentally expanded classical thermodynamics. He illuminated how such structures actively harness and dissipate energy, creating stable patterns and order from seemingly chaotic or turbulent conditions. This concept demonstrates that disorder (entropy) and irreversible processes are not merely destructive forces but can be integral drivers of creativity, adaptation, and the emergence of sophisticated, resilient systems. Dissipative structures include diverse phenomena such as cyclones, ecosystems, biological organisms, and even human societies—each continuously transforming energy and resources to maintain coherence and adaptability amidst constant change (Prigogine & Stengers, 1984).

Dissipative structures function similarly to a thriving city that is continuously absorbing energy and resources to sustain growth and complexity. Just as urban areas flourish through constant exchanges of goods, information, and culture, dissipative structures form intricate patterns of order precisely because of their openness to energy and matter flowing through them.

Prigogine's revolutionary insights also illustrate the vital role of irreversibility in the development of complexity. Irreversible processes ensure that dissipative structures evolve uniquely, guided by historical conditions and environmental interactions, making their evolutionary pathways inherently unpredictable. This perspective emphasizes the importance of understanding systems within their real-world contexts, highlighting complexity and unpredictability as intrinsic and valuable characteristics of natural and technological systems alike (Prigogine & Stengers, 1984).

Ilya Prigogine's theory of dissipative structures reveals how systems under far-from-equilibrium conditions can reorganize into higher states of order. Rather than resisting instability, open systems channel flows of energy and matter, exporting entropy into their environment. This process creates the possibility for new structures to emerge.

Figure 4.2 illustrates this dynamic with curving flows of input and output, highlighting how disruption and irreversibility fuel self-organization.

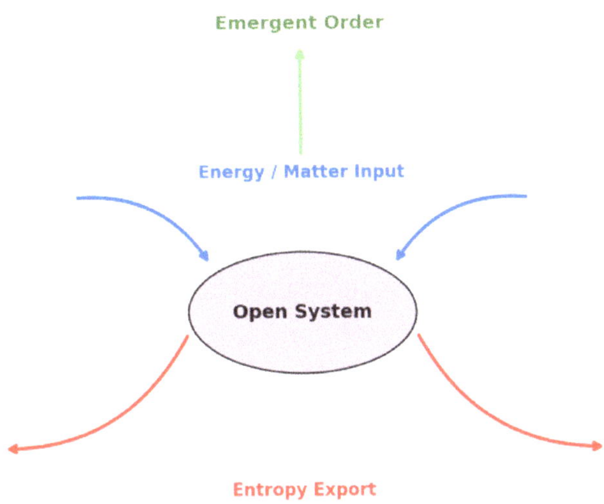

Figure 4.2. Dissipative structures: energy flows, entropy export, and emergent order. Adapted from Prigogine & Stengers (1984).

Note. The figure presents Prigogine's concept of dissipative structures as a flow-based system. Blue arrows represent incoming energy and matter that drive the system. Red arrows represent exported entropy, reflecting irreversible processes that prevent collapse. The upward green arrow represents emergent order, symbolizing new organizational forms. This emphasizes that resilience and adaptability stem from reorganization under conditions of instability, not from the avoidance of disruption.

Practical Relevance of Prigogine's Theory

Prigogine's concept of dissipative structures has profound implications for modern computational technologies, especially in artificial intelligence and quantum computing frameworks. Neural networks embody dissipative structures as they continuously adapt and reorganize based on dynamic data exchanges, enhancing their predictive capabilities and adaptability. Quantum computing similarly exemplifies Prigogine's theories, navigating complex quantum interactions and irreversibility, developing robust computational architectures capable of handling constant change and uncertainty. These insights inform the development of adaptive, resilient computational systems, capable of navigating and innovating within rapidly changing technological landscapes (Nielsen & Chuang, 2010; Preskill, 2018).

Blockchain networks also embody dissipative structures, continually evolving through decentralized interactions and consensus mechanisms, demonstrating resilience and adaptability. Much like a vibrant community marketplace that thrives through dynamic exchanges of ideas and resources, blockchain networks continually adapt and self-organize, creating stable and innovative patterns amidst continuous change.

Quantum computing further exemplifies these principles, characterized by constant interaction and energy exchanges at the quantum level, resulting in highly dynamic, non-equilibrium conditions. Quantum systems, similar to dissipative structures, exhibit spontaneous complexity and adaptation, driven by quantum phenomena such as entanglement, superposition, and decoherence. By leveraging Prigogine's theoretical insights, researchers and technologists can better understand and design quantum systems capable of effectively managing complexity, irreversibility, and inherent uncertainty. Such guidance is vital in crafting computational architecture that remains resilient and adaptive amidst continual technological and environmental changes (Nielsen & Chuang, 2010; Preskill, 2018).

Philosophical Significance of Prigogine's Insights

Prigogine's pioneering concepts challenge traditional deterministic views, embracing complexity, irreversibility, and uncertainty as inherent components of reality. Philosophically, his insights align closely with Bateson's holistic perspective, fostering deeper ecological awareness, adaptability, and ethical responsibility. By emphasizing uncertainty as a creative and productive force, Prigogine encourages us to view unpredictability not as an obstacle but as an essential catalyst for innovation, resilience, and ecological mindfulness. This philosophical shift has profound implications, urging ethical stewardship and thoughtful engagement with technology and ecological systems, emphasizing interconnectedness and the dynamic adaptability necessary for sustainable human advancement (Prigogine & Stengers, 1984).

Prigogine's philosophical contributions encourage a deeper ethical and ecological sensitivity, emphasizing our shared responsibility in navigating complex technological landscapes. His holistic perspective inspires resilience, adaptability, and creative innovation, guiding us toward responsible technological stewardship and thoughtful ecological engagement. Thus, his insights foster a deeper appreciation for complexity, urging us to thoughtfully engage with technology and nature, recognizing the profound interconnectedness and adaptive potential inherent within complex systems (Prigogine & Stengers, 1984).

Reflecting personally on Bateson and Prigogine's insights, I've grown to appreciate complexity not as a challenge to control but as an opportunity for growth, resilience, and innovation guiding our ethical responsibilities toward more adaptive and thoughtful technological stewardship

Synergy and Integration: Bateson, Prigogine, and the Complexity Paradigm

Delving deeply into the theoretical contributions of Gregory Bateson and Ilya Prigogine reveals profound synergies that significantly advance our understanding of complexity. Bateson's systemic thinking, particularly his conceptualization of feedback loops and relational interconnectedness, beautifully complements Prigogine's pioneering ideas about dissipative structures and emergent complexity. Both scholars underscore that complex systems are fundamentally interconnected and characterized by dynamic interactions that spontaneously generate intricate patterns and behaviors. Bateson's insights remind us that communication and systemic feedback are essential forces driving the evolution and adaptation of systems, whereas Prigogine illuminates how systems spontaneously self-organize into structured complexity precisely because they exist far from equilibrium (Bateson, 1972; Prigogine & Stengers, 1984).

This intellectual integration offers a compelling narrative on how complexity naturally emerges, evolves, and stabilizes within dynamic and ever-changing environments. Recognizing Bateson's feedback loops alongside Prigogine's dissipative structures encourages a holistic understanding that complexity is not an anomaly or threat but rather an intrinsic aspect of natural and technological systems. Their combined insights help us better appreciate the delicate balance between stability and innovation, predictability and surprise, encouraging us to manage technological and ecological challenges with wisdom, adaptability, and ethical sensitivity. Together, Bateson and Prigogine provide us with profound conceptual tools and philosophical guidance, fostering responsible stewardship and thoughtful engagement with complex adaptive systems in artificial intelligence, quantum computing, and broader ecological and social contexts.

Practical and Ethical Implications Moving Forward

The integration of Bateson's systemic thinking and Prigogine's theories on dissipative structures presents significant practical and ethical implications for the future of technological governance and organizational management. Effectively applying their integrated insights necessitates adopting adaptive governance frameworks, characterized by flexibility, continuous learning, and responsiveness. Organizations must embrace robust interpretability frameworks that enable transparency and ethical accountability in AI-driven technologies and quantum computing environments. These interpretative tools provide essential clarity, enabling stakeholders to understand how complex systems evolve and make decisions, ensuring technology aligns with societal values and ethical norms (Floridi & Cowls, 2019).

In today's rapidly advancing world of artificial intelligence where innovations such as self-driving cars and AI-powered healthcare diagnostics are becoming commonplace the need for flexible and responsive governance is more critical than ever. Much like a city's transportation system continually adjusts traffic lights and routes to prevent congestion, our approach to governing AI must also dynamically evolve. This adaptability allows us to swiftly address ethical challenges, including unintended algorithmic biases and threats to individual privacy, ensuring these advanced technologies serve humanity safely and responsibly.

Moreover, proactive ethical oversight and risk management strategies become critically important as systems become increasingly autonomous and interconnected. Organizations must recognize systemic interdependencies, regularly evaluating technological impacts on social, ecological, and economic environments. This continuous evaluation helps identify potential ethical dilemmas, mitigate biases, and ensure responsible technological deployment. Dynamic adjustments to governance policies and procedures, informed by ongoing monitoring and stakeholder feedback, further enhance systemic resilience and ethical responsiveness (Cohen et al., 2024).

Integrating Bateson's and Prigogine's insights underscores our collective responsibility in navigating complex technological landscapes. Their profound philosophical perspectives guide us toward embracing complexity with adaptability, resilience, and ecological sensitivity. By recognizing our interconnectedness within broader systemic contexts, organizations and individuals can foster sustainable technological advancements, ensuring that innovation not only enhances human capabilities but also promotes ethical integrity, ecological sustainability, and societal well-being.

The adaptive governance loop illustrates the iterative cycle of monitoring, interpreting, deciding, intervening, verifying, and learning within complex systems. This framework emphasizes how governance is not a linear process but a dynamic feedback-driven cycle. Surrounding thematic domains—including interpretability and transparency, dissipative structures, Bateson's feedback loops, AI and quantum applications, outcomes, stakeholders and values, and ethical oversight and risk—each provide critical perspectives that shape and are shaped by the governance process. Arrows within the model depict the continuous bidirectional flow of information, underscoring the interconnected and evolving nature of adaptive decision-making. Figure 4.1 presents this conceptual model, integrating insights from complexity theory, cybernetics, and technological governance.

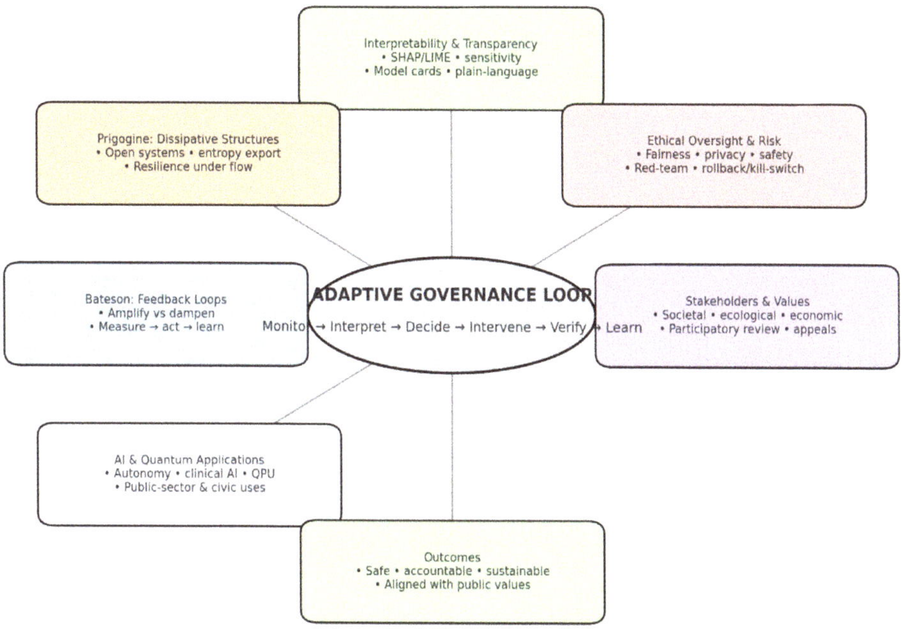

Figure 4.3. *Adaptive governance loop. Adapted from Bateson (2000/1972), Prigogine & Stengers (1984), and Floridi & Cowls (2019).*

Note. This figure depicts the adaptive governance loop as a cyclical process of monitoring, interpreting, deciding, intervening, and verifying. Surrounding domains—interpretability and transparency, dissipative structures, feedback loops, AI and quantum applications, outcomes, stakeholders and values, and ethical oversight and risk—provide critical inputs and constraints that shape governance decisions. The continuous bidirectional flow of influence reflects the interconnected, evolving nature of decision-making in complex systems.

Conclusion

By deeply engaging with Gregory Bateson's and Ilya Prigogine's groundbreaking insights, we profoundly enrich our understanding of complexity, interconnectedness, and the adaptability inherent in complex systems. Bateson's systemic thinking, with its profound recognition of interconnected feedback loops, fosters a deepened appreciation of how every action, communication, and interaction within a system can resonate far beyond its immediate context. This awareness guides us toward embracing holistic perspectives rather than isolated, linear approaches, enabling us to more thoughtfully navigate the intricate web of interactions that characterize modern technological, ecological, and social systems.

Similarly, Prigogine's pioneering work on dissipative structures and non-equilibrium thermodynamics invites us to recognize complexity and unpredictability as integral components of natural and technological processes. By understanding that order and complexity spontaneously emerge within dynamic, far-from-equilibrium environments, we can better appreciate and harness the creative potential of uncertainty and irreversibility. Prigogine's theories teach us that instead of seeking rigid control over complex systems, we should cultivate resilience, adaptability, and an ongoing openness to emergent possibilities, equipping us with valuable philosophical insights for responsibly engaging with rapidly evolving technological landscapes.

Integrating Bateson's and Prigogine's perspectives offers powerful philosophical and practical tools for addressing the complexities and ethical challenges inherent in modern technology and governance. Their combined legacy emphasizes the necessity of adaptive governance frameworks, capable of dynamic evolution in response to ongoing technological, ecological, and social changes. By continuously reevaluating and refining our governance approaches based on evolving insights and stakeholder feedback, we enhance our ability to navigate the ethical, social, and environmental complexities that arise with advanced technological systems such as artificial intelligence and quantum computing.

Moreover, embracing Bateson's and Prigogine's ideas helps us maintain a firm ethical foundation, ensuring that technological advancements reflect and uphold human values, promote societal well-being, and prioritize ecological sustainability. Their insights remind us of our shared responsibility to thoughtfully steward technology in ways that harmonize human progress with ecological integrity and social equity. By cultivating an awareness of our interconnectedness and systemic interdependencies, we are better positioned to ensure that technological progress serves broader humanistic goals rather than narrow interests.

In essence, the profound insights of Bateson and Prigogine inspire a humanistic, systemic, and ecologically sensitive approach to technology, emphasizing adaptability, resilience, and ethical integrity. As we continue advancing technologically, their pioneering contributions provide essential philosophical and practical guidance, equipping us to responsibly navigate complexity, embrace uncertainty, and ensure technology's role remains aligned with our shared human aspirations and ecological responsibilities.

Reflecting on these pioneers' insights provides me not just academic knowledge but also practical wisdom. Their ideas encourage an appreciation of complexity's beauty and creativity, inspiring greater responsibility and humility in our technological engagements.

Chapter 5: Murray Gell-Mann and Claude Shannon – Complexity, Information, and Adaptive Systems

Introduction

As we journey deeper into the intriguing and interconnected landscape of complexity, our exploration has already uncovered invaluable insights from chaos theory, quantum computing, genetic algorithms, and systems thinking. Much like explorers charting uncharted territory, we have discovered how seemingly simple interactions can lead to extraordinary complexity and how small changes can ripple outward to produce significant, sometimes unpredictable consequences. Having laid this robust foundation, we now turn our attention to two remarkable visionaries whose groundbreaking work enriches our understanding even further: Murray Gell-Mann and Claude Shannon.

Murray Gell-Mann, a pioneering physicist and Nobel laureate, invites us to recognize complexity as something intrinsically natural, intuitive, and essential. He envisioned the world as a vast network of interactions, akin to an intricate tapestry where individual threads weave together to form an elegant and coherent pattern. Gell-Mann's notion of complex adaptive systems reveals the remarkable capacity of simple elements to spontaneously self-organize into sophisticated structures. Imagine a bustling rainforest ecosystem: each organism, from the smallest insect to towering trees, operates independently, yet their collective interactions generate a stable, diverse, and resilient environment. Similarly, Gell-Mann's concepts help us appreciate how economic markets, human societies, and technological systems continuously adapt, evolving naturally toward greater coherence and resilience through their complex interactions.

Complementing Gell-Mann's insights, Claude Shannon, widely acknowledged as the father of information theory, offers profound clarity into how information shapes complexity itself. Shannon perceived information not merely as data, but as a meaningful measure of uncertainty and surprise. He eloquently described information as an unexpected twist in a compelling story, captivating precisely because of its unpredictability. Shannon's concept of entropy vividly portrays how uncertainty and variability form the very essence of effective communication and innovation. Picture a storyteller who masterfully balances predictability with unexpected surprises, continuously engaging their audience. In the same vein, Shannon's insights illuminate how information theory underpins communication networks, data storage systems, cryptographic security, and modern artificial intelligence, profoundly influencing how we manage complexity and uncertainty in today's digital age.

Together, the theories and contributions of Gell-Mann and Shannon not only bridge physics, complexity science, and information theory but also provide crucial philosophical and practical tools for responsibly navigating today's advanced technological environments. Their combined insights inspire us to embrace complexity and uncertainty not as threats, but as opportunities for growth, creativity, and resilience. As we delve deeper into their transformative ideas, we will explore real-world examples, compelling case studies, and intuitive analogies that clarify how these foundational theories profoundly shape the governance, innovation, and ethical stewardship of contemporary technology.

Murray Gell-Mann: Complexity and Adaptive Systems

Biography and Academic Contributions

Murray Gell-Mann (1929–2019), celebrated for his extraordinary intellectual curiosity and groundbreaking scientific achievements, left an enduring legacy that spans theoretical physics, complexity science, and interdisciplinary scholarship. Born and raised in New York City, Gell-Mann was recognized early on for his extraordinary analytical abilities and relentless pursuit of knowledge. This passion propelled him to earn his doctorate in physics from MIT, laying the foundation for his influential career that reshaped our understanding of the fundamental building blocks of nature and complex adaptive systems.

Awarded the Nobel Prize in Physics in 1969 for his discovery and classification of elementary particles known as quarks, Gell-Mann's early contributions fundamentally redefined our understanding of matter at the subatomic level. Yet, his insatiable curiosity soon drew him beyond traditional physics toward broader inquiries about how complexity and order spontaneously emerge from simpler interactions. Driven by his expansive vision, he co-founded the renowned Santa Fe Institute, an innovative research hub dedicated explicitly to the interdisciplinary exploration of complexity science. Under his guidance, the institute became a vibrant intellectual ecosystem, fostering collaborations that bridged fields as diverse as biology, economics, psychology, and computation.

Throughout his extensive career, Gell-Mann continually sought meaningful connections across disciplines, championing the belief that profound insights often arise at the intersections of different fields. His landmark book, "The Quark and the Jaguar," beautifully encapsulates his interdisciplinary spirit, illustrating parallels between elementary particle physics and the adaptive strategies observed in biological ecosystems, cultural evolution, and human decision-making processes. For instance, just as quarks combine and interact to create complex atomic structures, Gell-Mann observed how humans and societies evolve through diverse interactions and collective behaviors, generating sophisticated social systems and cultural innovations.

Gell-Mann's integrative approach to complexity not only challenged traditional disciplinary boundaries but also provided essential philosophical insights into adaptability, resilience, and interconnectedness. His legacy reminds us of our innate human capacity for innovation, adaptability, and collaborative exploration. By embracing complexity as an intrinsic and enriching aspect of life, Gell-Mann’s insights encourage us to thoughtfully engage with the unpredictable and interconnected world around us, guiding us toward sustainable, adaptive, and ethically mindful technological advancements.

Key Principles: Complex Adaptive Systems

Murray Gell-Mann's theory of Complex Adaptive Systems (CAS) provides powerful insights into how intricate and sophisticated patterns naturally emerge from simple, local interactions among numerous independent components. Rather than relying on rigid top-down control, CAS theory highlights the spontaneous, bottom-up emergence of complexity, stability, and resilience. To humanize this concept, consider the dynamics of a lively marketplace: each vendor operates independently, responding directly to customer preferences and adjusting prices, quality, and availability. Without any centralized coordination, this vibrant ecosystem naturally adjusts to demand, creating patterns of stability and adaptation that ensure the marketplace thrives and endures through changing economic conditions.

Similarly, Gell-Mann recognized that complexity in natural ecosystems, like tropical rainforests or coral reefs, arises spontaneously through countless decentralized interactions. In these environments, individual species continuously adapt their behavior based on local interactions finding food, avoiding predators, and engaging in mutually beneficial relationships. Collectively, these interactions create an ecological equilibrium that is not only incredibly rich and diverse but also resilient, capable of withstanding significant disturbances or environmental changes without collapsing.

This principle is vividly exemplified by ant colonies, where individual ants operate without centralized instructions yet collectively build sophisticated colonies, forage efficiently, and adapt dynamically to environmental challenges. Each ant responds directly to local cues, such as chemical trails or food availability, and collectively these individual interactions produce remarkable coordination, resilience, and adaptability at the colony level.

Extending these insights into human organizational structures, Gell-Mann's CAS theory helps illuminate why decentralized, adaptive organizations often thrive in turbulent, rapidly changing environments. For instance, innovative technology firms or agile startups typically employ flat, decentralized decision-making structures, empowering individuals and small teams to respond swiftly and flexibly to shifting market conditions, customer preferences, and technological advances. This adaptability creates robust organizational systems capable of enduring unpredictability and leveraging opportunities for growth and innovation.

Philosophically, the CAS framework advocates for humility, adaptability, and ethical responsibility, emphasizing our interconnectedness with broader social, ecological, and technological systems. Recognizing that complexity arises naturally from decentralized interactions encourages us to adopt governance and ethical frameworks that embrace flexibility, transparency, and continuous learning. In doing so, we can more effectively manage the inherent uncertainty and complexity of contemporary systems whether they're ecological, economic, technological, or social, fostering sustainability and ethical stewardship.

Gell-Mann's concept of Complex Adaptive Systems underscores a profound lesson: embracing complexity and adaptability enables us to navigate uncertainty not as an obstacle but as an opportunity for resilience, innovation, and meaningful growth.

Murray Gell-Mann's concept of Complex Adaptive Systems (CAS) highlights how complex behaviors emerge from the interactions of simple, independent agents without centralized control. Such systems adapt dynamically, responding to environmental pressures through localized interactions that collectively form resilient, self-organizing structures.

Figure 5.1 illustrates this concept by depicting agents interacting within a network, where emergent patterns arise from decentralized connections rather than top-down coordination.

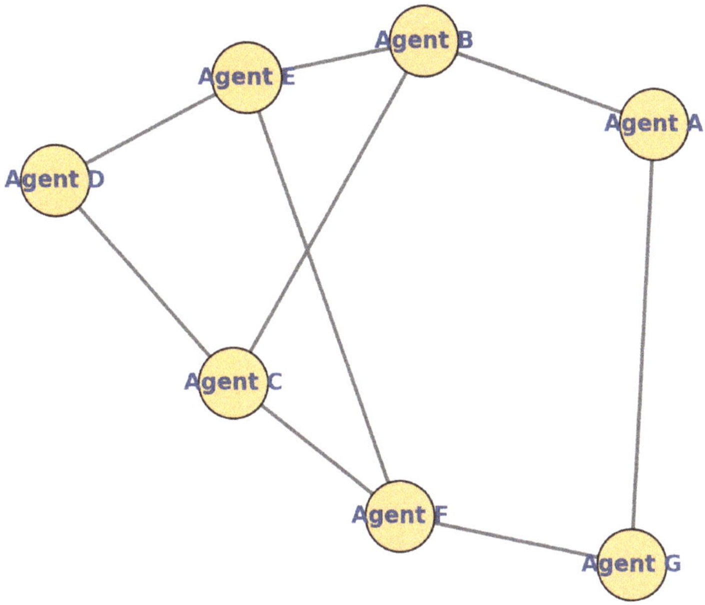

Figure 5.1. *Complex Adaptive System (CAS) network. Adapted from Gell-Mann (1994).*

Note. The figure represents a complex adaptive system, where independent agents interact locally, producing emergent patterns and systemic resilience. Such networks are evident in ecological systems, economies, and social structures. Adapted from Gell-Mann's principles of complexity described in The Quark and the Jaguar.

Complex Adaptive Systems (CAS) often evolve toward highly clustered, triangular networks. These triads emerge because agents interacting locally with two others are likely to form a closed loop, creating resilience and redundancy. In ecosystems, social networks, and markets, triangular relationships enhance stability by providing multiple pathways for interaction and adaptation. Figure 5.2 illustrates this principle by depicting agents connected through overlapping triangles, demonstrating how local clustering contributes to global system resilience and self-organization.

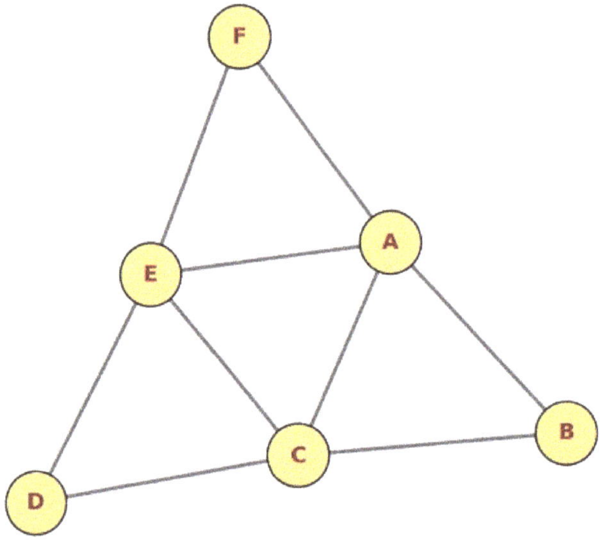

Figure 5.2. *Complex Adaptive System: Triangular network clustering. Adapted from Gell-Mann (1994).*

Note. This figure highlights how consistent triangular (triadic) structures emerge in complex adaptive systems. Such clustering provides redundancy and resilience, as multiple connections stabilize interactions even if one link fails. This property is evident in ecological food webs, social communities, and economic exchange networks. Adapted from Gell-Mann's framework of complexity in The Quark and the Jaguar.

Practical Applications

Complex Adaptive Systems (CAS) principles, articulated eloquently by Murray Gell-Mann, extend far beyond theoretical science, profoundly impacting various real-world domains including ecology, economics, organizational leadership, and technological innovation. The CAS framework provides practical tools that allow us to understand, predict, and effectively manage complex interactions and dynamics across diverse settings.

In ecology, CAS principles are crucial for managing environmental conservation and sustainability efforts. Consider a rainforest ecosystem, where biodiversity and ecosystem stability emerge from countless decentralized interactions among species, soil nutrients, rainfall patterns, and climate conditions. Conservation biologists and ecologists use CAS principles to create effective conservation strategies, recognizing that supporting biodiversity and ecosystem resilience relies not on top-down controls but on facilitating natural interactions and adaptations. For example, the reintroduction of wolves into Yellowstone National Park illustrates CAS principles in action; the wolves' return triggered a cascade of interactions, positively impacting vegetation, river stability, and numerous other species. This restoration demonstrated how decentralized ecological interactions drive emergent complexity and resilience, underscoring the importance of embracing natural adaptive processes in environmental management (Ripple & Beschta, 2012).

In the realm of economics, CAS offers valuable insights into how markets evolve and how companies adapt to continuous uncertainty and competition. Markets, composed of diverse participants such as consumers, businesses, regulatory bodies interact dynamically without central orchestration, leading to spontaneous adaptations and innovations. Consider the technology industry, where startups continuously innovate by adapting rapidly to consumer preferences, technological breakthroughs, and competitive pressures. The rise of streaming services like Netflix exemplifies this principle vividly. Initially, Netflix adapted swiftly from a mail-order DVD rental business to online streaming by closely responding to consumer preferences, technological advancements, and competitive market pressures. Its decentralized, agile organizational structure allowed it to innovate continuously and maintain resilience amidst rapid technological and market changes, effectively applying CAS principles in business strategy (McCord, 2017).

CAS principles also offer profound practical insights into organizational theory and leadership. Organizations that thrive amidst complexity often adopt decentralized decision-making structures, empowering individuals and teams to respond flexibly and rapidly to changing circumstances. The agile software development methodology demonstrates this concept well. Agile teams operate through iterative cycles, dynamically adjusting strategies based on real-time feedback and continuous learning. This decentralized approach fosters adaptability, innovation, and resilience within the organizational system, reflecting CAS principles directly. Such organizations recognize that navigating uncertainty effectively involves embracing complexity, rather than attempting rigid top-down control, promoting adaptability and ongoing innovation (Cockburn & Highsmith, 2001).

Furthermore, CAS concepts significantly influence technological innovation and artificial intelligence development. Neural networks and machine learning systems illustrate adaptive complexity vividly. For instance, autonomous vehicle systems rely on decentralized sensor inputs including cameras, lidar, radar, and GPS. Each sensor independently analyzes and interacts with complex real-world conditions. These decentralized interactions enable vehicles to adapt in real-time, creating robust, flexible, and innovative driving strategies. Tesla's self-driving vehicles exemplify this practical application, showcasing how decentralized information flows and adaptive interactions create sophisticated emergent behaviors that effectively navigate real-world complexity (Endsley, 2019).

The practical relevance of CAS extends broadly across diverse fields, offering powerful tools for understanding, managing, and leveraging complexity effectively. Embracing CAS principles allows organizations, ecosystems, economic markets, and technological systems to navigate uncertainty gracefully, fostering innovation, resilience, and sustainable adaptation. By adopting a humanistic perspective grounded in adaptability and interconnectedness, we can responsibly steward complex systems in ways that enhance human flourishing, societal well-being, and ecological sustainability.

Case Study: The Resilient Economic Systems

An illuminating example of Complex Adaptive Systems (CAS) in action is the resilience displayed by certain economic systems during and after financial downturns. A key factor that determines an economy's ability to withstand and rebound from crises is its adaptability or more specifically, how rapidly and effectively it responds to unexpected disruptions. Resilient economic systems exhibit decentralized decision-making, dynamic feedback loops, and diverse economic structures, enabling swift adaptations that lead to stronger recoveries.

Consider the Scandinavian economic model, particularly Sweden's response to the 2008 global financial crisis. Rather than imposing strictly centralized control measures, Sweden embraced decentralized decision-making across various economic sectors. Its policy frameworks supported adaptability, flexibility, and local responsiveness, enabling businesses and financial institutions to rapidly adjust strategies based on real-time conditions. Moreover, Sweden's robust social safety nets and diversified economy further provided a stabilizing influence, ensuring resilience and quick recovery from the crisis. By leveraging decentralized governance and adaptive feedback loops, Sweden exemplifies how complex adaptive principles can foster economic resilience and sustainability (Bergman & Hutchison, 2015).

In contrast, nations with heavily centralized control or rigid economic structures found recovery slower and more challenging. For instance, economies overly reliant on singular industries or inflexible governance structures experienced prolonged disruptions, highlighting vulnerabilities that emerge from limited adaptability and insufficient feedback mechanisms. The Greek economy during the European debt crisis provides a poignant illustration; heavily centralized decision-making, limited economic diversification, and delayed policy responses significantly hampered recovery efforts, prolonging economic hardship (Papadimitriou et al., 2013).

Furthermore, economic resilience through CAS principles can also be observed at the corporate level. Companies employing adaptive business strategies and decentralized decision-making consistently outperform competitors during economic shocks. For instance, during the COVID-19 pandemic, firms like Amazon and Zoom thrived precisely because of their flexible, decentralized approaches to decision-making and rapid responsiveness to market changes. Amazon dynamically adjusted supply chains and logistics operations to meet surging demand, while Zoom quickly scaled its infrastructure to support increased global usage. Their adaptability illustrates CAS principles effectively, showing how decentralized structures and real-time responsiveness create resilience and growth even amid disruption (Yeganeh, 2021).

Thus, the practical implications of CAS in economic contexts highlight the critical importance of fostering decentralized governance structures, economic diversity, and robust feedback loops. Economies and organizations built upon these adaptive principles demonstrate greater resilience and capacity to thrive, even in the face of severe disruptions. By embracing CAS insights, policymakers, business leaders, and communities can cultivate more resilient, responsive, and sustainable economic systems capable of navigating future uncertainties with flexibility and resilience.

Philosophical Implications

Murray Gell-Mann's profound insight into complex adaptive systems invite a philosophical shift in how we perceive uncertainty, complexity, and interconnectedness. Rather than viewing the world through the lens of predictable, linear cause-and-effect relationships, Gell-Mann encourages us to embrace the intrinsic unpredictability and emergent creativity that arise naturally from complex interactions. This philosophical transformation requires moving beyond conventional deterministic viewpoints where outcomes are considered entirely predictable if all initial conditions are known to recognizing and valuing uncertainty as an essential and enriching aspect of reality.

A compelling analogy illustrating this philosophy can be found in the art of improvisational jazz. Each musician brings individual creativity and unpredictability to the performance. Rather than following a rigid, predetermined musical script, the ensemble navigates uncertainty together, dynamically adapting to spontaneous cues and interactions. In this scenario, uncertainty and unpredictability are not threats but rather powerful sources of creativity, innovation, and emotional resonance. Likewise, Gell-Mann's philosophical perspective underscores the importance of embracing complexity as a source of continuous innovation, adaptation, and evolution.

Furthermore, Gell-Mann's philosophy promotes a deeper appreciation for interconnectedness within natural and human-made systems. His insights remind us of the profound ways in which ecosystems, economies, and social communities are interconnected, operating not in isolation but as integral components of broader adaptive networks. For instance, the COVID-19 pandemic revealed starkly how interconnected global health, economics, and ecological stability truly are decisions in one region rapidly reverberate globally. By acknowledging and respecting these interdependencies, policymakers, organizational leaders, and individuals can adopt more thoughtful, holistic strategies for adaptive governance and ethical stewardship of technological and ecological systems (Walker et al., 2020).

Gell-Mann's emphasis on adaptability and resilience further extends to our ethical responsibilities. His work invites reflection on how adaptability can serve as a guiding principle for ethical decision-making in increasingly complex and unpredictable environments. Ethical frameworks grounded in adaptability and resilience promote proactive responsiveness to emerging challenges, guiding leaders and institutions to remain flexible, innovative, and ethically responsible amidst constant change. For example, ethical considerations in artificial intelligence, such as algorithmic transparency and fairness, benefit profoundly from an adaptive perspective, emphasizing continuous learning, iteration, and responsiveness rather than static guidelines (Floridi & Cowls, 2019).

Embracing Gell-Mann's philosophy of complexity equips us with the cognitive and ethical tools necessary for navigating contemporary technological, ecological, and social challenges. By viewing complexity and uncertainty as opportunities for innovation and growth, we foster a humanistic approach characterized by humility, adaptability, and continuous learning. Gell-Mann's insights thus provide philosophical encouragement to explore uncertainty courageously, embracing complexity as a source of creativity, resilience, and sustainable advancement for the betterment of humanity and the planet.

Claude Shannon: Information, Entropy, and Uncertainty

Biography and Academic Contributions

Claude Shannon (1916–2001) stands out as one of the twentieth century's most influential thinkers, celebrated for pioneering information theory and reshaping our understanding of communication, data, and complexity. Born in Petoskey, Michigan, Shannon's insatiable curiosity and innate creativity were evident early in life, paving the way for a distinguished academic career marked by groundbreaking insights and interdisciplinary innovation. After completing degrees at the University of Michigan and MIT, Shannon joined Bell Laboratories, a renowned innovation hub where he would profoundly transform communication technologies and computational sciences.

Shannon's seminal 1948 publication, "A Mathematical Theory of Communication," revolutionized how scientists and engineers conceptualize information. His groundbreaking work introduced the concept of information entropy, fundamentally changing our understanding of data, uncertainty, and communication. Shannon envisioned information as something far richer than mere data. He saw it as the reduction of uncertainty, analogous to a detective uncovering a clue to solve a mystery or a writer carefully crafting plot twists to captivate an audience. This intuitive, human-centered view emphasized that effective communication thrives precisely because of the careful management of uncertainty, unpredictability, and novelty.

His foundational insights significantly influenced not only telecommunications but also the development of computing, cryptography, and artificial intelligence. Shannon's theory provided the intellectual bedrock for practical innovations, including data compression algorithms, secure encryption protocols, and modern machine learning techniques. For example, digital encryption today utilizes Shannon's insights by deliberately introducing randomness and entropy, ensuring secure data transmission and protecting information privacy in an increasingly interconnected world.

Beyond his technical contributions, Shannon was also deeply interested in how information shapes human creativity, decision-making, and societal dynamics. His playful inventions, such as a mechanical mouse navigating mazes, showcased his belief in creativity, experimentation, and curiosity as fundamental drivers of innovation and learning. Shannon's multidisciplinary vision and playful experimentation continue to inspire engineers, researchers, and philosophers, underscoring the value of embracing uncertainty and complexity as creative and enriching aspects of life.

Claude Shannon's remarkable legacy goes beyond technological innovations, offering profound philosophical insights into how we communicate, innovate, and navigate uncertainty. His work challenges us to appreciate the rich interplay between order and unpredictability, guiding us to responsibly manage complex systems with humility, creativity, and ethical mindfulness.

Fundamental Concepts: Information and Entropy

Claude Shannon's groundbreaking concept of information entropy transformed how we understand and measure uncertainty and complexity in information systems. To humanize this complex idea, imagine walking through a dense forest path for the first time. Each turn presents unexpected sights and sounds, keeping you alert and engaged. Similarly, Shannon perceived information not merely as static data but as a dynamic measure of uncertainty, the extent to which the outcome or content of a message cannot be predicted beforehand. The greater the unpredictability or surprise, the higher the informational value. In this sense, Shannon highlighted unpredictability as a core attribute of meaningful information, proposing that it is precisely the surprise element that makes communication genuinely engaging and insightful (Shannon, 1948).

Shannon's theory also offers an illuminating analogy in the realm of music composition. When listening to a new musical piece, what often captivates listeners is not just harmony, but the unexpectedness of melody and rhythm. The listener's uncertainty about what comes next creates intrigue and emotional engagement. Shannon entropy captures this essence mathematically, emphasizing that information becomes meaningful when it reduces uncertainty or adds novelty and surprise. In communication, whether through stories, music, or data exchanges, unpredictability and entropy create deeper connections and more impactful interactions (Shannon, 1948).

In project management and risk management contexts, this concept can be paralleled with the way teams assess and respond to uncertainty in complex projects. Just as a musical composition's unexpected elements keep the audience engaged, unforeseen risks and emerging information can significantly influence project outcomes. For example, in large-scale infrastructure projects, the discovery of unexpected regulatory changes or supply chain disruptions introduces "informational surprises" that alter the course of planning and execution. High-entropy scenarios where many outcomes are possible require adaptive planning, scenario analysis, and responsive communication to maintain project alignment.

Similarly, in risk management, identifying and quantifying uncertain events (such as shifting market conditions, geopolitical changes, or unforeseen stakeholder concerns) transforms uncertainty into actionable insight. By reducing the "entropy" of the situation through structured analysis, decision-makers can reallocate resources, revise timelines, or adjust strategies, enhancing the project's resilience and likelihood of success.

Claude Shannon's concept of entropy in information theory (Shannon, 1948) provides a powerful analogy for understanding risk management. In this framework, entropy, in Shannon's sense, reflects the fog of multiple potential outcomes before clarity emerges through information. Risk management processes, such as data collection and analysis, serve to reduce entropy, enabling more informed decisions and optimized allocation of resources.

Figure 5.3 illustrates this analogy, showing how information gathering reduces uncertainty and improves decision-making outcomes.

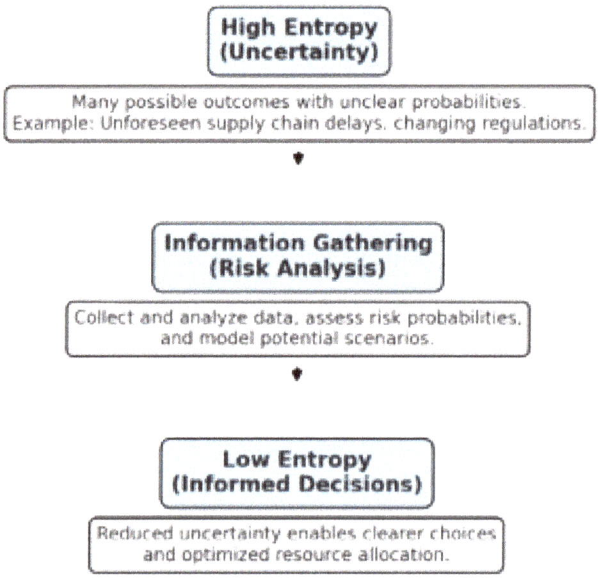

Figure 5.3. *Analogy between Shannon's Entropy and Risk Management.*

Note. Shannon reframed entropy as the uncertainty in communication. Today, this translates into the ambiguity leaders face in decision-making until data reduces the fog. Figure created by the author (2025) to illustrate the relationship between Shannon's entropy and uncertainty reduction in risk management processes.

Shannon's principles are fundamental across various modern technological domains, including artificial intelligence, cryptography, and data science. Information entropy serves as a foundational tool in digital communication, enabling engineers to optimize information encoding and transmission efficiency. For example, file compression technologies such as JPEG for images or MP3 for audio rely on Shannon's entropy calculations to minimize data redundancy, effectively reducing file sizes while preserving essential information quality. By identifying and compressing predictable patterns, these technologies highlight entropy's practical relevance in managing uncertainty and complexity in everyday digital interactions (Cover & Thomas, 2006).

Shannon's ideas also intersect seamlessly with complexity and chaos theory. Complex adaptive systems, whether natural ecosystems or computational networks, inherently rely on uncertainty as a driving force for evolution and innovation. Uncertainty facilitates adaptation, encouraging systems to evolve through continuous experimentation and exploration. Consider the example of evolutionary biology, where genetic mutations introduce unpredictability, fostering adaptive traits and species diversification. Similarly, Shannon entropy quantifies how uncertainty fuels adaptive innovation in technology and communication, underlining the intrinsic value of unpredictability within dynamic, evolving systems (Gleick, 2011).

Shannon's entropy challenges deterministic views by underscoring uncertainty and unpredictability as not only inevitable but also essential for growth and creativity. It encourages us to embrace complexity, unpredictability, and surprise as opportunities rather than obstacles. From a humanistic standpoint, Shannon's concept invites reflection on how uncertainty enriches human experience, creativity, and communication. By recognizing unpredictability as a natural and valuable aspect of life and technology, Shannon's entropy theory promotes adaptability, ethical responsiveness, and innovation rooted in continuous learning and exploration.

In summary, Shannon's fundamental concepts of information and entropy offer profound insights into how uncertainty, complexity, and unpredictability drive meaningful communication, innovation, and adaptive growth. By appreciating the creative potential embedded within uncertainty, we become better equipped to responsibly steward technology, enhance human creativity, and foster resilient, adaptive societies.

Practical Relevance

Claude Shannon's groundbreaking ideas have deeply influenced our practical engagement with modern technology, significantly shaping innovations in communication, computing, artificial intelligence, and cybersecurity. Shannon's foundational insights into information entropy directly translate into the effectiveness of various technologies that permeate everyday life, enabling efficient and meaningful information exchange and management.

Consider modern data compression as a fundamental aspect of how we store, share, and process information. Imagine packing for a long journey where you must carefully decide what to take along, prioritizing essentials and eliminating redundancy. Similarly, data compression algorithms leverage Shannon's entropy to distinguish critical information from redundant data. These algorithms reduce file sizes by recognizing predictable patterns and removing unnecessary repetition, making digital storage and data transmission incredibly efficient. Common formats such as JPEG for images and MP3 for audio files owe their compactness and quality preservation directly to Shannon's principles, emphasizing the practical relevance of entropy in everyday technology (Cover & Thomas, 2006).

Beyond compression, Shannon's principles profoundly shape communication technologies, ensuring clear and efficient data transmission even under challenging conditions. Wireless networks, satellite communications, and cellular technologies regularly rely on information entropy to optimize signal transmission. For instance, consider satellite communication systems that must transmit clear signals over vast distances amidst noise and interference. Shannon's theories guide engineers in designing communication protocols that dynamically adjust transmission rates, error correction, and data encoding to maintain clarity and efficiency, even when signals encounter significant environmental disruptions (Sklar, 2001).

In the realm of cybersecurity, Shannon entropy has essential practical implications, particularly in cryptography. Secure encryption methods, such as those used in online banking or private messaging, rely heavily on principles derived from Shannon's work. High entropy, or unpredictability, is deliberately introduced into cryptographic keys and protocols, making them incredibly resistant to unauthorized access. This application of Shannon's insights ensures that private and sensitive information remains secure, highlighting entropy's fundamental role in maintaining privacy and data security in our increasingly digital world (Paar & Pelzl, 2009).

Quantum computing represents another significant frontier where Shannon's theories provide practical guidance. Quantum systems, characterized by inherent uncertainty and probabilistic behaviors, require highly sophisticated communication protocols that can manage unpredictability effectively. Quantum cryptography, quantum key distribution, and quantum error correction methods directly utilize Shannon's concepts to ensure that quantum data transmission remains accurate and efficient, despite the fundamental uncertainties intrinsic to quantum mechanics. Researchers and engineers rely on entropy-based principles to innovate new quantum protocols, enhancing security, reliability, and adaptability within emerging quantum computing infrastructures (Nielsen & Chuang, 2010; Preskill, 2018).

Moreover, Shannon's principles significantly underpin artificial intelligence systems. Machine learning algorithms leverage entropy measures to manage uncertainty, optimize decision-making processes, and enhance predictive accuracy. For example, decision tree algorithms utilize entropy calculations to choose optimal paths for decision-making, allowing AI models to adapt dynamically to complex, real-world scenarios. Such approaches enable AI systems to operate effectively across diverse applications, from personalized recommendation systems and healthcare diagnostics to autonomous vehicles and real-time market analysis (Russell & Norvig, 2020).

Shannon's foundational theories serve as essential cornerstones in practical technological advancements, from everyday digital communications to groundbreaking quantum and artificial intelligence innovations. His insights into information entropy remind us that effectively managing uncertainty and complexity is central not just to technological efficiency, but also to fostering meaningful, secure, and innovative interactions within an increasingly interconnected world.

Case Study: Cryptography and Cybersecurity

Cryptographic systems exemplify Shannon's information entropy principles. Secure encryption algorithms deliberately introduce high entropy, making encoded data appear random and unpredictable. These principles secure data against unauthorized access, forming the backbone of modern cybersecurity practices, and illustrating the ongoing practical significance of Shannon's foundational theories. For example, the Advanced Encryption Standard (AES) uses complex substitution and permutation operations to maximize entropy, ensuring that even if an attacker intercepts the encrypted message, the data appears as an indecipherable stream of random bits without the correct decryption key.

Philosophical Significance

Claude Shannon's groundbreaking insights into information theory reach far beyond technical applications, resonating deeply with philosophical questions about human cognition, creativity, and ethical engagement with technology. His perspective, emphasizing the inherent value of uncertainty and unpredictability, invites us to reconsider our traditional views on complexity and control. Shannon prompts us to understand that complexity and uncertainty are not merely barriers to be managed or eliminated, but rather powerful sources of creativity, innovation, and genuine human experience.

Philosophically, Shannon's concept of entropy enriches our understanding of human cognition and creativity. Consider the process of artistic creation whether composing music, writing literature, or crafting visual arts. Artists rely heavily on unpredictability and surprise; their work captivates precisely because it defies expectations and offers novel interpretations. Shannon's theory elegantly quantifies this dynamic, helping us see creativity as fundamentally driven by uncertainty and surprise. Thus, embracing uncertainty, rather than fearing or avoiding it, becomes a philosophical principle that encourages creative exploration and continuous discovery (Shannon, 1948; Gleick, 2011).

Moreover, Shannon's work highlights the philosophical value of adaptability and resilience in managing complexity. As we navigate an increasingly information-rich and technologically sophisticated world, embracing Shannon's insights encourages adaptability and responsive decision-making. Analogously, navigating a complex landscape without a predetermined path requires ongoing adaptation and openness to unexpected routes and outcomes. Philosophically, this teaches us that resilience emerges not through rigid planning, but through flexible responsiveness and the ability to continuously learn and adapt (Taleb, 2012).

From an ethical standpoint, Shannon's theory carries significant implications for how we responsibly manage information and technological innovation. By emphasizing uncertainty and complexity as integral and valuable, Shannon advocates for ethical frameworks that prioritize transparency, privacy, and accountability. For example, the modern proliferation of data-intensive technologies such as social media platforms, personalized recommendation systems, and smart devices has raised critical ethical questions about privacy and information control. Shannon's philosophical viewpoint underscores the ethical importance of transparency in communication and technology, ensuring that users clearly understand how information is managed, secured, and shared. Ethical technology stewardship, therefore, becomes rooted in embracing uncertainty not as a hindrance but as an opportunity for responsible innovation and deeper human connection (Floridi & Cowls, 2019).

Furthermore, Shannon's philosophy invites reflection on our broader societal responsibilities. As technological systems grow increasingly complex and autonomous, there is a pressing need to ensure these technologies align with ethical values, societal well-being, and ecological sustainability. His principles remind us that complexity and unpredictability demand ethical vigilance, continuous learning, and adaptive governance. They prompt us to consider carefully how technological advancements affect human dignity, societal cohesion, and ecological health, urging us to steward information technologies responsibly, transparently, and ethically (Russell & Norvig, 2020).

Shannon's philosophical insights offer a profound perspective on human engagement with technology, emphasizing adaptability, resilience, ethical awareness, and creative innovation. By embracing uncertainty and complexity, we cultivate deeper appreciation, meaningful connections, and responsible technological stewardship, reflecting our shared humanistic commitment to ethical integrity, societal flourishing, and ecological sustainability.

Synergy and Integration: Gell-Mann, Shannon, and Complexity Science

Integrating Murray Gell-Mann's complex adaptive systems (CAS) with Claude Shannon's principles of information entropy provides a profound and enriched perspective on complexity, information, and adaptive evolution. Both visionaries illuminate how dynamic interactions, unpredictability, and continuous feedback create and sustain intricate, sophisticated structures and behaviors. By harmonizing their ideas, we gain deeper insights into how complexity and information management co-evolve, enabling systems such as natural, technological, and societal to adapt gracefully and thrive within ever-changing environments.

To humanize this integrated perspective, consider a thriving metropolis like New York City, where complexity emerges naturally through continuous interactions among millions of individuals. The city embodies Gell-Mann's CAS principles through decentralized decision-making enabling individual citizens, small businesses, public services, and various organizations to independently adapt to their local circumstances. Simultaneously, it reflects Shannon's insights into entropy and information management, as the continuous flow of information through transportation networks, communication systems, and economic exchanges creates a resilient and innovative urban environment. Like ecosystems that balance diversity and adaptation, such cities continually reinvent themselves, demonstrating robustness and flexibility amid dynamic change and uncertainty.

In technological contexts, the synergy of Gell-Mann and Shannon is equally compelling. Consider social media platforms, which are complex adaptive systems that thrive by processing vast amounts of information and feedback. These platforms continuously adapt to user interactions, adjusting content and recommendations through decentralized feedback loops and entropy-based information algorithms. Facebook and Twitter exemplify how complexity and entropy jointly facilitate adaptation and innovation. By embracing uncertainty represented by Shannon's entropy, platforms remain dynamic, responsive, and innovative, reflecting Gell-Mann's principles of complexity through decentralized, adaptive interactions.

Furthermore, the combination of Gell-Mann's complexity science and Shannon's entropy provides powerful insights for ethical governance and transparency. In complex adaptive systems, managing uncertainty and complexity ethically requires transparent and adaptable governance frameworks. For instance, consider the governance of AI systems deployed in healthcare. These systems continuously adapt by processing dynamic medical data, patient interactions, and clinical feedback. Transparent governance, underpinned by Shannon's principles of information clarity and Gell-Mann's adaptability, ensures ethical decision-making, patient privacy, and effective treatment outcomes. Such frameworks encourage ethical accountability, continuous learning, and adaptability, essential for managing complexity responsibly in dynamic healthcare environments.

From a philosophical perspective, integrating Gell-Mann and Shannon encourages us to embrace complexity, uncertainty, and interconnectedness as valuable and enriching aspects of our existence. Rather than attempting rigid control over complex systems, their combined insights prompt us to view complexity as a source of creativity, growth, and resilience. They guide us to adopt adaptive strategies that welcome uncertainty, seeing unpredictability as a fertile ground for continuous innovation and ethical mindfulness.

The powerful synergy of Murray Gell-Mann and Claude Shannon offers profound philosophical and practical guidance, equipping us to navigate complexity with adaptability, transparency, and ethical responsibility. Their integrated perspectives illuminate the path toward responsible innovation, sustainable technological advancement, and meaningful human engagement with the complex systems that shape our world.

Conclusion

By thoughtfully embracing the visionary contributions of Murray Gell-Mann and Claude Shannon, we achieve a richer, more nuanced appreciation of complexity, adaptability, and ethical responsibility within modern technological and ecological contexts. The combined legacies of these two pioneering thinkers illuminate a pathway toward understanding how complexity and uncertainty are not merely challenges to manage, but rather essential sources of creativity, innovation, and meaningful human connection.

Gell-Mann's complexity theory invites us to recognize how vibrant, resilient structures and systems emerge naturally through simple yet dynamic interactions. Imagine a thriving community where innovation and collaboration blossom organically not through centralized control, but through spontaneous interactions among diverse participants. Such communities continuously adapt and innovate precisely because they embrace complexity and uncertainty as inherent to their growth and resilience. Likewise, Shannon's groundbreaking insights into entropy and information remind us that unpredictability and uncertainty are fundamental drivers of meaningful communication, creativity, and adaptability. Think of a memorable story or a captivating melody, where unexpected turns and variations enhance engagement and emotional depth. Shannon's principles highlight how uncertainty enriches human experience and innovation, reinforcing the importance of flexibility and adaptability within our increasingly interconnected world.

Integrating Gell-Mann's and Shannon's insights equips us with essential tools for responsibly navigating and managing advanced technologies such as artificial intelligence, quantum computing, and complex adaptive systems. The agile organization, which thrives in today's turbulent and dynamic marketplaces, exemplifies this practical wisdom clearly. Companies embracing decentralized decision-making, continuous adaptation, and ethical responsiveness consistently outperform those adhering to rigid, centralized structures. This adaptability fosters robust innovation and ethical accountability, allowing organizations to navigate uncertainty and complexity with agility and resilience (Cockburn & Highsmith, 2001).

Ethically, adopting the integrated insights of Gell-Mann and Shannon underscores our collective responsibility to steward technological innovation mindfully, transparently, and ethically. As technologies become more sophisticated and impactful, it becomes imperative to maintain clear ethical frameworks, ensuring transparency, fairness, and accountability in every innovation. Consider the rapid advancements in artificial intelligence such as AI-driven decision-making in healthcare, autonomous transportation, and algorithmic governance demands adaptive, ethically responsible stewardship to safeguard human dignity, social equity, and ecological sustainability (Floridi & Cowls, 2019).

By embracing the profound philosophical and practical contributions of Murray Gell-Mann and Claude Shannon, we cultivate a deeper understanding and appreciation for complexity, interconnectedness, adaptability, and ethical responsibility. Their insights offer invaluable guidance, enabling us to foster technological innovation that aligns closely with humanistic values and contributes positively to societal well-being and ecological sustainability. By valuing complexity and uncertainty as integral and enriching aspects of reality, we empower ourselves to responsibly and creatively navigate the complexities of the modern world, creating a future characterized by resilience, innovation, and ethical stewardship.

Chapter 6: Norbert Wiener and Heinz von Foerster—Cybernetics, Communication, and Observing Complexity

Introduction

Our journey through the multifaceted landscape of complexity has thus far revealed remarkable insights from pioneering thinkers, each enriching our understanding of how intricate patterns and innovative solutions spontaneously emerge from simple interactions. We began by examining Henri Poincaré's foundational work on chaos theory and unpredictability, followed by Edward Lorenz's powerful demonstration of sensitive dependence on initial conditions, popularly known as the butterfly effect. We then delved into John Holland's revolutionary insights on genetic algorithms, highlighting how complex systems naturally evolve and adapt, and Stuart Kauffman's compelling explorations into self-organization, underscoring how order emerges spontaneously without centralized guidance.

In Chapter 5, we integrated Murray Gell-Mann's complex adaptive systems (CAS) and Claude Shannon's groundbreaking information theory. Together, these visionaries further illuminated how complexity, adaptability, and communication underpin our understanding of advanced technological systems, emphasizing the profound interplay between uncertainty, creativity, and innovation.

Now, as we progress into Chapter 6, we introduce two additional visionary scholars whose profound contributions significantly deepen our appreciation of complexity through cybernetics and the philosophy of observation. Norbert Wiener, often hailed as the father of cybernetics, profoundly reshaped our understanding of communication, feedback, and control within both machines and living organisms. Wiener's groundbreaking work established the foundational principles of cybernetics, emphasizing how dynamic feedback mechanisms enable systems to adapt, communicate, and maintain equilibrium.

Complementing Wiener's foundational cybernetics, Heinz von Foerster pioneered the development of second-order cybernetics, shifting our perspective to include the role of the observer within observed systems. Von Foerster's insights dramatically enriched our comprehension of complexity by highlighting how observers inevitably influence the systems they study, underscoring the active role humans play within complex adaptive interactions. By integrating Wiener's and von Foerster's groundbreaking contributions, we further illuminate the philosophical dimensions of complexity, emphasizing adaptability, ethical mindfulness, and reflective awareness as central principles guiding responsible technological innovation and ecological stewardship.

In this chapter, we will explore how Wiener and von Foerster's cybernetic theories offer powerful tools for navigating modern technological challenges, shaping ethical decision-making frameworks, and deepening our philosophical appreciation of complexity as a source of innovation, resilience, and meaningful human connection.

Norbert Wiener: Cybernetics and Communication

Biography and Academic Contributions

Norbert Wiener (1894–1964) was a remarkable figure whose groundbreaking insights fundamentally reshaped our understanding of complex systems, communication, and control mechanisms. Born in Columbia, Missouri, Wiener's extraordinary intellectual trajectory began early in life, displaying a rare gift for mathematics and scientific inquiry that was nurtured by supportive mentorship and rigorous education. His academic path was notably diverse, spanning disciplines such as mathematics, engineering, philosophy, biology, and social sciences. Wiener's interdisciplinary ethos embodied his belief that profound insights emerge not in isolated silos but through active exploration across multiple domains.

Wiener earned his doctorate from Harvard University at just 18 years old, launching a lifelong academic journey characterized by relentless curiosity and interdisciplinary innovation. As a young mathematician, he was particularly intrigued by how complex systems maintain stability and adapt effectively to changing environments through continuous communication and feedback. This fascination laid the groundwork for his development of cybernetics, a groundbreaking interdisciplinary field examining communication, control, and regulation within both living organisms and mechanical systems.

During World War II, Wiener's theoretical insights found practical application as he contributed significantly to wartime research on guided missile systems. Through this experience, he closely observed parallels between mechanical control mechanisms and biological systems, particularly the dynamic feedback processes enabling precision and adaptation. These insights prompted Wiener to formalize the foundational principles of cybernetics, eloquently articulated in his seminal 1948 work, Cybernetics: Or Control and Communication in the

Animal and the Machine. This groundbreaking publication profoundly influenced scientific and philosophical understandings of how dynamic feedback loops, information processing, and communication enable adaptive stability within complex systems. Wiener positioned cybernetics around control and communication, anticipating today's real-time dashboards for organizational oversight. (Wiener, 1948).

Wiener's cybernetics theory rapidly transcended traditional disciplinary boundaries, influencing fields as diverse as robotics, artificial intelligence, cognitive science, organizational theory, and sociology. His work underscored the crucial role of communication and information flow in shaping systems' behaviors, adaptations, and interactions. Wiener emphasized the ethical implications of technological advancements, advocating strongly for human-centered and ethically responsible innovation. He recognized that technological progress, while beneficial, carried significant ethical responsibilities, urging scientists, technologists, and policymakers to remain mindful of technology's impacts on human dignity, privacy, and society.

Moreover, Wiener's interdisciplinary approach extended to his philosophical contributions. He argued compellingly with humility, ethical reflection, and continuous learning in technological and scientific advancement. He saw technology not merely as a tool but as an integral extension of human consciousness, urging thoughtful consideration of its social, ethical, and ecological implications. His influential philosophical perspective significantly shaped contemporary discussions around technology ethics, information privacy, and responsible innovation, guiding subsequent generations toward more ethically mindful and adaptive technological engagements.

Today, Wiener's legacy endures vividly in numerous contemporary technological and organizational practices. Cybernetic principles underlie innovations such as adaptive robotics, automated decision-making systems, and dynamic organizational management approaches. His philosophical insights continue to inspire ethical reflection and adaptive governance frameworks, ensuring that technology aligns meaningfully with human values and societal well-being.

Through his pioneering contributions, Norbert Wiener profoundly transformed our understanding of complexity, communication, and ethical responsibility, leaving an enduring intellectual legacy that continues to guide ethical innovation and adaptive stewardship in our increasingly interconnected and technologically sophisticated world.

Fundamental Concepts: Feedback, Control, and Communication

At the core of Norbert Wiener's cybernetic theory lies the insightful recognition of how feedback loops, communication, and adaptive control are foundational to maintaining stability and enabling complex systems to thrive amid constant change. Wiener envisioned feedback loops as vital processes through which systems continuously monitor their environments and internal conditions, dynamically adapting their behavior to sustain equilibrium and optimal performance.

To appreciate this, consider the analogy of the human body's temperature regulation an exquisite example of a biological feedback loop. When external temperatures rise, sensors within the human body detect increased heat, prompting mechanisms such as sweating and vasodilation to lower body temperature back to equilibrium. Conversely, in cold conditions, the body shivers and reduces blood flow to extremities to conserve heat. Wiener's feedback loops function similarly: systems continually adjust and recalibrate based on incoming information, ensuring resilience and adaptability in the face of unpredictable circumstances (Wiener, 1948; Galison, 1994).

Moreover, Wiener's emphasis on communication underscores the essential role that information flow plays within adaptive systems. Communication, in Wiener's view, is akin to a dynamic dialogue where information circulates continuously between components of a system and its external environment, enabling effective adaptation and stability. A modern organizational example is a responsive supply chain. Suppliers, manufacturers, distributors, and consumers communicate in real-time, constantly adjusting to demand fluctuations, disruptions, or market shifts. Just as a harmonious orchestra relies on clear, ongoing communication between conductors and musicians to adapt rhythm and harmony, effective communication within complex adaptive systems enables precise adjustments, coherent responses, and dynamic equilibrium (Conway & Siegelman, 2005).

Price escalation is a significant challenge in project management, requiring continuous monitoring and effective communication across multiple stakeholders. Building on Norbert Wiener's principles of communication and feedback, the price escalation monitoring communication loop provides a framework for integrating market data, supplier input, procurement insights, and managerial oversight. This ensures that information flows dynamically, enabling timely responses to cost fluctuations and supporting informed decision-making. Figure 6.1 illustrates how feedback loops connect procurement teams, suppliers, contractors, project managers, financial controllers, and market data in a coordinated monitoring system.

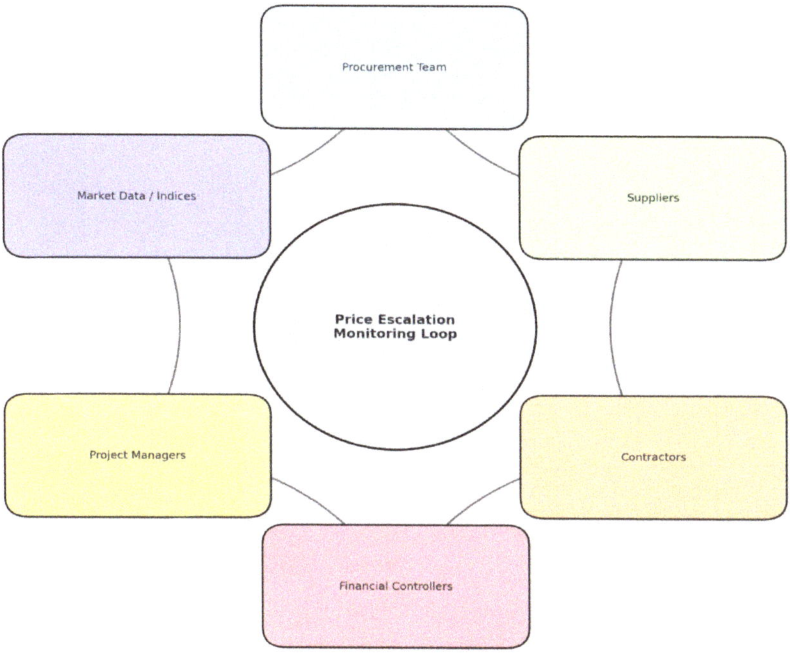

Figure 6.1. *Price escalation monitoring communication loop in project management.*

Note. Figure created by the author (2025) to visualize the application of Wiener's communication and feedback principles to price escalation monitoring in complex project management contexts. The diagram shows how key stakeholders—including procurement teams, suppliers, contractors, project managers, financial controllers, and market data sources—interact in a continuous loop of information exchange to anticipate and respond to cost fluctuations.

Wiener's concept of adaptive control is especially powerful in technological applications, particularly in robotics and automation. Imagine an autonomous drone navigating complex terrain: it continuously receives feedback from its sensors such as cameras, lidar, and GPS, and uses that information to adapt flight paths and obstacle avoidance strategies dynamically. This constant interaction between feedback and control enables the drone to maintain stability, adaptability, and responsiveness, effectively illustrating Wiener's cybernetic principles in practice. A compelling real-world example is NASA's Ingenuity helicopter drone, deployed on Mars, which operates in an environment with thin atmosphere, extreme temperature variations, and unpredictable wind patterns. To function effectively, Ingenuity relies on adaptive control loops that process continuous feedback from onboard sensors, making real-time adjustments to rotor speed, navigation, and stability to compensate for environmental challenges. Such adaptive control is fundamental to modern robotics, autonomous vehicles, and industrial automation systems, reflecting the enduring relevance of Wiener's insights (Hayles, 1999).

Wiener's fundamental concepts challenge traditional notions of centralized control, advocating for a decentralized, adaptive approach built on continuous feedback and transparent communication. His ideas invite humility, acknowledging that complex systems cannot be entirely predicted or rigidly managed. In this view, adaptive responsiveness, continuous learning, and open information sharing become essential for effective management and ethical responsibility. These principles resonate strongly in organizational leadership, governance frameworks, and technological ethics, emphasizing that adaptive control, clear communication, and constant feedback loops are critical to achieving sustainable innovation and ethical stewardship (Galison, 1994).

Wiener's concepts of feedback, control, and communication also reveal how complex systems maintain equilibrium, adapt to change, and drive innovation over time. Applying these foundational cybernetic principles equips us to better navigate and manage complexity, ensuring that technological progress remains aligned with ethical standards, societal well-being, and ecological sustainability.

Practical Applications

Norbert Wiener’s cybernetic principles extend widely into diverse practical domains, including technology, economics, organizational management, healthcare, and even social policy. These principles have profoundly shaped modern advancements, highlighting how continuous feedback, dynamic adaptation, and effective communication foster resilience and innovation across various fields.

In technology, particularly robotics and automation, Wiener's cybernetic concepts have proven indispensable. Consider modern drones used in agriculture: these unmanned aerial vehicles continuously gather real-time feedback from their environment including weather conditions, soil quality, crop health to dynamically adjust their flight paths, camera angles, and spraying patterns. This process enables precise farming techniques, optimizes resource use, and enhances crop yields, reflecting the effectiveness of cybernetic feedback loops in practical scenarios (Wolfert et al., 2017).

Another compelling example is the field of healthcare robotics. Surgical robots, such as the da Vinci surgical system, demonstrate Wiener's principles vividly. Surgeons remotely control robotic arms, continuously receiving precise feedback on tissue resistance, position accuracy, and physiological responses. This dynamic exchange of information allows surgeons to adapt their movements swiftly, ensuring safer procedures and improved patient outcomes. The precision and adaptability of these robotic systems reflect Wiener’s foundational insights into adaptive control and communication (Marescaux & Diana, 2015).

In economics, Wiener’s cybernetic insights play a pivotal role in developing adaptive economic policies and resilient financial systems. Modern financial markets, with their complex web of transactions, information exchanges, and feedback loops, embody cybernetic principles. Central banks, such as the U.S. Federal Reserve, continuously monitor economic indicators such as employment rates, inflation, and market confidence, to adjust interest rates and monetary policy dynamically. These adjustments resemble Wiener's feedback loops, aiming to stabilize economic fluctuations, foster market confidence, and mitigate the impacts of economic crises (Sornette, 2017).

At the organizational level, cybernetics significantly influences adaptive leadership and management practices. Agile organizations exemplify these principles effectively, using continuous feedback and communication to adapt quickly to changing market conditions. Companies like Spotify and Netflix thrive by embracing cybernetic principles, empowering decentralized teams to make responsive decisions based on real-time feedback, customer preferences, and technological shifts. This decentralized, feedback-driven approach enables rapid innovation, adaptability, and resilience within competitive market environments (Cockburn & Highsmith, 2001).

Moreover, cybernetic principles profoundly impact social policy and governance frameworks, particularly in crisis management and urban planning. For instance, during public health crises like the COVID-19 pandemic, adaptive governance approaches, informed by real-time data feedback and continuous communication, enabled swift policy adjustments, effective resource allocation, and resilient community responses. Similarly, smart cities leverage cybernetic principles to continuously adjust traffic flow, manage energy resources, and enhance urban resilience through real-time communication and adaptive responses to citizens' needs (Kummitha & Crutzen, 2017).

These practical applications highlight the importance of adaptive thinking, transparent communication, and ethical responsiveness in managing complexity and uncertainty. Wiener’s cybernetic approach invites leaders, policymakers, and innovators to embrace feedback, adaptability, and continuous learning as the foundation for effective decision-making, innovation, and sustainable development across a wide range of contexts.

Norbert Wiener's cybernetic principles have shown remarkable relevance across decades, shaping advancements in technology, economics, organizational management, healthcare, and governance. Applying his adaptive insights allows us to cultivate innovation, resilience, and ethical stewardship—ensuring that the systems and technologies we build remain aligned with core ethical standards, societal well-being, and long-term sustainability.

Philosophical Implications

At the philosophical heart of Norbert Wiener's cybernetic theory lies a profound ethical vision advocating for adaptability, transparent communication, and a deep sense of accountability within technological innovation. Wiener's approach challenges traditional paradigms of technology as merely neutral tools, instead highlighting technology's profound ethical dimensions and its interconnectedness with human values, dignity, and society.

Wiener passionately believed that adaptability that enhanced our capacity to respond flexibly and ethically to emerging challenges, formed a cornerstone of responsible technological advancement. Consider an agile dancer performing improvisational choreography, continuously adapting movements to music, partners, and audience reactions. This dancer embodies Wiener's philosophy of adaptability, demonstrating responsiveness, creativity, and thoughtful integration of feedback into performance. Likewise, Wiener argued that ethical technology should dynamically adapt to societal needs and environmental changes, aligning itself with evolving human contexts and values rather than imposing rigid, inflexible solutions (Wiener, 1950).

Transparent communication, a critical component of Wiener's cybernetic philosophy, underscores the ethical importance of clarity, openness, and honest information-sharing within technological systems. As technology grows increasingly complex, transparency becomes paramount in safeguarding privacy, ensuring fairness, and maintaining trust. Imagine healthcare technology, such as AI-driven diagnostic tools; transparent communication ensures that patients clearly understand how data is processed, empowering them with meaningful information and preserving autonomy. Wiener strongly advocated transparency as a core ethical principle, ensuring technology serves human interests and respects personal dignity and agency (Floridi & Cowls, 2019).

Wiener's philosophy also emphasizes accountability as foundational in technological innovation. Accountability means recognizing and embracing our responsibilities for technological consequences, including potential impacts on privacy, societal well-being, and ecological sustainability. Wiener's cybernetic perspective, therefore, promotes continuous ethical reflection, evaluation, and recalibration of technological strategies. For example, the ethical development of artificial intelligence, particularly in high-stakes domains like autonomous driving, necessitates clear mechanisms of accountability. Developers, organizations, and policymakers must regularly evaluate AI systems, transparently disclose decision-making processes, and promptly address ethical concerns, reflecting Wiener's emphasis on adaptive accountability (Russell & Norvig, 2020).

Further, Wiener's philosophical insights encourage a deeper appreciation for the interconnectedness between humans, technology, and nature. His cybernetic perspective promotes a holistic understanding, recognizing that technology does not exist in isolation but profoundly influences human experiences and ecological systems. Ethically mindful technological innovation, informed by Wiener's philosophy, prioritizes ecological balance, human welfare, and sustainable stewardship, carefully considering broader societal impacts and responsibilities. Wiener urges us to reflect continually on our interconnectedness, promoting humility, adaptability, and responsible innovation within our technologically sophisticated society (Galison, 1994).

Norbert Wiener's philosophical legacy profoundly enriches our understanding of technology's ethical implications, advocating adaptability, transparency, accountability, and interconnectedness as central principles guiding responsible technological innovation. By embracing his insights, we commit ourselves to ethical mindfulness, adaptive responsiveness, and humanistic stewardship, ensuring that technological advancements enhance human dignity, societal harmony, and ecological sustainability.

Heinz von Foerster: Second-Order Cybernetics and Observing Systems

Biography and Academic Contributions

Heinz von Foerster (1911–2002) was an influential Austrian American scientist, thinker, and philosopher whose groundbreaking contributions to cybernetics fundamentally reshaped our understanding of complexity, cognition, and systems theory. Born in Vienna, Austria, von Foerster's early intellectual environment was shaped by vibrant interdisciplinary dialogues, providing a fertile foundation for his unique and innovative perspectives. This vibrant milieu encouraged him to integrate diverse fields including physics, philosophy, biology, cognitive science, and information theory, reflecting his belief in holistic inquiry as essential for grasping complexity and human experience.

In the mid-20th century, von Foerster emigrated to the United States, joining the University of Illinois, where he established the

Biological Computer Laboratory (BCL). Under his visionary leadership, the BCL emerged as a pioneering hub of interdisciplinary research, fostering collaboration among scientists from various backgrounds. Here, von Foerster advanced the concept of second-order cybernetics, profoundly challenging traditional perspectives by emphasizing the critical role observers play within the systems they study (von Foerster, 2003).

While traditional cybernetics viewed observers as detached from the observed phenomena, von Foerster's innovative approach integrated human consciousness directly into systemic interactions. His second-order cybernetics highlights that observers are not passive or neutral; rather, they actively shape and influence the systems they investigate. To illustrate, consider a filmmaker documenting an unfolding social event: their presence, choices, and interactions inevitably affect the event itself, shaping not only the narrative captured but also influencing how events unfold in real time. Von Foerster's perspective thus underscores the profound interconnectedness and mutual influence between observers and observed systems (von Glasersfeld, 2002).

Heinz von Foerster's pioneering insights extended beyond theoretical science, influencing diverse fields such as cognitive psychology, sociology, education, and organizational theory. His concept of observing systems found practical application in education, where recognizing learners as active participants reshapes pedagogical methods toward more collaborative and student-centered approaches. Similarly, in therapeutic contexts, von Foerster's second-order cybernetics inspires therapists to acknowledge and reflect upon their active roles within therapeutic interactions, enhancing the quality and effectiveness of therapy through greater self-awareness and relational sensitivity (Glanville, 2004).

Von Foerster's insights carry profound implications for understanding human cognition, perception, and ethical responsibility. His emphasis on the observer's active role aligns with constructivist philosophies, suggesting that knowledge is actively built through individual experiences and interactions rather than passively received. This perspective encourages humility and ethical mindfulness, recognizing the significant ways individuals shape and influence the realities they perceive and construct. By fostering reflective awareness, adaptability, and ethical responsibility, von Foerster's work deepens our understanding of complexity, cognition, and human relationships (Glasersfeld, 2002).

Heinz von Foerster's enduring legacy is evident in contemporary discussions around complexity, communication, and ethical technology use. His innovative second-order cybernetics continues to guide adaptive governance, organizational management, and technological innovation, emphasizing transparency, accountability, and ethical reflection. For example, in participatory urban planning projects, city governments have applied second-order cybernetic principles by actively involving residents, business owners, and community organizations in iterative decision-making processes. This approach recognizes the community as both the observer and participant, allowing local knowledge, values, and lived experiences to shape the evolving design of policies and infrastructure. Ultimately, von Foerster's visionary contributions offer essential philosophical and practical insights, guiding us toward responsible engagement with complexity, human consciousness, and adaptive technological advancement, enriching both human experience and societal well-being.

Observer–Participant Loop in Second-Order Cybernetics (Participatory Urban Planning Example)

The figure below illustrates the cyclical relationship between four key stages in participatory governance: Community Stakeholders,

Feedback, Policy & Decisions, and Implementation. Arrows indicate the continuous flow of information and influence, demonstrating von Foerster's principle that observers are active participants in shaping the systems they engage with. In the urban planning example, community members provide feedback that informs policy and project decisions, which are then implemented and monitored, leading to further stakeholder engagement.

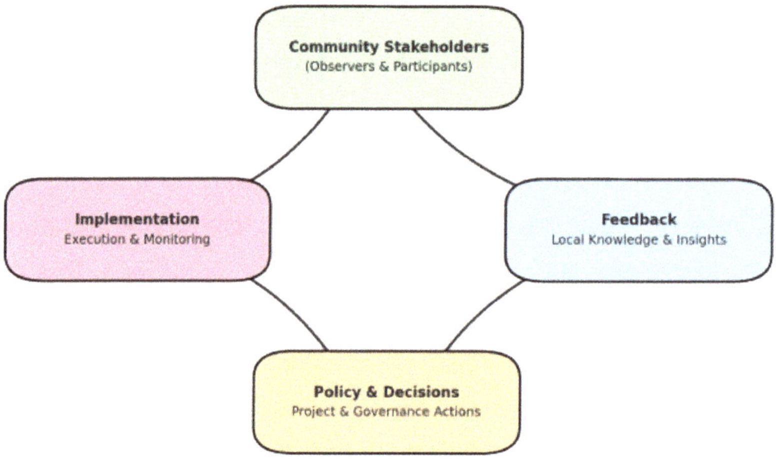

Figure 6.2. *Observer-participant loop in second-order cybernetics (participatory urban planning example).*

Note. Figure created by the author (2025) to depict the application of second-order cybernetic principles to participatory urban planning, emphasizing the iterative exchange between observers and the systems they influence.

Fundamental Concepts: Observing Systems and Second-Order Cybernetics

Heinz von Foerster significantly expanded our understanding of cybernetics through his concept of second-order cybernetics, an innovative perspective that places the observer actively within the system being observed. In traditional cybernetics, observers were typically considered neutral and objective, standing apart from the systems they studied. Von Foerster's groundbreaking idea challenges this conventional stance, arguing instead that observers are inevitably intertwined with, and influential upon, the systems they observe. This revolutionary shift in perspective profoundly reshapes our understanding of complexity and interaction, suggesting that observing is not merely passive recording but an active, participatory act that shapes outcomes and meaning.

To visualize this clearly, consider the analogy of a teacher interacting with students in a classroom. The teacher's behaviors, choices, attitudes, and presence inherently influence students' reactions, learning experiences, and classroom dynamics. The teacher is not merely a neutral observer but actively contributes to shaping the environment being studied and influenced. Similarly, second-order cybernetics emphasizes that scientists, researchers, and theorists are active participants who shape the systems they observe. Their questions, interpretations, biases, and interactions significantly affect the phenomena being observed, creating dynamic feedback loops between observer and observed (Glanville, 2004).

In practical contexts, von Foerster's second-order cybernetics profoundly impacts fields such as organizational management, therapy, education, and communication. For instance, consider a business consultant conducting organizational assessments. The consultant's interactions through interviews, feedback, and suggestions do not simply gather objective data but can also alter employee perceptions, attitudes, and behaviors. These changes, in turn, shape the consultant's assessments and recommendations. By acknowledging the observer's role, organizations gain deeper insights, foster greater trust, and encourage reflective awareness, enabling adaptive management and effective organizational development (von Glasersfeld, 2002).

In therapeutic practices, second-order cybernetics underscores the relational dynamics between therapists and clients. Therapists are not merely detached observers of their clients' conditions; their presence, empathy, communication style, and therapeutic strategies profoundly shape clients' experiences, responses, and therapeutic outcomes. Recognizing this interplay fosters therapeutic relationships characterized by mutual respect, trust, and reflective awareness, enhancing therapeutic effectiveness and promoting meaningful client growth (Anderson & Goolishian, 1992).

Von Foerster's concept also profoundly enriches educational methodologies. Teachers, educators, and facilitators become mindful observers who continuously reflect on their influence upon students' learning processes. Educational settings inspired by second-order cybernetics embrace interactive, student-centered approaches, empowering students as active participants in shaping their own learning journeys. This philosophical stance promotes continuous learning, adaptability, and reflective practice, creating educational environments characterized by mutual engagement, innovation, and growth (Doll, 2008).

Second-order cybernetics challenges traditional notions of objectivity and neutrality, prompting deep ethical reflection on observation, interaction, and the construction of knowledge. Von Foerster reframes complexity not as something external to be observed from a distance, but as an inherently relational phenomenon shaped by human perception, interaction, and communication. His perspective encourages humility, ethical responsibility, and reflective awareness, recognizing that observing systems requires active ethical engagement, accountability, and adaptability within interconnected environments (von Foerster, 2003).

A clear example of these principles can be found in conflict mediation processes. Here, facilitators do not act as neutral, detached arbiters; instead, they recognize that their presence, questions, and framing of issues influence the tone, direction, and possible outcomes of the dialogue. By actively engaging with participants and reflecting on their own influence, mediators embody second-order cybernetic thinking—treating the mediation process as a co-constructed reality rather than an objective, one-sided evaluation.

Von Foerster's second-order cybernetics also offers powerful conceptual tools that underscore the observer's active and influential role within complex adaptive systems. Applying these principles fosters reflective awareness, ethical responsibility, and a commitment to continuous learning, ensuring that our interactions, whether in scientific research, education, organizational leadership, or therapeutic contexts, remain adaptive, attentive, and ethically grounded.

Practical Applications

Second-order cybernetics, introduced by Heinz von Foerster, holds significant practical implications across diverse domains such as education, organizational management, and therapeutic practices. By highlighting the active role of observers within systems, this approach reshapes our understanding and practices in various fields, leading to more effective, adaptive, and ethically responsible outcomes.

In educational settings, second-order cybernetics inspires a transformative approach to teaching and learning. Rather than viewing students as passive recipients of knowledge, this approach acknowledges learners as active participants who co-create educational experiences alongside educators. Imagine a classroom as an interactive workshop, where students and teachers collaborate actively, exchanging ideas, asking questions, and jointly constructing knowledge. This dynamic collaboration empowers learners, fostering critical thinking, adaptability, and lifelong learning. Educational methods such as inquiry-based learning and project-based learning exemplify this second-order cybernetic approach, engaging students deeply in active learning processes where their perspectives, questions, and feedback continuously reshape and enrich educational experiences (Doll, 2008).

Organizational management and leadership practices also benefit profoundly from second-order cybernetics. In traditional hierarchical organizations, employees may be viewed merely as passive components performing predefined roles. However, second-order cybernetics emphasizes that employees are active observers and participants whose insights, interactions, and experiences significantly shape organizational outcomes. Consider innovative companies adopting a holacracy or agile methodology—these organizations empower employees at all levels to actively observe, reflect, and adapt strategies based on real-time feedback and interactions. Such approaches foster adaptability, resilience, and collective innovation, allowing organizations to navigate uncertainty and market fluctuations effectively. By valuing employees as active, reflective participants, second-order cybernetics transforms leadership styles toward inclusive, adaptive, and collaborative practices (Laloux, 2014).

Therapeutic practices similarly benefit from the insights of second-order cybernetics. In traditional therapy models, therapists might perceive themselves as external observers diagnosing and treating passive clients. Second-order cybernetics challenges this perspective, highlighting the therapist's active role in shaping therapeutic interactions and outcomes. Consider a family therapy session: the therapist's questions, reflections, and communication style significantly influence family dynamics and conversations, actively reshaping the therapeutic interaction. Acknowledging this active participation encourages therapists to adopt a more reflective, adaptive stance, focusing on collaborative conversations and mutual understanding rather than hierarchical prescriptions. This relational approach enhances therapeutic efficacy, deepens trust, and fosters more meaningful, enduring therapeutic outcomes (Anderson & Goolishian, 1992).

Moreover, second-order cybernetics has practical relevance in fields like social services and community development. Practitioners in these areas who recognize their active role as observers and influencers become more attuned to how their interactions shape community dynamics. For example, community facilitators organizing public consultations actively shape community dialogue through their communication methods, facilitation strategies, and framing of issues. Embracing second-order cybernetics prompts these facilitators to maintain transparency, adaptability, and ethical awareness, ensuring community engagement remains responsive, inclusive, and aligned with local values and needs (Midgley & Richardson, 2007).

The practical applications of second-order cybernetics extend widely, reshaping education, organizational leadership, therapeutic practices, and community engagement. By embracing the observer's active role, this approach fosters deeper reflective awareness, adaptability, ethical mindfulness, and meaningful collaboration across diverse practical contexts, significantly enhancing effectiveness, innovation, and societal well-being.

Philosophical Implications

Heinz von Foerster's second-order cybernetics introduces profound philosophical shifts in how we understand knowledge, objectivity, and ethical engagement within complex systems. By explicitly acknowledging the observer's role as inseparable from the observed phenomenon, von Foerster fundamentally challenges traditional, objective stances in scientific inquiry, urging us instead toward a reflective, relational understanding of complexity and observation.

Von Foerster's insights resonate with constructivist epistemologies, emphasizing that knowledge is actively constructed through the observer's experiences, interactions, and interpretations. Imagine two travelers exploring an unfamiliar city—each traveler's experiences, perceptions, and interpretations differ profoundly based on their unique interests, backgrounds, and interactions with local residents. Similarly, von Foerster posits that reality is not passively discovered but actively constructed through each observer's unique perspectives and interactions. This stance fosters humility, reminding us that our understanding of complex phenomena is inherently subjective, partial, and contextually shaped, prompting continuous reflection and openness to multiple perspectives (von Glasersfeld, 2002).

Von Foerster's philosophy also emphasizes ethical accountability, particularly in scientific and technological practices. Recognizing that observers influence outcomes encourages scientists, engineers, and policymakers to critically reflect on their roles and responsibilities. Consider artificial intelligence and automated decision-making systems. Developers inevitably shape these technologies based on their values, assumptions, and design choices, profoundly affecting human experiences and societal outcomes. Von Foerster's philosophy highlights the ethical imperative of acknowledging these influences transparently, ensuring responsible technological innovation that respects privacy, human dignity, and social justice (Floridi & Cowls, 2019).

Moreover, von Foerster's philosophical insights advocate for adaptive engagement with complexity. Rather than attempting rigid control or static certainty, his second-order cybernetics encourages adaptability, flexibility, and continual learning. For instance, effective organizational leadership in today's rapidly changing world relies on adaptive responsiveness rather than fixed strategies. Leaders who embrace von Foerster's philosophy become adept at continuously assessing their actions and adapting strategies based on real-time feedback, stakeholder interactions, and evolving circumstances. This adaptive approach fosters organizational resilience, innovation, and sustainable development, reflecting the ethical mindfulness and flexibility central to von Foerster's philosophical perspective (Glasersfeld, 2002).

In educational and therapeutic contexts, von Foerster's philosophy similarly emphasizes reflective awareness and ethical mindfulness. Teachers and therapists who recognize their active roles as observers within educational and therapeutic interactions gain deeper self-awareness and ethical responsibility. By continuously reflecting on their practices and interactions, these professionals become more attuned to ethical implications, power dynamics, and relational complexities, enhancing effectiveness, trust, and mutual respect within their professional engagements (Anderson & Goolishian, 1992).

Heinz von Foerster's philosophical contributions offer profound insight into the nature of knowledge, objectivity, and ethical responsibility within complex adaptive systems. By embracing reflective awareness, ethical accountability, and adaptability, we can navigate complexity with humility, openness, and ethical mindfulness, ensuring technological innovation, scientific inquiry, and social engagement remain aligned with humanistic values and societal well-being.

Synergy and Integration: Wiener, von Foerster, and Complexity Science

The integrated insights of Norbert Wiener and Heinz von Foerster create a profound synergy, deepening our appreciation and understanding of complexity, communication, and observation. By bridging Wiener's foundational concepts of cybernetic feedback and communication with von Foerster's innovative approach to second-order cybernetics, we discover valuable perspectives on how complexity arises dynamically from continuous interactions among observers, systems, and their environments.

Consider the analogy of a jazz ensemble improvising together: Wiener's principles resemble musicians continuously listening and responding to each other, dynamically adapting their notes, rhythm, and tempo based on real-time feedback. Von Foerster, in contrast, emphasizes that each musician is not merely responding passively, but actively shaping the collective performance by their interpretations, emotions, and creative impulses. The ensemble's resulting performance is thus not pre-scripted or predictable but emerges uniquely each time through mutual responsiveness and active participation. This rich interplay exemplifies how Wiener's and von Foerster's combined perspectives reveal complexity as arising naturally and creatively from dynamic interactions between systems and observers (Glanville, 2004; Wiener, 1948).

In practical terms, the integration of Wiener's cybernetics with von Foerster's second-order cybernetics holds profound implications for adaptive governance and organizational decision-making. Effective governance of complex systems such as managing a large metropolitan city or guiding a multinational corporation requires acknowledging that leaders and policymakers are active participants whose choices significantly influence systemic outcomes. By embracing Wiener's adaptive communication and feedback mechanisms alongside von Foerster's observer-centered insights, organizations can foster transparency, adaptability, and ethical responsiveness. For example, agile organizational frameworks that encourage continuous feedback, reflective practice, and decentralized decision-making can dynamically adjust strategies to effectively navigate rapidly changing market conditions, technological shifts, or societal expectations (Cockburn & Highsmith, 2001).

This synergistic perspective has significant ethical implications for technological innovation and responsible stewardship. Wiener's emphasis on ethical accountability and transparent communication aligns closely with von Foerster's philosophy of reflective observation, highlighting our active role in shaping technological and societal outcomes. Consider the ethical governance of artificial intelligence technologies, where continuous adaptation, transparency, and stakeholder involvement are critical. By applying these integrated cybernetic principles, technologists, policymakers, and communities collaboratively develop ethical frameworks that continuously adapt, promoting fairness, accountability, and transparency in AI-driven decision-making (Floridi & Cowls, 2019).

The combined view challenges traditional notions of objective detachment and rigid control, instead emphasizing a holistic, relational understanding of complexity. Recognizing that observers actively shape observed systems encourages humility, adaptability, and ongoing reflection, enriching our philosophical appreciation of complexity and interconnectedness. Such insights highlight the profound ways in which humans, technology, and nature continuously influence each other, underscoring our ethical responsibility to steward complexity mindfully and sustainably.

The synergy of Wiener's and von Foerster's cybernetic insights equips us with powerful tools for navigating complexity, fostering innovation, and promoting ethical responsibility. By recognizing complexity as a dynamic, co-created phenomenon arising from interactions among observers, systems, and environments, we embrace adaptability, transparency, and continuous ethical reflection, ensuring that technological advancements align closely with humanistic values, ecological sustainability, and societal well-being.

Synergy and Integration: Wiener, von Foerster, and Complexity Science. Figure 6.3 illustrates the conceptual integration of Norbert Wiener's principles of cybernetic feedback and communication with Heinz von Foerster's second-order cybernetics and emphasis on the observer's role. The central synergy highlights dynamic complexity emerging from continuous interactions between observers, systems, and environments. From this integration flow two major domains: (1) practical applications such as adaptive governance and organizational decision-making, and (2) ethical implications including AI governance, transparency, and accountability. Arrows indicate the directional flow of ideas and their influence on both practical and ethical domains.

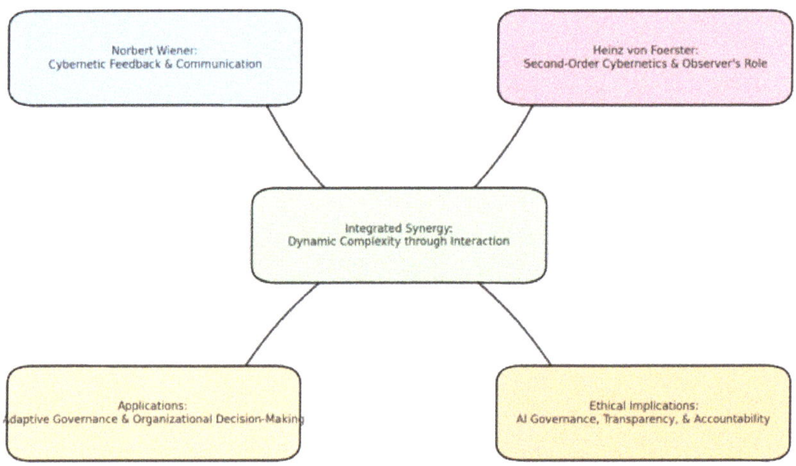

Figure 6.3. *Synergy and integration: Wiener, von Foerster, and complexity science.*

Note. Figure created by the author (2025) to depict the integration of Wiener's and von Foerster's cybernetic principles, illustrating their combined relevance to complexity science, adaptive governance, and ethical technology stewardship.

Practical and Ethical Implications Moving Forward

The integrated insights of Norbert Wiener and Heinz von Foerster profoundly influence how we approach practical and ethical decision-making in governance, technology, and societal interactions. Their cybernetic theories emphasize the importance of adaptability, transparent communication, and ethical reflection, offering invaluable practical frameworks for effectively managing complexity, uncertainty, and dynamic interactions in our modern world.

In governance contexts, Wiener and von Foerster's insights encourage adaptive policymaking and responsive leadership, promoting continuous reflection and iterative learning processes. For instance, governments and public institutions facing global challenges such as climate change, public health crises, or economic disruptions benefit significantly from embracing cybernetic principles. By fostering decentralized decision-making, continuous feedback, and adaptive strategies, governance frameworks become more responsive, resilient, and ethically accountable. A practical example includes adaptive urban planning initiatives, where city planners and community members collaboratively adapt policies based on real-time environmental data, public feedback, and evolving community needs. Such approaches enhance resilience, ensuring effective responsiveness and transparent governance that aligns closely with public interests and ethical standards (Walker et al., 2020).

In technological innovation, the practical implications of Wiener's and von Foerster's combined insights are equally profound. Technology developers, organizations, and researchers must continually reflect on their active roles as observers and participants within technological systems. Ethical frameworks guided by cybernetic principles ensure that innovations such as artificial intelligence, autonomous vehicles, and smart technologies are developed transparently, ethically, and adaptively. For example, the development of self-driving cars relies heavily on adaptive algorithms continuously informed by real-time feedback from human users, regulatory oversight, and societal values. This cybernetic approach fosters technological innovation that remains aligned with human dignity, ethical standards, and societal well-being, promoting transparency, accountability, and continuous ethical reflection (Floridi & Cowls, 2019).

Within organizational contexts, Wiener's and von Foerster's principles significantly reshape ethical leadership practices. Leaders who acknowledge their active roles as observers and influencers within organizational systems become more reflective, transparent, and adaptive. Consider organizations embracing agile methodologies: leadership and teams engage in continuous reflection, adaptive decision-making, and transparent communication. Ethical considerations have become central to organizational culture, promoting accountability, mutual respect, and ongoing learning. Companies that adopt this approach such as Patagonia or Zappos are widely recognized for their adaptability, ethical transparency, and robust innovation, highlighting the practical relevance of cybernetic insights for organizational resilience and sustainability (Laloux, 2014).

In societal contexts, the ethical implications of cybernetic theories underscore the importance of continuous learning, adaptability, and transparent communication. Community's engaging in participatory governance initiatives exemplify these principles vividly. Citizen science projects, where community members actively engage in data collection and environmental monitoring, reflect Wiener's and von Foerster's cybernetic perspectives. Participants become active observers and agents, continuously informing and adapting community policies and environmental management strategies. This participatory approach ensures greater ethical accountability, transparency, and responsiveness to community needs, fostering resilience and sustainability within local communities (Bonney et al., 2014).

Wiener's and von Foerster's insights invite us to embrace complexity and uncertainty as enriching and productive elements, guiding us toward adaptive, ethical mindfulness. By fostering reflective awareness, continuous adaptation, and transparent communication, their principles equip us with practical tools for navigating complex adaptive systems ethically and sustainably. Their combined cybernetic perspectives encourage us to view technology and complexity as opportunities for responsible innovation, humanistic growth, and ecological stewardship, ensuring technological advancement remains aligned closely with societal values, ethical standards, and the common good.

Conclusion

In exploring the pioneering ideas of Norbert Wiener and Heinz von Foerster, we have significantly enriched our understanding of complexity, communication, and observation, opening new pathways toward adaptability and reflective engagement. Their groundbreaking contributions illuminate how deeply interconnected our actions, technologies, and ecological systems truly are, guiding us toward more ethically responsible and human-centered innovation.

By embracing Wiener's foundational cybernetic principles, we recognize that feedback loops and adaptive communication are integral to maintaining equilibrium and resilience across diverse systems. Wiener encourages us to see complexity as a dynamic conversation or a continuous exchange of information, adaptation, and response. His insights offer us powerful tools for navigating uncertainty, urging us to embrace adaptability, transparency, and ethical mindfulness. Through Wiener's perspective, complexity becomes a vibrant, continuous process of dialogue and mutual responsiveness, enriching our capacity for innovation and ethical stewardship (Wiener, 1948).

Similarly, Heinz von Foerster's profound contributions to second-order cybernetics remind us of our active and influential role within observed systems. His philosophy challenges traditional notions of objectivity, underscoring the observer's responsibility in shaping the realities they perceive and engage with. By acknowledging our role as active participants rather than passive spectators, von Foerster inspires a more reflective and ethically conscious approach. His insights encourage us to continually reflect on how our actions, decisions, and communications profoundly influence the complex systems we study, manage, and innovate (von Foerster, 2003).

Together, Wiener and von Foerster's visionary insights equip us with profound philosophical and practical frameworks, enabling us to thoughtfully navigate complexity in governance, technology, education, and ethical decision-making. Their combined perspectives advocate for continuous learning, adaptability, ethical transparency, and reflective awareness as foundational principles guiding responsible technological advancement. By embracing complexity as an inherent, enriching aspect of life and innovation, we become better equipped to manage technology in ways that truly serve humanity, promote societal well-being, and sustain ecological balance.

Moving forward, these pioneering insights encourage us to adopt adaptive governance frameworks, fostering transparent communication and reflective ethical oversight. Organizations, educators, policymakers, and technologists inspired by Wiener and von Foerster can create innovative solutions that remain responsive, ethically responsible, and deeply aligned with humanistic values. Such approaches ensure that technological innovation does not merely pursue advancement for its own sake, but genuinely enhances human dignity, societal flourishing, and ecological sustainability.

The enduring legacies of Norbert Wiener and Heinz von Foerster challenge us to meet complexity not with rigid control, but with humility, adaptability, and ethical mindfulness. Their contributions remind us that the systems we design, influence, and inhabit are inseparable from our own actions, perceptions, and responsibilities. By applying their insights, we do more than navigate complexity—we become active stewards of it, shaping its trajectory through reflection, creativity, and collaborative innovation. This approach reframes technology and complexity as living conversations between humanity, society, and the environment, urging us to design futures where progress is measured not only in technical achievement, but in the depth of our care for one another and the planet we share.

Chapter 7: Warren McCulloch and Ross Ashby—Neural Networks, Cybernetics, and the Complexity of Cognition

Introduction

Our exploration of complexity has taken us on a profound intellectual journey, beginning with the fascinating unpredictability of chaos theory and the enigmatic world of quantum mechanics, moving through adaptive systems shaped by cybernetics, and into the deeply reflective realm of observation and human cognition. Each step along this journey has illuminated how intricately connected and dynamically adaptive our natural, technological, and social systems truly are. As we delve deeper into complexity science, it becomes increasingly clear that understanding complexity is not merely an academic endeavor; rather, it is central to navigating and thriving in an ever-changing, interconnected world.

In this chapter, we introduce two pioneering visionaries whose innovative contributions further enrich our appreciation of complexity, adaptability, and cognitive science: Warren McCulloch and Ross Ashby. Warren McCulloch, an influential neuroscientist and thinker, revolutionized our comprehension of human cognition and artificial intelligence through his seminal work on neural networks. By bridging biological neural functions with computational logic, McCulloch opened pathways for advancements that remain foundational to contemporary artificial intelligence and cognitive computing.

Ross Ashby, equally groundbreaking in his contributions to cybernetics, provided profound insights into the dynamics of adaptive complexity through his pioneering concepts of homeostasis and the "Law of Requisite Variety." Ashby's influential ideas underscore the critical importance of maintaining adaptive responsiveness and sufficient internal complexity to navigate external challenges effectively. His work continues to profoundly shape our understanding of complexity management, organizational resilience, and ethical governance.

Through exploring the pioneering contributions of McCulloch and Ashby, this chapter deepens our practical, philosophical, and ethical understanding of complexity. We will uncover how McCulloch's innovative neural theories illuminate contemporary practices in artificial intelligence, cognitive science, and robotics, and how Ashby's cybernetic insights enrich our approaches to adaptive organizational management, systemic resilience, and ethical decision-making.

By integrating the visionary insights of McCulloch and Ashby, we gain powerful tools for managing complexity effectively, ethically, and in ways that prioritize human values. Their contributions not only guide technological innovation and organizational adaptability but also inspire us to engage thoughtfully and reflectively with complexity, recognizing it not as a burden but as an opportunity for creativity, resilience, and meaningful innovation. This chapter illustrates how these two pioneering minds continue to profoundly influence our contemporary engagement with adaptive complexity, ethical responsibility, and sustainable technological advancement, guiding us toward a more resilient, innovative, and human-centered future.

Warren McCulloch

Biography and Academic Contributions

Warren Sturgis McCulloch (1898–1969), born in Orange, New Jersey, was an exceptionally influential figure whose pioneering ideas dramatically reshaped our understanding of neuroscience, cognition, artificial intelligence, and philosophy. Gifted with remarkable intellectual versatility, McCulloch's early academic pursuits took him through diverse fields, beginning with philosophy at Yale University and later medicine and neuroscience at Columbia University. His multidisciplinary background provided him with a unique vantage point, fostering deep curiosity about the intricate interplay between the brain's neural structures and logical reasoning.

Throughout his distinguished career, McCulloch remained deeply committed to understanding the complexities of human cognition and consciousness, believing strongly in the power of interdisciplinary inquiry. His collaboration with the young logician Walter Pitts at the University of Illinois in the early 1940s marked a watershed moment. This collaboration synthesized biology, mathematics, and logic, giving birth to the concept of logical neurons. Neurons understood not merely as biological entities but as logical, computational units capable of performing simple, binary operations.

The landmark paper published by McCulloch and Pitts in 1943, "A Logical Calculus of Ideas Immanent in Nervous Activity," revolutionized our understanding of neural function by formally introducing the idea of neurons as logical operators. To illustrate this idea, consider a bustling city intersection where traffic lights efficiently control the flow of cars. Just as traffic lights operate through simple logical instructions, including green signals "go," and red signals "stop." McCulloch and Pitts envisioned neurons as similarly performing basic logical operations, enabling complex cognitive processes through simple interactions and computations.

Their groundbreaking work laid essential foundations for modern artificial intelligence, inspiring subsequent developments in neural network architectures, machine learning, and cognitive computing. McCulloch's logical neuron theory significantly influenced the early development of computers and artificial intelligence systems, helping scientists conceptualize how machines could replicate human-like cognition and learning through logical and computational structures.

Beyond artificial intelligence, McCulloch's influence also extended into philosophy and cognitive neuroscience, sparking deeper philosophical inquiries into human consciousness, identity, and ethics. His interdisciplinary perspective invited philosophers, neuroscientists, and ethicists to reconsider traditional boundaries between human cognition and artificial intelligence, raising profound questions about consciousness, self-awareness, and ethical responsibility in artificial systems. By demonstrating the deep connection between neural structures, logical reasoning, and computational processes, McCulloch fostered broader philosophical discussions about what it means to be human in an increasingly technological world.

McCulloch's legacy continues to inspire interdisciplinary research and innovation today, emphasizing the importance of crossing traditional academic boundaries and embracing holistic, collaborative approaches. His work encourages modern researchers, neuroscientists, technologists, and philosophers alike to continue exploring the profound connections between biological cognition, logical reasoning, and computational intelligence, always maintaining ethical mindfulness and a human-centered approach to innovation.

In summary, Warren McCulloch's pioneering insights and interdisciplinary vision significantly enriched our understanding of cognition, neuroscience, and artificial intelligence, providing critical foundations that continue to shape modern science, technology, and philosophy.

Fundamental Concepts: Neural Networks and Logical Neurons

At the core of Warren McCulloch's innovative contribution lies his groundbreaking conceptualization of neurons as logical computing units. McCulloch, collaborating closely with Walter Pitts, advanced a revolutionary perspective: the idea that biological neurons operate much like computational logic gates, receiving various inputs and producing precise outputs based on specific conditions. This elegant analogy bridged the previously distant worlds of biological neuroscience and digital computation, laying the critical foundation for what would eventually become the field of artificial neural networks.

To better understand McCulloch's logical neuron concept in a humanistic way, consider a large traffic intersection controlled by traffic lights. Each traffic light receives input including signals from timers, sensors embedded in the road detecting vehicle presence, and pedestrian buttons indicating crossing requests. These inputs are processed using logical rules to determine precise outputs, such as when lights change or pedestrian crossings activate. Similarly, McCulloch and Pitts imagined biological neurons as logical processors, receiving various sensory inputs, integrating and processing them based on certain logical rules, and generating clear output signals. This insight allowed neuroscientists and computer scientists to understand neural functionality in terms of logical operations and computational processes, significantly deepening our comprehension of cognition and information processing in biological and artificial systems (McCulloch & Pitts, 1943).

The elegance of McCulloch's neural model is that it captures how complex cognitive functions, and intelligent behaviors emerge from relatively simple interactions among neurons. Consider again the analogy of musicians in an orchestra: each musician individually produces simple notes, yet together they create complex symphonies. Similarly, logical neurons individually perform simple binary operations, yet collectively form sophisticated networks capable of learning, recognizing patterns, and making decisions. This collective interaction is fundamental to cognitive processes like memory, perception, and decision-making, providing valuable insights into how human cognition and artificial intelligence might function similarly (Churchland & Churchland, 1990).

This fundamental concept of logical neurons directly paved the way for the development of artificial neural networks (ANNs) or computational structures now extensively used in machine learning, robotics, pattern recognition, and artificial intelligence. Modern deep learning architectures, which power contemporary AI applications such as voice recognition, autonomous vehicles, medical diagnostics, and image processing, rely directly on McCulloch's foundational ideas. Each computational neuron in these artificial neural networks mimics McCulloch's logical neuron, processing inputs to produce logical outputs, collectively forming systems capable of learning, adapting, and exhibiting intelligent behaviors (Russell & Norvig, 2020).

McCulloch-Pitts Logical Neuron Concept: From Biological Analogy to Modern AI

Figure 7.1 illustrates Warren McCulloch and Walter Pitts' conceptualization of the neuron as a logical computing unit. The top section uses a traffic light analogy, where inputs such as vehicle presence sensors, pedestrian crossing buttons, and timers feed into a logical neuron that determines the output signal (changing lights or activating crossings). The middle section employs an orchestra analogy, where individual musicians producing simple notes represent individual neurons, and their coordinated performance symbolizes the complex outputs of neural networks. The bottom section links these analogies to modern artificial neural networks used in deep learning, pattern recognition, and robotics, showing the conceptual continuity from McCulloch and Pitts' model to contemporary AI systems.

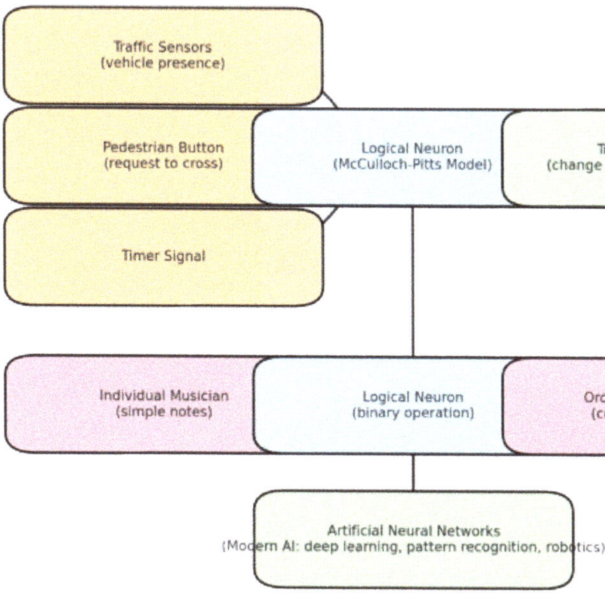

Figure 7.1. *McCulloch-Pitts logical neuron concept: From biological analogy to modern AI.*

Note. Figure created by the author (2025) to demonstrate how McCulloch and Pitts' logical neuron concept can be explained through relatable analogies and its connection to present-day artificial neural network applications.

McCulloch's concepts carry profound implications for our philosophical understanding of cognition and consciousness. By conceptualizing neurons as logical computational units, McCulloch's work challenges traditional views of human cognition as something inherently mysterious or purely biological. Instead, it frames cognition as fundamentally logical and computational, encouraging deeper philosophical reflections on consciousness, cognition, and ethical implications in artificial intelligence development. This philosophical perspective encourages us to responsibly and thoughtfully engage with AI systems, mindful of their cognitive parallels and potential implications for human society and ethical governance (Churchland & Churchland, 1990).

McCulloch's foundational insights into neural networks and logical neurons have profoundly shaped contemporary understanding and innovation in neuroscience, cognitive science, artificial intelligence, and robotics. By illustrating how simple logical operations collectively form complex cognitive functions, his pioneering contributions underscore the inherent interconnectedness and adaptability within biological and technological systems, fostering deeper appreciation and ethical mindfulness in our ongoing engagements with complexity and cognition.

Practical Applications: Influence on AI, Cognitive Science, and Robotics

The pioneering theoretical foundations laid by Warren McCulloch continue to significantly influence contemporary practical applications across fields such as artificial intelligence (AI), cognitive science, and robotics. McCulloch's logical neuron framework, conceptualized in collaboration with Walter Pitts, provided the critical groundwork upon which modern artificial neural networks were constructed, enabling revolutionary advancements in computational technology, machine learning, and adaptive robotics.

In the field of artificial intelligence, modern deep learning systems, central to technologies such as voice assistants, recommendation engines, and natural language processing, are fundamentally rooted in McCulloch's early insights. For example, consider today's facial recognition technologies: neural networks analyze complex patterns of pixels to identify individuals rapidly and accurately, similar to how McCulloch envisioned logical neurons processing information. Each artificial neuron processes input data, pixels from images, and collectively, these interactions produce sophisticated recognition patterns. This technology, now prevalent in personal devices, security systems, and social media platforms, demonstrates the tangible, practical impact of McCulloch's foundational neural network concepts (Goodfellow, Bengio, & Courville, 2016).

From McCulloch-Pitts Logical Neurons to Modern Deep Learning: Facial Recognition Example. Figure 7.2 traces the conceptual and practical evolution from Warren McCulloch and Walter Pitts' 1943 model of the neuron as a logical computing unit to contemporary deep learning systems used in facial recognition technologies. The diagram begins with the foundational McCulloch-Pitts model, progresses to modern artificial neural networks, and then focuses on a facial recognition workflow. In this workflow, pixel data from images or videos are processed through multiple layers of artificial neurons for feature extraction and pattern recognition, producing an output such as an identified individual or classification result. This progression illustrates the enduring relevance of McCulloch's conceptual framework to present-day AI applications, including voice assistants, security systems, and social media platforms.

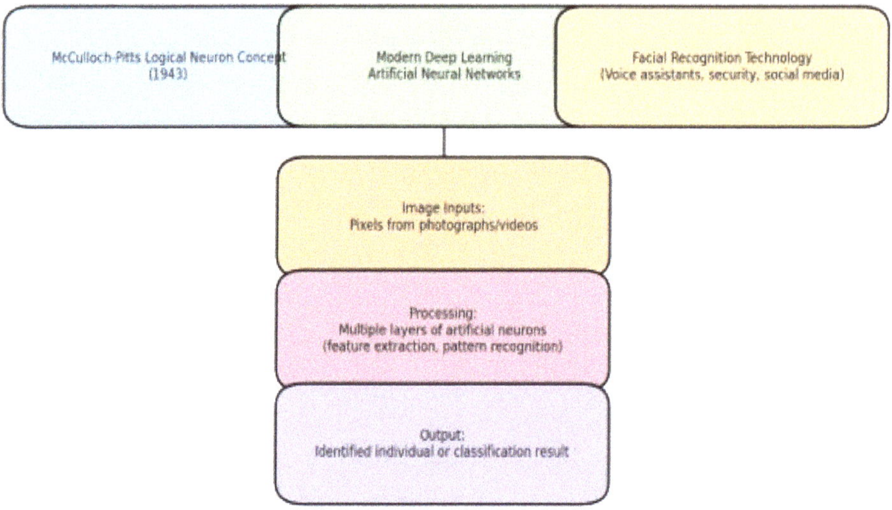

Figure 7.2. *From McCulloch-Pitts logical neurons to modern deep learning: Facial recognition example.*

Note. Figure created by the author (2025) to illustrate the connection between McCulloch and Pitts' logical neuron model, modern deep learning architectures, and practical applications in facial recognition technology.

Similarly, McCulloch's insights have significantly impacted cognitive modeling and the broader field of cognitive science. His neuron-as-logical-unit concept provided a computational framework that allows researchers to model human cognitive processes such as perception, memory, and decision-making. For example, computational models of human cognition now simulate how people process language or recognize patterns, guiding both psychological research and practical applications in education and skill development. Cognitive tutoring systems, widely used in educational technology, utilize neural network-based models influenced by McCulloch's theories to adaptively guide students through personalized learning experiences, illustrating practical relevance and effectiveness (Anderson et al., 1995).

In robotics, McCulloch's theoretical concepts have enabled significant advancements in adaptive and autonomous robotic systems. Consider autonomous vehicles navigating complex urban environments: neural network architectures, directly inspired by McCulloch's logical neurons, continuously process real-time data from sensors including cameras, lidar, radar, to make precise driving decisions. These robots dynamically adjust steering, speed, and braking, adapting flexibly and safely to traffic conditions, pedestrians, and unexpected obstacles. Similarly, robotics in healthcare such as robotic surgical assistants leverage neural networks to adaptively respond to subtle feedback from surgical environments, improving precision, patient outcomes, and safety during complex medical procedures (Panchmatia et al., 2018).

Furthermore, McCulloch's foundational insights profoundly influenced intelligent robotics used in exploration and logistics. Robots deployed for planetary exploration like Mars rovers use neural network architectures to autonomously navigate unfamiliar terrains, analyzing environmental data and making real-time decisions. In logistics, intelligent warehouse robots employ adaptive neural networks to manage inventory, optimize pathways, and enhance operational efficiency. These real-world examples highlight how McCulloch's theoretical contributions directly shape practical robotic solutions that improve exploration capabilities and logistical efficiency, reflecting genuine human-centered innovation (Kober et al., 2013).

Thus, Warren McCulloch's groundbreaking ideas continue to inform practical innovations across artificial intelligence, cognitive science, and robotics. His visionary theoretical foundations guide contemporary technologies, enhancing their adaptability, effectiveness, and ethical responsiveness. By embracing and furthering McCulloch's neural frameworks, we continue developing intelligent, adaptive systems that profoundly enhance human capabilities, improve societal well-being, and foster responsible technological advancement.

Philosophical Implications: Human Cognition, Consciousness, and Ethics

Warren McCulloch's groundbreaking insights extend far beyond the boundaries of technology and computation, significantly enriching our philosophical perspectives on human cognition, consciousness, and ethical responsibility within artificial intelligence. By conceptualizing neurons as logical computational units, McCulloch challenged long-held assumptions about human thought processes as pure biological phenomena. This revolutionary approach invites us to reconsider cognition and consciousness in more integrated terms, recognizing both biological and computational aspects as integral to understanding the human mind.

McCulloch's contributions prompt profound reflections on the nature of consciousness itself. Traditionally, consciousness has been viewed as a uniquely human attribute, inherently tied to subjective experiences and emotional awareness. McCulloch's computational view invites us to explore consciousness through the lens of emergent complexity, much like how a mosaic's beauty arises not from isolated tiles, but through their intricate and collective arrangement. This perspective encourages deeper philosophical inquiries into whether artificial systems, capable of replicating complex cognitive tasks, might someday achieve a form of consciousness, and if so, what ethical implications would arise from such a development (Dennett, 1991).

McCulloch's approach offers valuable insights into the ethical implications of cognitive enhancement and human-computer interactions. His work underscores the responsibility inherent in developing technologies that increasingly emulate human intelligence. For example, consider the rapid advancements in brain-computer interfaces, neural implants, and cognitive enhancement technologies. These innovations pose profound ethical questions about autonomy, identity, and the boundary between human cognition and artificial augmentation. McCulloch's philosophical perspective encourages reflective awareness and ethical responsibility, emphasizing that technological developments should remain sensitive to human dignity, privacy, and individual agency (Clark, 2003).

McCulloch's interdisciplinary perspective urges careful consideration of the moral responsibilities in creating intelligent systems. As artificial intelligence systems become increasingly sophisticated, closely mirroring human cognitive processes, critical ethical considerations arise regarding transparency, accountability, and fairness. Ethical questions about AI-driven decision-making such as automated healthcare diagnostics, autonomous vehicles, and algorithmic governance require thoughtful reflection informed by philosophical insights such as McCulloch's. For instance, in autonomous vehicle technology, ethical decision-making about accident prevention and passenger safety is deeply influenced by understanding cognitive processes and consciousness. McCulloch's conceptual framework offers crucial philosophical insights, encouraging ethical transparency, continuous reflection, and adaptive governance to guide responsible AI innovation (Floridi & Cowls, 2019).

McCulloch's integration of biology and computation also prompts deeper inquiries into human identity and the nature of intelligence itself. By highlighting cognition as computational, McCulloch challenges notions of human uniqueness, prompting discussions on the relationship between biological intelligence and artificial systems. Such philosophical exploration encourages humility and adaptability, recognizing that intelligence, consciousness, and cognition are complex phenomena shaped by both biological evolution and technological innovation (Churchland & Churchland, 1990).

Warren McCulloch's pioneering insights offer profound philosophical and ethical frameworks guiding our interactions with artificial intelligence, cognitive science, and technological advancement. By embracing his interdisciplinary perspectives, we cultivate greater ethical mindfulness, reflective awareness, and humanistic responsibility, ensuring that our technological innovations align closely with human dignity, societal values, and ecological sustainability.

Synergy and Integration: Linking Biological and Artificial Intelligence

Warren McCulloch's visionary integration of neural science and computational logic illuminates powerful synergies that bridge the intricate worlds of biological cognition and artificial intelligence. By observing natural biological systems, particularly the human brain's unparalleled complexity and adaptability, McCulloch provided foundational insights that continue to guide the design and development of intelligent computational systems. His pioneering approach emphasizes that artificial intelligence is most effectively understood not as an isolated technological advancement, but as an extension and reflection of our biological heritage, cognitive patterns, and adaptive strategies.

To humanize this synergy, consider the analogy of biomimicry in architecture: architects carefully study nature's designs including beehives, termite mounds, and coral reefs to inspire sustainable, efficient, and aesthetically beautiful human-built environments. Similarly, McCulloch's approach encourages researchers and technologists to observe biological neural systems closely, understanding how neurons communicate, adapt, and collectively produce complex cognitive behaviors. These biological insights inform artificial neural networks, ensuring that technological innovations closely mimic biological adaptability, flexibility, and creativity. For example, deep learning architecture used today in image recognition or natural language processing directly draw inspiration from the human brain's neural structures, reflecting McCulloch's early interdisciplinary integration of biology and computational logic (Goodfellow, Bengio, & Courville, 2016).

The synergy McCulloch established between biological cognition and artificial intelligence profoundly shapes innovative technological applications. For instance, advanced robotic systems employed in disaster response or search-and-rescue missions rely on neural networks inspired by human cognitive processing. These robots analyze complex environmental data, adaptively navigating through unpredictable scenarios by continually learning and adjusting their strategies. Similarly, medical diagnostic systems leveraging neural networks for image analysis and patient assessment closely replicate human diagnostic reasoning, ensuring accurate, adaptive healthcare decisions. These examples vividly illustrate how McCulloch's integrative insights translate directly into tangible, ethically mindful innovations, significantly improving human well-being and safety (Russell & Norvig, 2020).

McCulloch's synergistic perspective profoundly enriches our ethical engagement with artificial intelligence technologies. By closely aligning artificial systems with biological cognition, we become more ethically aware of AI's implications for privacy, autonomy, and human dignity. This integrated approach fosters continuous ethical reflection, transparency, and adaptive governance in AI development and implementation. For instance, developers of autonomous vehicles must closely consider human cognition, ethics, and adaptive decision-making patterns, ensuring these technologies act ethically and responsively in complex, real-world situations. McCulloch's foundational ideas thus encourage developers, researchers, and policymakers to ensure technological advancements remain deeply connected to human values and societal ethics (Floridi & Cowls, 2019).

McCulloch's integration of biological and computational perspectives prompts deeper reflections on human identity, consciousness, and cognitive enhancement. This synergy challenges us to rethink traditional distinctions between humans and machines, emphasizing our interconnectedness and mutual influence. It encourages humility, adaptability, and ethical mindfulness, recognizing artificial intelligence not as separate from human cognition but as an extension and reflection of our shared cognitive legacy. By embracing this integrated perspective, we foster greater understanding, ethical responsibility, and adaptive innovation, enriching our philosophical appreciation of complexity, consciousness, and intelligence.

The powerful synergy McCulloch introduced between biological cognition and artificial intelligence provides profound philosophical, practical, and ethical insights. His visionary integration continues guiding responsible technological innovation, emphasizing adaptability, transparency, and ethical stewardship. By closely observing and integrating biological insights into technological advancements, we ensure AI technologies remain deeply aligned with humanistic values, societal well-being, and ecological sustainability, creating a thoughtful and adaptive future for humanity and technology alike.

Ross Ashby

Biography and Academic Contributions

Ross Ashby (1903–1972), born in London, England, emerged as one of the most influential thinkers in the fields of cybernetics, psychiatry, and systems theory. His diverse academic journey, deeply rooted in interdisciplinary exploration, allowed him to offer profound insights that bridged human cognition, biology, and technological complexity.

Ashby’s multifaceted approach was characterized by his belief that understanding complex systems required insights from multiple perspectives, blending psychiatry, biology, and mathematical rigor to uncover the deeper principles of adaptation, control, and stability within both natural and artificial systems.

Initially trained in psychiatry, Ashby’s early clinical experiences at the Burden Neurological Institute in Bristol profoundly shaped his curiosity regarding the adaptive behavior of living systems. Driven by a desire to understand how organisms maintain stability amidst changing conditions, he transitioned into cybernetics and systems theory, which offered frameworks to explore these adaptive processes systematically. His unique integration of psychiatry and cybernetics provided groundbreaking insights into how living organisms, including humans, maintain equilibrium, adapt effectively, and thrive despite unpredictable environmental changes (Ashby, 1956; Pickering, 2010).

Ashby's pivotal contributions to cybernetics are encapsulated in his influential books, An Introduction to Cybernetics (1956) and Design for a Brain (1960). These works introduced foundational concepts such as homeostasis and the "Law of Requisite Variety." Ashby's notion of homeostasis explored how complex systems self-regulate and maintain stability, dynamically responding to environmental fluctuations and internal disruptions. To illustrate homeostasis in relatable terms, consider a busy airport managing hundreds of flights, passengers, and logistical challenges daily. The airport continuously adapts schedules, personnel, and resources, maintaining smooth operations despite unexpected disruptions such as weather delays or flight cancellations. This continual adaptive management embodies Ashby’s homeostatic principles, emphasizing how systems dynamically sustain equilibrium through continuous feedback and adaptation (Ashby, 1956).

Ashby's Concept of Homeostasis: Enhanced Airport Feedback Loop. Figure 7.3 illustrates Ross Ashby's principle of homeostasis using the analogy of airport operations. The external environment—including variables such as weather, passenger demand, and air traffic regulations—interacts with the airport operations system, which manages schedules, personnel, and logistics. Feedback mechanisms monitor delays, allocate resources, and make real-time adjustments. These components work together to maintain homeostasis, ensuring smooth operations despite disruptions. Orange dashed arrows represent continuous feedback loops, highlighting the dynamic, synergistic interactions and constant adjustments required to sustain stability in complex adaptive systems.

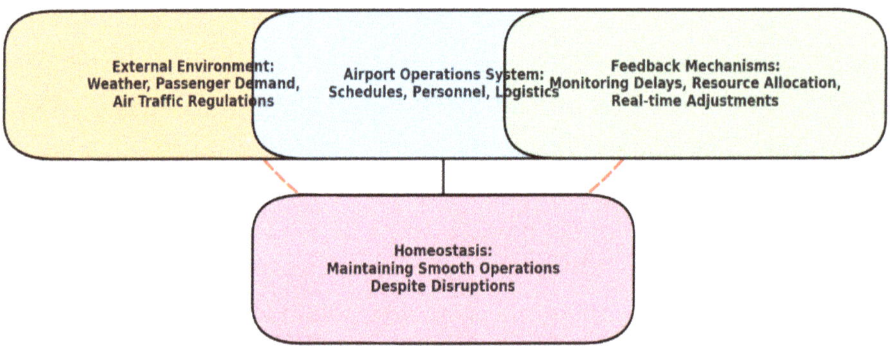

Figure 7.3. *Ashby's concept of homeostasis: Enhanced airport feedback loop.*

Note. Figure created by the author (2025) to visually demonstrate Ashby's homeostasis principle through a real-world analogy, emphasizing the role of feedback loops in maintaining stability and adaptability in complex systems.

Ashby's "Law of Requisite Variety" provides a critical cybernetic principle, stating that a system's internal complexity must match or exceed the complexity of its external environment to maintain effective control and adaptation. Consider the analogy of a skilled football team adapting dynamically during a challenging match. To effectively respond to the opposing team's diverse strategies, the team must possess sufficient internal versatility and variety, and players skilled in various positions, flexible tactics, and adaptive teamwork. Similarly, Ashby argued that successful adaptive management within complex systems, whether organizational, technological, or ecological, depends on internal complexity, responsiveness, and flexibility, allowing systems to match and effectively handle external challenges (Ashby, 1960; Espejo & Harnden, 1989).

Ashby's ideas profoundly influenced practical applications across diverse fields, including organizational theory, ecological management, technological innovation, and adaptive governance frameworks. His insights directly informed methodologies such as agile management practices and adaptive policy frameworks, emphasizing responsiveness, flexibility, and continuous learning in managing complexity effectively. Ashby's interdisciplinary contributions continue to shape contemporary practices, ensuring that organizations and technological systems remain resilient, adaptive, and ethically responsible in navigating complex, dynamic environments.

Ashby's cybernetic theories encourage us to embrace complexity and adaptability as intrinsic elements of reality. He advocated for humility, ethical mindfulness, and ongoing reflection in managing technological and organizational complexity, underscoring the importance of adaptive responsiveness and ethical accountability in societal development. Ashby's legacy thus inspires continued philosophical reflection, ethical stewardship, and practical innovation, providing robust frameworks for effectively navigating and responsibly managing complexity in our interconnected world.

Fundamental Concepts: Law of Requisite Variety and Homeostasis

Among Ross Ashby's most influential contributions to cybernetics are two closely interconnected concepts: the "Law of Requisite Variety" and the principle of homeostasis. Both concepts provide profound insights into how complex adaptive systems dynamically maintain stability, adaptability, and resilience within changing environments.

Ashby's "Law of Requisite Variety" articulates a fundamental cybernetic principle: the internal complexity and adaptability of any system must match or exceed the complexity it encounters in its external environment. In simpler terms, the more variety or unpredictability the environment presents, the more diverse, flexible, and adaptable the system itself must be to maintain effective control. Imagine a seasoned orchestra conductor faced with unexpected changes during a live performance like a soloist deviating from a score or sudden technical difficulties. To manage these complexities, the conductor must possess sufficient internal variety of expertise, flexibility, and rapid responsiveness to smoothly adapt, ensuring harmony and coherence among the musicians. Ashby argues that complex systems, whether organizational, ecological, or technological, similarly require sufficient internal diversity and adaptability to handle diverse external conditions effectively (Ashby, 1956).

In organizational contexts, the Law of Requisite Variety significantly influences management practices and decision-making structures. Businesses operating in turbulent and unpredictable markets benefit from cultivating internal flexibility, decentralized decision-making, and diverse expertise. For example, during economic fluctuations or market disruptions, companies with adaptive organizational structures such as agile teams empowered to make rapid decisions can effectively respond to external complexity. Organizations like Amazon and Google illustrate this principle vividly: they continuously adapt to market dynamics through decentralized decision-making, diverse internal expertise, and real-time responsiveness, effectively matching external complexity with internal adaptability (Beer, 1972; Laloux, 2014).

Ashby's principle of homeostasis complements this concept, describing the ability of systems to maintain stability through dynamic feedback loops and internal adjustments. Homeostasis is the adaptive equilibrium achieved when a system continuously senses environmental changes, responding through internal adjustments to preserve stability and functionality. Consider the human body's regulatory systems: maintaining body temperature, blood pressure, or blood sugar levels despite external variations. These physiological processes rely on continuous feedback and adaptive adjustments, ensuring internal equilibrium and resilience. Ashby's homeostasis similarly highlights how technological and organizational systems maintain stability through adaptive responsiveness to continuous feedback from their environments (Ashby, 1960).

In technological systems, the principle of homeostasis informs the design of adaptive artificial intelligence and automation technologies. Autonomous vehicles illustrate this vividly by continuously adjusting their driving behavior, speed, and steering in response to real-time traffic conditions, obstacles, and environmental feedback. These technological systems maintain operational stability, performance, and safety precisely because they dynamically adapt to changing external conditions, embodying Ashby's homeostatic principles in practical applications (Russell & Norvig, 2020).

Ashby's concepts significantly enrich our understanding of complexity, adaptability, and ethical stewardship. His insights encourage us to embrace complexity not as a barrier to overcome but as a valuable opportunity for ongoing learning, ethical reflection, and adaptability. Ashby advocates for humility, acknowledging that effective control or management requires openness to continuous feedback, adaptive responsiveness, and sufficient internal complexity to address external challenges ethically and responsibly (Pickering, 2010).

Ashby's fundamental cybernetic concepts, the Law of Requisite Variety and homeostasis, provide powerful tools for effectively managing complexity, fostering adaptability, and maintaining ethical mindfulness. By embracing these principles, we can ensure that our organizations, technologies, and societal systems remain resilient, responsive, and ethically engaged, effectively navigating complexity and uncertainty with creativity, innovation, and thoughtful stewardship.

Practical Applications: Organizational Adaptability, Governance, and Management

Ross Ashby's influential cybernetic principles have profound practical relevance for modern organizational management, governance frameworks, and strategic leadership. His emphasis on adaptive systems, requisite variety, and homeostatic balance guides contemporary organizations toward resilience, flexibility, and sustained innovation amidst uncertainty.

In today's rapidly evolving business environment, organizations face complex and unpredictable challenges from market fluctuations and technological advancements to global disruptions like economic crises or pandemics. Ashby's cybernetic insights are highly practical, emphasizing the necessity for organizations to cultivate internal flexibility and adaptive governance structures. Successful organizations do not merely withstand external pressures; they continuously adapt their internal strategies, decision-making processes, and organizational structures to match external complexities. For instance, companies employing agile methodologies such as rapid iteration, decentralized decision-making, and continuous feedback loops demonstrate Ashby's principles vividly, adapting quickly to changing market demands and uncertainties.

Consider, for example, the organizational adaptability demonstrated by Amazon during the COVID-19 pandemic. Facing unprecedented global disruptions, supply-chain uncertainties, and rapidly changing customer demands, Amazon leveraged decentralized decision-making structures, extensive real-time data feedback, and adaptive logistical management practices. This approach allowed the company to swiftly adjust inventory, logistics, and distribution strategies, maintaining high operational effectiveness and customer satisfaction despite significant external complexity. Amazon's practical adaptation demonstrates how Ashby's cybernetic principles effectively guide organizational responsiveness and resilience in real-world scenarios (Kraus et al., 2020).

Similarly, governance frameworks in both corporate and public sectors benefit profoundly from Ashby's adaptive insights. Effective governance in dynamic, complex environments necessitate real-time feedback, transparent communication, and adaptive decision-making structures. Public governance institutions responding effectively to large-scale challenges such as climate change, pandemics, or economic volatility employ decentralized decision-making and real-time adaptive strategies guided by Ashby's principles. For instance, governance responses to COVID-19 in New Zealand involved adaptive, transparent communication strategies, real-time data analysis, and decentralized management approaches. This enabled effective coordination and rapid adaptation, successfully mitigating the pandemic's impacts while maintaining public trust, transparency, and adaptive governance practices (Hartley & Jarvis, 2020).

Organizational management practices also significantly reflect Ashby's insights into requisite variety and homeostasis. Successful management in complex industries, such as technology or healthcare, emphasizes internal variety and flexibility to adapt effectively to external market dynamics. Consider healthcare organizations facing rapid technological advancements, regulatory changes, and evolving patient needs. Adopting decentralized management structures, cross-functional teams, and continuous feedback mechanisms effectively adapt services, patient care models, and organizational strategies. Mayo Clinic exemplifies this adaptive approach, employing continuous feedback loops, interdisciplinary teamwork, and decentralized decision-making to manage complexity effectively, enhancing patient outcomes and organizational resilience (Berry & Seltman, 2008).

Ashby's practical insights emphasize adaptability, ethical responsibility, and transparency as essential elements of effective organizational governance and management. Organizations guided by Ashby's cybernetic principles foster a culture of continuous learning, ethical mindfulness, and responsive adaptability. This culture ensures decisions remain aligned with societal values, stakeholder interests, and ecological sustainability, promoting ethical innovation and responsible stewardship within complex adaptive environments (Laloux, 2014).

Ross Ashby's practical contributions provide invaluable guidance for managing organizational complexity, governance challenges, and strategic innovation effectively. By adopting adaptive, decentralized governance structures, continuous feedback mechanisms, and transparent communication practices, organizations remain resilient, innovative, and ethically responsible, effectively navigating uncertainty and complexity within our interconnected world.

Philosophical Implications: Complexity, Adaptation, and Ethical Stewardship

Ross Ashby's cybernetic philosophy invites us to profoundly reconsider traditional perspectives on complexity, adaptability, and ethical responsibility. At the heart of Ashby's insights lies an essential philosophical shift from rigid, control-focused thinking toward embracing adaptive responsiveness and ethical mindfulness. His innovative concepts encourage us to view complexity not as something to dominate or simplify, but as a meaningful aspect of reality to be engaged with humility, adaptability, and ethical care.

Ashby's philosophy challenges traditional notions of command-and-control management, prompting deeper reflection on the intrinsic complexity and uncertainty of natural, organizational, and technological systems. Imagine a gardener carefully tending a complex garden ecosystem. Instead of imposing rigid control that would attempt to force plants to grow in predetermined ways, the gardener recognizes that thriving ecosystems naturally maintain balance through dynamic interactions among diverse species and changing environmental conditions. Similarly, Ashby's philosophy encourages us to embrace complexity as inherently adaptive and responsive, requiring continuous observation, adjustment, and flexible strategies to navigate effectively. This approach fosters humility, acknowledging the limits of our understanding and control, while emphasizing continuous learning and adaptive management in our interactions with complex systems (Ashby, 1956; Beer, 1972).

In practical philosophical terms, Ashby's concepts encourage ethical stewardship and transparent governance in technological and organizational contexts. By emphasizing the alignment of internal adaptability with external complexity, Ashby underscores the importance of ethical accountability, transparency, and continuous responsiveness. Ethical stewardship entails carefully considering how organizational decisions and technological innovations impact society, individuals, and ecological systems. For instance, organizations developing artificial intelligence technologies must continuously adapt their internal governance, ensuring transparency, fairness, and ethical responsibility as external societal expectations evolve. Ashby's philosophy thus encourages ongoing reflection and adaptive responsiveness, promoting ethical mindfulness in the face of technological complexity (Floridi & Cowls, 2019).

Ashby's philosophical insights extend profoundly to environmental ethics and sustainability, encouraging adaptive approaches to ecological stewardship. As global environmental challenges, such as climate change and biodiversity loss, grow increasingly complex, Ashby's concepts become crucial. Effective environmental management demands adaptive governance and responsive decision-making that continuously align internal strategies with external ecological complexities. Organizations and governments implementing adaptive policies such as flexible conservation strategies, dynamic renewable energy initiatives, and community-responsive environmental planning embody Ashby's philosophy, reflecting ethical stewardship, ecological sustainability, and ongoing responsiveness to environmental complexity (Walker et al., 2020).

Ashby's emphasis on internal adaptability highlights the philosophical importance of diversity, inclusivity, and pluralism within organizations and governance structures. To manage external complexities effectively, organizations must foster diverse internal perspectives, skills, and experiences, enabling adaptive responses to emerging challenges. This philosophical stance promotes inclusivity and ethical responsibility, recognizing that adaptability and resilience arise from diverse contributions, continuous learning, and transparent communication among various stakeholders (Laloux, 2014).

Ashby's cybernetic philosophy offers profound insights into ethically navigating complexity, adaptability, and uncertainty in contemporary society. By embracing adaptive responsiveness, humility, and ethical stewardship, we cultivate resilience, creativity, and humanistic responsibility. Ashby's philosophical legacy thus inspires us to engage thoughtfully and ethically with complex adaptive systems, ensuring our technological innovations and organizational practices remain deeply aligned with human values, societal well-being, and ecological sustainability.

Synergy and Integration: Practical Tools for Managing Technological Complexity

Ross Ashby's cybernetic principles offer an essential foundation for practical and ethical management of complexity in contemporary technological, organizational, and ecological systems. By integrating his insights, we obtain valuable tools and frameworks to navigate complexity adaptively, ethically, and effectively, enabling responsive decision-making and innovative problem-solving within rapidly changing environments.

Ashby's emphasis on the "Law of Requisite Variety" provides clear guidance for practical management strategies. Consider the example of modern crisis response teams, such as those handling natural disasters or public health emergencies. These teams confront complex, unpredictable situations requiring swift decision-making and flexible responsiveness. According to Ashby's law, their internal adaptability, including the variety of strategies, skills, communication channels, and decision-making processes must match or exceed the complexity and unpredictability they face externally. By fostering diverse expertise, decentralized decision-making, and adaptive feedback mechanisms, crisis teams effectively manage emergencies, reduce harm, and improve recovery outcomes. Ashby's cybernetic principle thus provides essential guidance, ensuring practical strategies remain responsive, adaptable, and effective in complex real-world scenarios (Comfort, 2007)

Ashby's Law of Requisite Variety: Dynamic Management in Complex Systems.

Figure 7.4 illustrates Ross Ashby's principle of the Law of Requisite Variety using a practical systems framework. External complexity—including unpredictable challenges such as natural disasters, public health crises, climate shifts, and market volatility—interacts with an organizational system containing diverse skills, expertise, communication channels, and adaptive strategies. This interaction leads to effective response and stability, characterized by harm reduction, resilience, recovery, and sustained operations. The feedback and continuous adaptation component ensure ongoing learning, resource reallocation, and policy refinement. The magenta arrows represent the feedback loops that enable constant adaptation and resilience in complex environments.

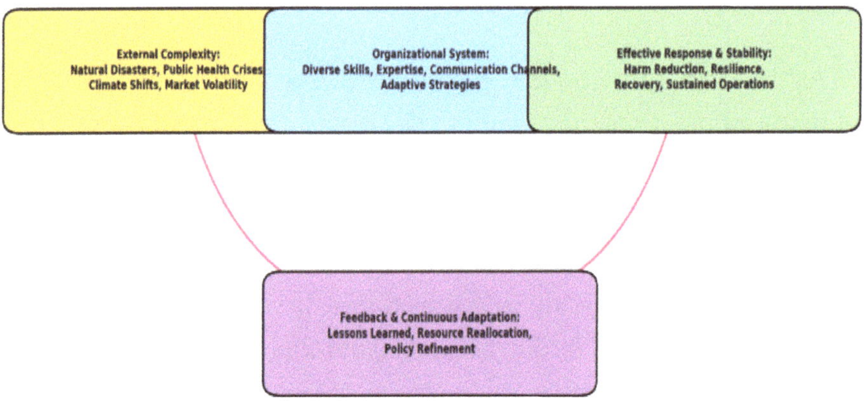

Figure 7.4. Ashby's law of requisite variety: Dynamic management in complex systems.

Note. Figure created by the author (2025) to visually demonstrate Ashby's Law of Requisite Variety with a focus on organizational and technological adaptability, continuous feedback, and responsive governance in complex systems.

Ashby's cybernetic insights significantly enrich adaptive management strategies in technological innovation. Agile development methodologies in software engineering illustrate this vividly: teams constantly gather feedback from users, markets, and stakeholders, adapting strategies rapidly to meet changing demands and conditions. Companies adopting agile principles, such as Spotify and Atlassian, exemplify this adaptive responsiveness, maintaining flexibility, innovation, and resilience. Ashby's cybernetic principles underpin these practices, highlighting the importance of continuous feedback, variety, and adaptation to effectively manage technological complexity and innovation (Cockburn & Highsmith, 2001).

In ecological and environmental management, Ashby's cybernetic tools are increasingly crucial for managing complex environmental challenges and sustainability efforts. Adaptive ecosystem management practices rely on continuously monitoring environmental changes, dynamically adjusting conservation strategies based on real-time feedback. For instance, adaptive approaches in water resource management address climate variability by continuously adjusting policies and practices to changing conditions, ensuring effective resource sustainability and ecosystem health. Ashby's practical cybernetic tools like feedback loops, adaptive variety, and transparent communication guide these environmental management strategies, fostering resilience and sustainability within complex ecological systems (Holling, 2001).

Ashby's cybernetic principles provide essential practical tools for ethical governance of advanced technologies, especially artificial intelligence and autonomous systems. Ethical AI governance frameworks depend on maintaining internal adaptability, diversity of expertise, transparent decision-making processes, and continuous ethical reflection. Organizations developing AI systems use Ashby's principles to continually assess, adjust, and refine their ethical strategies, ensuring alignment with societal values and human-centered objectives. For instance, ethical AI guidelines adopted by companies like Google and Microsoft leverage adaptive governance, transparency, and ongoing ethical reflection, embodying Ashby's practical principles to manage technological complexity responsibly (Floridi & Cowls, 2019).

Ashby's insights underscore the critical importance of adaptive flexibility, transparency, and ethical responsibility within complex technological and organizational systems. Practical integration of his cybernetic principles encourages us to embrace complexity and uncertainty not as threats, but as valuable opportunities for ongoing learning, innovation, and responsible governance. Ashby's approach fosters ethical mindfulness, continuous reflection, and adaptive stewardship, ensuring technological advancements and organizational innovations remain closely aligned with humanistic values, societal well-being, and ecological sustainability.

In summary, integrating Ashby's cybernetic principles provides robust practical tools and strategies for effectively managing technological, organizational, and environmental complexity. By cultivating internal adaptability, continuous feedback, ethical transparency, and reflective governance, we ensure that our interactions with complex systems remain responsive, ethical, and deeply human-centered. Ashby's enduring legacy guides our practical and philosophical approaches, empowering us to navigate complexity thoughtfully, ethically, and sustainably in today's interconnected world.

Conclusion

Through our exploration of Warren McCulloch and Ross Ashby, we have deepened our understanding of complexity, cybernetics, and the profound interconnections between biological cognition, technological innovation, and ethical responsibility. McCulloch's pioneering insights into neural networks provided a transformative perspective, illustrating that artificial intelligence and advanced computing are not isolated developments but rather extensions of human cognition, biology, and our innate drive toward understanding and innovation. His groundbreaking integration of neural science and computational logic reminds us that technological progress is profoundly intertwined with human curiosity, biological heritage, and our quest to replicate and extend human cognitive capacities.

Ross Ashby's foundational cybernetic principles, particularly the Law of Requisite Variety and the concept of homeostasis, have significantly advanced our practical and philosophical grasp of adaptive complexity. Ashby's ideas highlight the importance of cultivating internal flexibility, variety, and adaptability in managing external complexities effectively, whether within organizational systems, technological environments, or ecological landscapes. His vision encourages us to approach complexity not merely as a threat or challenge, but as a rich source of possibilities, innovation, and ethical responsibility.

Together, the insights provided by McCulloch and Ashby underscore the necessity of embracing complexity through adaptive thinking, transparent communication, and continuous ethical reflection. Their philosophical legacy compels us to approach technological advancement and organizational management in ways that remain deeply aligned with human values, societal ethics, and ecological sustainability. By doing so, we actively foster adaptive leadership practices and ethical mindfulness, ensuring that our technological and organizational innovations genuinely contribute to human flourishing, societal harmony, and ecological balance.

The combined contributions of these visionary thinkers also inspire broader reflections on our contemporary responsibilities as stewards of technology, complexity, and ethical innovation. As we continue to develop advanced artificial intelligence, autonomous systems, and organizational strategies, the humanistic philosophies of McCulloch and Ashby remind us of our ethical obligations to ensure transparency, accountability, and adaptive governance. This thoughtful approach enables us to not merely manage complexity, but actively harness it as a source of creativity, resilience, and ethical responsibility.

Embracing the profound insights offered by McCulloch and Ashby equips us with powerful philosophical and practical tools for thoughtfully navigating complexity in the modern world. Their visionary contributions guide us toward adaptability, humility, and reflective awareness, emphasizing that complexity is not simply to be overcome or simplified, but rather engaged with ethically, adaptively, and creatively. By cultivating these values, we can responsibly manage complexity, foster sustainable innovation, and ensure that our technological and organizational practices remain profoundly connected to human dignity, societal well-being, and ecological sustainability—today, and for future generations.

Chapter 8: Stafford Beer and Niklas Luhmann—Managing Organizational and Social Complexity

Introduction

Continuing our exploration into the intricate and compelling domain of complexity, we increasingly recognize how essential interdisciplinary thought is for understanding modern challenges in organizations and societies. Complexity is more than an abstract scientific concept; it is the fabric of our daily lives, deeply embedded within organizational structures, societal interactions, and human experiences. In previous chapters, we traversed the groundbreaking realms of neural computation, cybernetic feedback loops, adaptive systems, and the active roles played by observers within complex environments. As our understanding deepens, each visionary contribution adds invaluable layers to our perspective, enabling us to navigate complexity more effectively, ethically, and adaptively.

In Chapter 8, we turn our attention to two pioneering scholars whose insights have profoundly shaped contemporary approaches to organizational resilience, systemic adaptation, and social dynamics: Stafford Beer and Niklas Luhmann. Stafford Beer, a visionary figure in cybernetics management, revolutionized organizational thinking through his development of the Viable System Model (VSM), providing a practical framework for achieving organizational adaptability and sustainability. Beer's innovative perspective illuminates how organizations, like living organisms, can continuously adapt to their environments, effectively managing complexity through responsive communication, adaptive decision-making, and internal variety.

Complementing Beer's organizational insights, Niklas Luhmann, an influential systems theorist, introduced profound perspectives on social complexity through his theory of autopoietic social systems. Luhmann's groundbreaking work encourages us to consider societies not merely as collections of individuals, but as self-organizing entities that continuously regenerate themselves through meaningful communication and internal interactions. His ideas enrich our understanding of how complexity emerges within social structures, influencing organizational communication, governance strategies, and systemic adaptability.

Together, Beer and Luhmann offer complementary yet distinct lenses through which we can explore complexity, organizational resilience, and ethical responsibility. By examining their theories, we gain essential tools for navigating organizational complexity, adaptive governance, and ethical innovation. Their integrated perspectives encourage us to approach complexity as a valuable source of creativity, innovation, and adaptability, guiding us toward sustainable and ethically mindful strategies within organizational and societal contexts. This chapter will explore the significant philosophical insights and practical applications emerging from Beer's and Luhmann's contributions, deepening our appreciation of how complexity shapes organizational structures, social systems, and ethical practices in our increasingly interconnected world.

Stafford Beer

Biography and Academic Contributions

Stafford Beer (1926–2002) was a visionary British theorist, practitioner, and consultant whose groundbreaking ideas significantly advanced our understanding of organizational systems, complexity management, and adaptive governance. Born in London, Beer's intellectual curiosity and interdisciplinary mindset guided his path through engineering, operations research, management theory, and cybernetics, reshaping our approach to managing organizational complexity and decision-making processes.

Beer began his career with a deep commitment to practical problem-solving and innovation in management practices. During his early years in industry, he recognized the pressing need for organizational adaptability and responsiveness amidst rapidly changing business environments. This realization led him to explore cybernetics, a discipline emphasizing communication, feedback loops, and adaptive control mechanisms as a practical framework for addressing complexity within organizational structures.

His seminal publications, notably Brain of the Firm and The Heart of Enterprise, provided innovative frameworks to understand how organizations could emulate biological organisms in adaptability, responsiveness, and self-organization. Beer's central contribution, the Viable System Model (VSM), emerged from his extensive experience and rigorous analysis of organizational structures, presenting an insightful model depicting organizations as living, adaptable entities. The VSM articulated the internal functions, communication flows, and adaptive mechanisms required for organizational viability and resilience in the face of external disruptions and uncertainties (Beer, 1972; Espejo & Harnden, 1989).

Stafford Beer was also notable for applying his theoretical ideas practically and innovatively, notably in Chile during the early 1970s, where he developed Project Cybersyn, an advanced technological system intended to help the Chilean government manage the national economy adaptively. Though short-lived due to political shifts, Project Cybersyn provided profound practical insights into applying cybernetic principles to governance, economic management, and organizational decision-making, reflecting Beer's commitment to leveraging technology and adaptive governance ethically and effectively (Medina, 2011).

Project Cybersyn Opsroom Interface

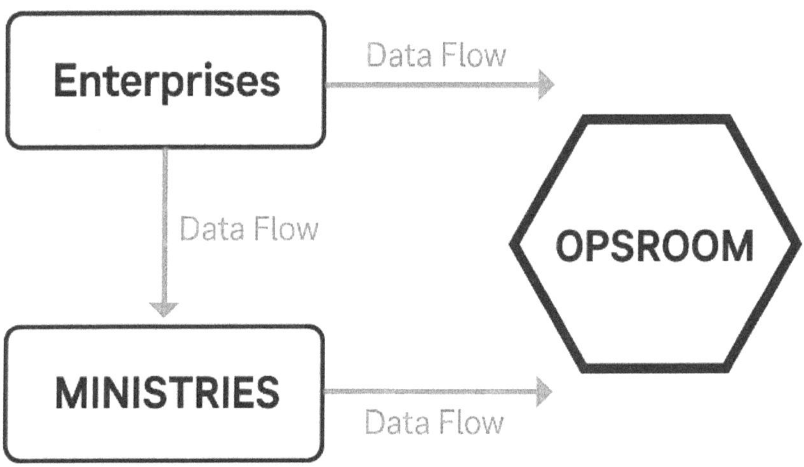

Figure 8.1. *Project Cybersyn Opsroom Interface.*

Note. Figure created by the author (2025) to illustrate the flow of economic data within Project Cybersyn in Chile during the early 1970s. Enterprises transmitted production and operational data to ministries, which then relayed consolidated information to the central Opsroom. This structure enabled real-time monitoring and decision-making, embodying Stafford Beer's cybernetic principles of adaptive governance.

Throughout his career, Beer continuously integrated interdisciplinary insights drawing from biology, psychology, engineering, and management to enrich his understanding and application of cybernetics. His adaptive philosophy emphasized that organizational resilience arises not through hierarchical, rigid control but through decentralized, flexible structures capable of rapid responsiveness to environmental complexity. Beer's unique approach continues to significantly influence contemporary management thinking, inspiring agile organizational practices, decentralized governance strategies, and adaptive leadership methodologies adopted by innovative organizations worldwide (Laloux, 2014).

Beer advocated for human-centered, ethical organizational practices, underscoring the profound responsibility leaders bear in shaping organizational cultures and decision-making processes. He believed strongly in transparency, accountability, and ongoing reflective practice, emphasizing that adaptability and ethical responsibility are fundamental to sustainable organizational success and resilience. His visionary contributions thus provide essential philosophical and practical tools, ensuring organizations and governance frameworks remain responsive, ethical, and deeply aligned with human values and societal well-being.

Stafford Beer's enduring legacy offers powerful insights into complexity management, adaptive governance, and ethical innovation. His humanistic approach, grounded in rigorous interdisciplinary scholarship and practical experience, continues to inspire contemporary leaders, researchers, and practitioners, guiding them toward more adaptive, resilient, and ethically responsible organizational practices and governance strategies.

Fundamental Concepts: Management Cybernetics and the Viable System Model (VSM)

Stafford Beer's innovative development of Management Cybernetics, particularly through the Viable System Model (VSM), offers a compelling and practical framework for understanding and navigating complexity within organizational settings. At its core, the VSM provides a structured approach for achieving adaptability, responsiveness, and long-term viability in organizational systems.

To grasp the intuitive essence of Beer's Viable System Model, consider the metaphor of a vibrant ecosystem, such as a rainforest. Within this ecosystem, numerous species and elements—trees, insects, birds, water sources—interact continuously, adapting their behaviors in response to changing environmental conditions like temperature, rainfall, and food availability. This ongoing adaptation, communication, and responsiveness maintain the rainforest's stability and ecological health. Similarly, Beer viewed organizations as dynamic, self-regulating entities that require continuous adaptation, effective internal communication, and flexible control mechanisms to maintain viability and respond effectively to external changes and complexities (Beer, 1972; Espejo & Reyes, 2011).

The VSM consists of multiple interrelated subsystems, each fulfilling critical roles and functions within an organization to ensure adaptive viability. These subsystems encompass operational activities, coordination processes, management decision-making, strategic planning, and policy governance. Beer emphasized the crucial importance of effective communication flows and feedback loops among these subsystems. Just as the human body's organs and systems such as nervous, circulatory, digestive interact dynamically, maintaining overall health and equilibrium, the VSM highlights that organizations require similarly effective interactions and adaptive responses between internal subsystems to sustain viability and manage external complexity (Espejo & Harnden, 1989).

The VSM emphasizes the concept of "variety" and internal complexity as essential components of organizational viability. According to Beer, successful organizations maintain sufficient internal diversity and flexibility to match and manage external challenges effectively, a principle aligning closely with Ashby's "Law of Requisite Variety." For example, adaptive organizations may employ decentralized decision-making processes, flexible resource allocation, and real-time feedback systems, ensuring internal variety matches external complexity. This dynamic alignment enables organizations to respond swiftly and adaptively to changing market demands, environmental challenges, or technological innovations, thereby sustaining organizational resilience and effective complexity management (Beer, 1972).

In contemporary organizational practices, the VSM significantly informs strategic management, adaptive governance, and leadership methodologies. Organizations adopting Beer's cybernetic principles, such as holacracy or agile frameworks, exemplify VSM's practical applications. These adaptive organizations encourage decentralized decision-making, continuous communication, and iterative learning processes, effectively responding to complex market dynamics, competitive pressures, and technological disruptions. Examples include companies like Zappos or Patagonia, where internal flexibility, continuous adaptation, and decentralized governance structures embody VSM principles, fostering innovation, responsiveness, and long-term organizational sustainability (Laloux, 2014).

Beer's VSM underscores the profound importance of adaptive governance, ethical transparency, and organizational humility. His cybernetic perspective promotes ethical mindfulness and continuous reflection, encouraging leaders and organizations to recognize complexity and uncertainty as opportunities for creative adaptation, responsible innovation, and continuous growth. By adopting VSM-inspired strategies, organizations can foster ethical accountability, transparency, and ongoing reflective practice, ensuring organizational activities remain closely aligned with humanistic values, societal well-being, and environmental sustainability (Beer, 1979; Pickering, 2010).

The Viable System Model offers powerful conceptual and practical tools, enabling organizations to navigate complexity thoughtfully, adaptively, and ethically. By integrating Stafford Beer's cybernetic insights, contemporary organizational leaders, policymakers, and innovators can effectively manage complexity, foster resilience, and promote responsible technological and organizational stewardship in our increasingly interconnected world.

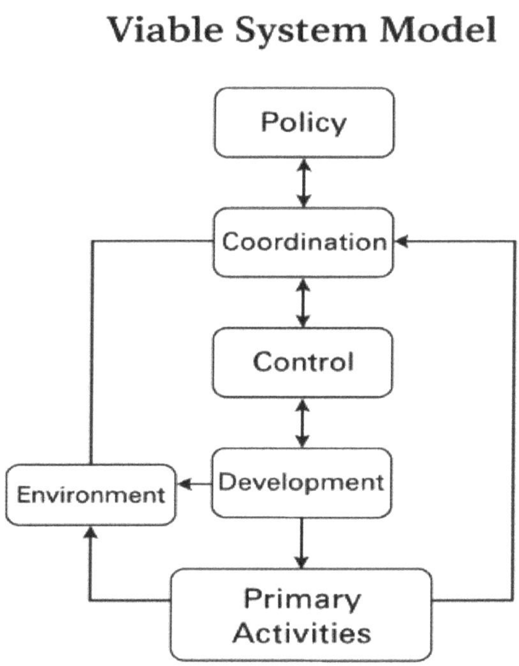

Figure 8.2. *Stafford Beer's Viable System Model (VSM).*

Note. The Viable System Model illustrates Stafford Beer's conceptualization of organizations as dynamic, adaptive systems composed of interconnected subsystems: Subsystem 1 (Primary Activities), Subsystem 2 (Coordination), Subsystem 3 (Control), Subsystem 4 (Development/Planning), and Subsystem 5 (Policy). Communication channels and feedback loops connect the subsystems to one another and to the external environment, ensuring viability and adaptability in complex conditions.

Practical Applications: Organizational Management, Strategic Governance, and Adaptive Leadership

Stafford Beer's Viable System Model (VSM) offers powerful, practical tools that have profoundly shaped modern approaches to organizational management, strategic governance, and adaptive leadership. By conceptualizing organizations as dynamic, responsive systems, Beer's principles guide leaders toward effective strategies for navigating complexity, uncertainty, and rapid change in today's interconnected environment.

Within organizational management, Beer's VSM strongly informs adaptive methodologies such as agile management and decentralized organizational structures. Agile organizations are characterized by flexibility, real-time responsiveness, and continuous feedback mechanisms—elements deeply rooted in Beer's cybernetic principles. Consider innovative technology firms like Netflix, where dynamic internal structures empower teams to rapidly respond to evolving market demands and user preferences. These organizations leverage continuous communication and real-time data insights to adapt strategies swiftly, fostering organizational resilience, innovation, and responsiveness even amid intense market volatility (Denning, 2018).

Strategic governance practices inspired by Beer's cybernetic principles profoundly shape organizational decision-making and responsiveness. Effective strategic governance involves continuous assessment of environmental complexity, ensuring internal strategies and decision-making processes align dynamically with external conditions. For example, global corporations navigating complex international markets, regulatory shifts, or disruptive technological innovations frequently employ strategic frameworks reflecting VSM principles. Companies like Unilever or LEGO exemplify adaptive strategic governance actively monitoring diverse external variables and adjusting internal strategies, processes, and resource allocations to remain resilient and responsive to global complexities (Beer, 1972; Espejo & Reyes, 2011).

In public administration and government institutions, Beer's VSM provides crucial insights for adaptive governance, policy formulation, and crisis management. During events such as the COVID-19 pandemic, governments that adopted adaptive governance strategies—characterized by decentralized decision-making, real-time data-driven responsiveness, and flexible resource allocation—demonstrated remarkable resilience and effectiveness. Countries like New Zealand exemplified Beer's adaptive governance principles by continuously assessing emerging data, communicating transparently with citizens, and dynamically adjusting policies to manage public health effectively. Such adaptive responsiveness, deeply rooted in cybernetic principles, ensures governance remains flexible, ethical, and effectively responsive to complex societal challenges (Hartley & Jarvis, 2020).

Beer's cybernetic concepts also directly influence adaptive leadership practices. Adaptive leadership involves leaders who continuously reflect, respond, and adjust strategies based on real-time feedback and changing circumstances. Adaptive leaders leverage diverse perspectives, decentralized decision-making, and transparent communication practices closely aligned with Beer's VSM. Organizations that cultivate adaptive leadership cultures like Patagonia or Atlassian demonstrate remarkable resilience and innovation, precisely because their leadership practices embody principles of flexibility, ethical accountability, and continuous learning (Heifetz et al., 2009).

Beer's practical applications encourage leaders, organizations, and governance frameworks to embrace complexity and uncertainty as valuable opportunities rather than mere obstacles. His principles foster deeper reflective awareness, ethical responsibility, and adaptability in decision-making processes. By recognizing organizations as viable, self-adapting systems, Beer's insights promote a human-centered approach that prioritizes ethical transparency, organizational resilience, and sustained innovation, ensuring that management and governance practices align closely with societal values and ecological sustainability (Laloux, 2014).

Stafford Beer's cybernetic principles offer essential practical tools and strategies for effective organizational management, strategic governance, and adaptive leadership. By embracing these principles, organizations and leaders can navigate complexity ethically, adaptively, and effectively, ensuring resilience, innovation, and long-term sustainability within complex adaptive systems.

Philosophical Implications: Autonomy, Organizational Resilience, and Ethical Responsibility

Stafford Beer's cybernetic approach offers profound philosophical insights that extend beyond practical organizational and technological strategies, enriching our deeper understanding of autonomy, resilience, and ethical accountability. At the core of Beer's philosophy is the recognition that complexity within organizational systems requires more than traditional top-down control; it demands adaptive flexibility, continuous learning, and genuine ethical mindfulness.

Central to Beer's philosophical perspective is the principle of autonomy. He emphasized that organizations, like living organisms, thrive when internal components have sufficient autonomy to adapt dynamically and respond proactively to challenges. Imagine a vibrant community garden: each gardener tends their own plots, exercising autonomy in decision-making regarding planting, watering, and care. Yet, they remain interconnected, learning from each other and collectively adapting to weather changes, pests, and environmental conditions. Similarly, Beer proposed that organizations function optimally when their internal structures and individuals have sufficient autonomy, enabling flexible, adaptive, and responsive governance to flourish in complex environments (Beer, 1979).

Beer's concept of organizational resilience further enriches his philosophical contributions. He viewed resilience not merely as organizational endurance but as an active capability to adapt, innovate, and thrive in the face of disruption and uncertainty. Philosophically, this emphasizes the importance of cultivating adaptive governance frameworks that can respond swiftly and creatively to external challenges, ensuring sustainable organizational vitality. For example, organizations that successfully navigated disruptions such as global financial crises or pandemics leveraged Beer's cybernetic principles—adaptive responsiveness, decentralized autonomy, and continuous feedback to sustain organizational effectiveness, stability, and ethical responsibility (Comfort, 2007).

Ethical responsibility, as emphasized by Beer, becomes deeply integral to organizational practices. His cybernetic philosophy challenges organizations to prioritize ethical mindfulness and continuous reflective practices in all decision-making processes. Ethical governance demands transparency, accountability, and responsiveness, aligning organizational actions with broader societal values and humanistic objectives. Consider organizations navigating the ethical implications of artificial intelligence such as bias, transparency, and privacy concerns. Beer's insights encourage organizations to proactively reflect on ethical considerations, continuously adopting strategies to ensure technological advancements remain ethically responsible, transparent, and deeply aligned with human-centered values (Floridi & Cowls, 2019).

Beer's philosophical approach underscores the necessity for continuous reflective awareness within organizational structures. Adaptive organizations thrive not just by responding to external complexity but by continuously reflecting upon their internal decision-making processes, ethical implications, and adaptive strategies. Organizations adopting Beer's cybernetic philosophy promote ongoing learning, reflective feedback loops, and internal ethical accountability. They foster cultures of transparency, continuous improvement, and adaptive innovation, ensuring organizational practices remain resilient, ethically responsible, and dynamically responsive to complex external conditions (Beer, 1979; Laloux, 2014).

Beer's philosophical insights offer a powerful framework for guiding ethical innovation, adaptive governance, and organizational resilience. By embracing autonomy, cultivating resilience, and fostering ethical mindfulness, organizations can navigate complexity thoughtfully and adaptively, ensuring practices remain deeply aligned with societal well-being, ecological sustainability, and ethical stewardship. Beer's enduring legacy continues to inspire contemporary organizational leaders, policymakers, and innovators, providing philosophical guidance that ensures complexity is managed effectively and ethically in today's interconnected world.

Synergy and Integration: Connecting Organizational Complexity to Technological Innovation

Integrating Stafford Beer's cybernetic insights with modern technological innovation significantly enhances our ability to manage complexity ethically and adaptively. Beer's Viable System Model (VSM) provides valuable frameworks for organizations to navigate complex technological environments, fostering resilience, ethical responsibility, and sustained innovation. By emphasizing internal adaptability, responsive feedback, and transparent governance, Beer's cybernetic principles empower organizations to integrate advanced technologies effectively, aligning technological advancement with humanistic values, ethical accountability, and societal well-being.

To illustrate this integration vividly, consider the analogy of an orchestra conductor guiding a performance of complex and dynamic music. The conductor continuously receives real-time feedback from musicians and audience reactions, adapting tempos, dynamics, and expression to ensure a harmonious, engaging performance. Similarly, organizations integrating Beer's cybernetic principles continuously adapt internal structures and technological strategies based on real-time feedback and ethical reflection. This approach allows organizations to effectively manage technological complexity, ensuring that advancements in fields such as artificial intelligence, data analytics, and automation remain deeply aligned with human-centered objectives and ethical considerations (Beer, 1972; Laloux, 2014).

Organizations successfully leveraging Beer's principles exemplify adaptive governance, responsive decision-making, and ethical stewardship in technological innovation. For example, major healthcare providers employing advanced AI-driven diagnostic systems utilize adaptive governance approaches inspired by Beer's VSM. These organizations continuously assess and adapt diagnostic algorithms based on patient feedback, clinical outcomes, and ethical considerations, ensuring technological innovations enhance patient care, protect privacy, and respect human dignity. By actively integrating cybernetic principles, such healthcare organizations effectively manage complexity, ensuring technological advancements remain adaptive, ethically transparent, and closely aligned with humanistic values (Topol, 2019).

Organizations employing cybernetic approaches to manage ecological sustainability and environmental innovation also demonstrate significant practical integration. Consider energy companies transitioning toward renewable energy solutions; these organizations must dynamically adapt technological innovations and internal processes based on continuous environmental data, regulatory shifts, and stakeholder feedback. Integrating Beer's adaptive management strategies and transparent communication approaches allows such companies to effectively manage ecological complexity, fostering innovation that remains ethically responsible, environmentally sustainable, and responsive to societal needs (Walker et al., 2020).

Beer's cybernetic principles provide valuable guidance for effective integration of AI technologies into organizational practices, particularly regarding ethical transparency and responsible innovation. Companies such as IBM and Microsoft have developed robust ethical governance frameworks for AI innovation, continuously adapting their technological practices based on real-time stakeholder feedback, ethical reflection, and adaptive decision-making. This integration of cybernetic principles ensures technological advancements remain accountable, fair, and aligned closely with societal well-being, human-centered values, and ecological sustainability (Floridi & Cowls, 2019).

Integrating Beer's cybernetic principles with technological innovation promotes ongoing reflection, adaptive responsiveness, and ethical stewardship. Organizations adopting this approach recognize that effective management of technological complexity requires continuous learning, transparent communication, and ethical mindfulness. Beer's insights encourage leaders and innovators to approach complexity not as something to be strictly controlled, but as a source of creative innovation, adaptive learning, and ethical responsibility.

The synergy between Beer's cybernetic principles and technological innovation equips organizations with powerful tools for effectively managing complexity, fostering ethical responsibility, and ensuring technological advancements enhance human flourishing, ecological sustainability, and societal resilience. By embracing adaptive governance, responsive innovation, and transparent ethical stewardship, organizations can thoughtfully navigate complex technological landscapes, creating meaningful, sustainable, and ethically mindful outcomes.

Niklas Luhmann

Biography and Academic Contributions

Niklas Luhmann (1927–1998), one of the most influential German sociologists and systems theorists, fundamentally transformed our understanding of social structures, complexity, and communication. Born in Lüneburg, Germany, Luhmann embarked on an intellectual journey that would profoundly shape sociology, philosophy, and systems theory. Initially trained in law, his curiosity soon led him to sociology and the study of complex social phenomena, prompting a profound intellectual shift that significantly enriched modern systems' thinking.

Luhmann's innovative scholarship is perhaps best exemplified in his groundbreaking concept of autopoiesis, originally a biological term introduced by Humberto Maturana and Francisco Varela and applied by Luhmann to describe self-producing, self-maintaining social systems. In landmark publications such as Social Systems (1995) and Introduction to Systems Theory (2012), Luhmann articulated the idea that societies and social systems continuously produce and reproduce themselves through internal communication processes and interactions. This concept revolutionized traditional sociology by illustrating that social complexity arises not from linear structures or fixed hierarchies, but from continuous, dynamic processes of self-production and adaptive communication (Luhmann, 1995, 2012).

Luhmann's extensive academic career was distinguished by his commitment to interdisciplinary scholarship, blending insights from sociology, philosophy, systems theory, and cognitive science. He served as a professor of sociology at Bielefeld University, where he cultivated an intellectual environment fostering critical discussions on social complexity, communication theory, and systemic adaptation. His lectures and publications attracted scholars across various disciplines, influencing diverse fields including organizational management, legal theory, political science, and even economics.

One of Luhmann's key intellectual contributions lies in his emphasis on communication as the foundational element of social systems. Luhmann posited that social systems do not consist primarily of individual human beings, but rather of ongoing communicative interactions. This unique approach challenged traditional views of sociology that prioritized individuals or institutions, highlighting instead the emergent properties arising from continuous interactions and communication patterns within societies. Luhmann's systemic approach to social dynamics significantly reshaped organizational theory, providing valuable frameworks to understand how organizations adaptively self-regulate through internal communication and interactions (Seidl & Becker, 2006).

Luhmann's scholarship also extended profoundly into philosophical explorations of complexity, autonomy, and ethical reflection within social systems. His autopoietic theory encouraged philosophers and social scientists to reconsider the ethical implications of systemic autonomy and self-organization. By understanding societies and organizations as autonomous, self-maintaining entities, Luhmann's philosophy highlighted the necessity of humility, adaptability, and ongoing ethical reflection within governance frameworks and organizational management (Luhmann, 1995; Moeller, 2006).

Throughout his prolific career, Luhmann authored numerous influential books and essays, profoundly shaping contemporary sociology, philosophy, and systems thinking. His enduring legacy is reflected in the continued influence of his ideas on adaptive governance strategies, organizational theory, communication practices, and social philosophy. By emphasizing complexity, autonomy, and ethical reflection as foundational principles guiding adaptive social systems, Luhmann's scholarly contributions continue to inspire scholars, practitioners, and policymakers globally.

Today, Niklas Luhmann's pioneering theories and intellectual contributions remain deeply relevant, providing essential philosophical and practical insights into social complexity, communication processes, and adaptive governance frameworks. His humanistic approach encourages ongoing reflection, adaptability, and ethical responsibility, enriching our capacity to navigate complexity effectively within organizational and societal contexts.

Fundamental Concepts: Autopoiesis, Social Systems, and Communication Theory

Central to Niklas Luhmann's profound insights into social complexity is his innovative use of the concept of autopoiesis, a term borrowed from biology and originally developed by biologists Humberto Maturana and Francisco Varela. Autopoiesis refers to the inherent capacity of a system to produce and maintain itself through continuous, internally generated processes. Applying this powerful biological metaphor to sociology, Luhmann described social systems as networks that reproduce by carrying conversations and decisions forward (Luhmann, 1995; Moeller, 2006).

To appreciate autopoiesis in an intuitive, humanistic manner, consider the vibrant culture of a community or a tradition, such as storytelling. Storytelling cultures sustain themselves by continually generating, sharing, and reshaping narratives. These narratives evolve through ongoing communication exchanges, adaptations to audience feedback, and the creation of new meanings that resonate across generations. Similarly, Luhmann's autopoietic theory conceptualizes social systems as continuously self-generating, autonomous entities that maintain their identity and coherence through dynamic interactions, communication, and meaning-making processes (Mingers, 2002).

At the heart of Luhmann's approach lies the belief that communication is not merely a transmission of information but a creative, self-organizing process through which social systems generate and maintain themselves. Communication creates meaning, shapes understanding, and facilitates adaptive responses to internal and external complexity. For instance, an organization facing rapid technological changes relies heavily on internal communication to adapt strategies, update internal structures, and align employee understanding with shifting environmental demands. This ongoing communication is not passive; it is inherently creative and adaptive, continuously regenerating organizational coherence and responsiveness to emerging challenges (Seidl & Becker, 2006).

Luhmann further highlights that social systems, through their autopoietic processes, develop distinct boundaries, identities, and autonomy. These boundaries are maintained through continuous communicative interactions, distinguishing the system from its environment while enabling responsive adaptation. A practical illustration is an educational institution: its identity, structure, and internal coherence depend on ongoing communication exchanges among teachers, students, administrators, and broader community members. Through these interactions, the institution continuously produces new meanings, adapts to societal expectations, and sustains its internal organization despite external complexities, exemplifying the self-producing and adaptive nature of social systems (Luhmann, 1995; Moeller, 2006).

Luhmann's concepts of autopoiesis and communication theory significantly challenge traditional views of social structures as rigid or static entities. His perspective underscores the inherent complexity, autonomy, and adaptability of social systems, emphasizing continuous reflective awareness and ethical responsibility. Social systems, according to Luhmann, do not merely respond to external stimuli passively; rather, they actively generate their own adaptive responses, continuously shaping their internal dynamics through communicative interactions and meaning-making processes. This philosophical shift highlights the necessity of fostering ethical mindfulness, adaptive governance, and transparent communication within organizations and social systems, ensuring alignment with societal values and humanistic objectives (Luhmann, 2012).

Luhmann's autopoietic theory and communication perspective offer profound insights into social complexity, enabling a deeper understanding of how societies, organizations, and institutions continuously regenerate themselves through internal processes. By recognizing communication as the core adaptive mechanism, Luhmann's theories guide our engagement with social systems toward transparency, adaptability, and ethical responsibility. Embracing these principles fosters organizational resilience, ethical stewardship, and sustainable innovation, ensuring our social structures remain responsive and human-centered within our increasingly complex and interconnected world. Figure 8.3 visualizes this relationship, showing communication as the self-sustaining core of social systems in interaction with their environment.

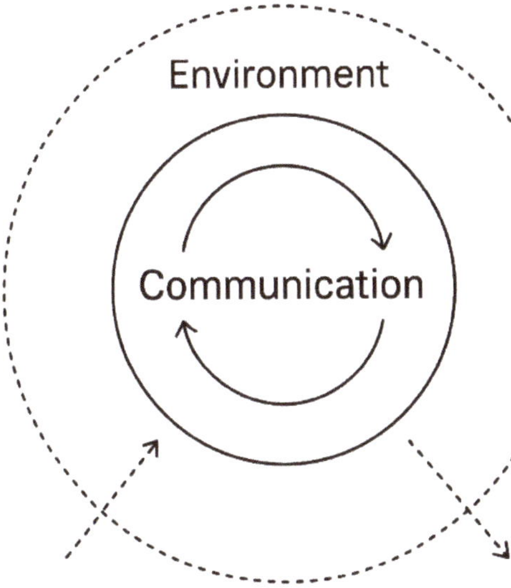

Figure 8.3. *Luhmann's Autopoietic Social System Model.*

Note. The model illustrates social systems as self-producing entities sustained through recursive communication. Communication is the generative mechanism that continuously reproduces the social system's identity and boundaries while distinguishing it from the environment. Dashed arrows indicate structural coupling with the environment, reflecting interaction without direct control.

Practical Applications: Organizational Communication, Social Dynamics, and Systemic Governance

Niklas Luhmann's insights into autopoietic social systems offer significant practical implications for enhancing organizational communication, understanding complex social dynamics, and designing effective governance frameworks. His ideas suggest that organizations and societies function most effectively when they recognize themselves as self-organizing systems, continuously adapting and evolving through internal communication and reflective interactions. These principles offer practical guidance for navigating today's complex organizational environments, societal challenges, and governance systems.

In the context of organizational communication, Luhmann's autopoietic theory emphasizes the critical importance of internal dialogues and continuous feedback loops. Organizations effectively utilizing these principles prioritize transparent, open, and responsive communication strategies, facilitating greater adaptability, resilience, and innovation. Consider successful companies such as Patagonia or Google, which encourage ongoing internal dialogue among teams, actively inviting and responding to feedback from employees and stakeholders. These communication practices reflect autopoiesis, continuously shaping organizational identity, enhancing responsiveness, and ensuring alignment with evolving market conditions and societal expectations. Such organizations not only foster adaptive innovation but also build internal coherence and resilience through meaningful communication practices (Seidl & Becker, 2006).

In addition, Luhmann's concepts offer profound practical tools for understanding and navigating complex social dynamics. Communities and social groups are increasingly faced with diverse, multifaceted challenges such as social inequality, public health crises, and environmental sustainability issues. Luhmann's perspective encourages stakeholders to recognize these social systems as autonomous entities that continuously regenerate and adapt through internal interactions and communication exchanges. Practical applications include participatory governance frameworks, community-based initiatives, and grassroots movements, where continuous dialogue, reflective interaction, and responsive communication significantly enhance collective problem-solving capacities. For instance, participatory budgeting initiatives empower community members through ongoing dialogue and reflective feedback, allowing local communities to adapt effectively to changing social needs and priorities (Cabannes, 2004).

Systemic governance frameworks also benefit profoundly from Luhmann's autopoietic principles, particularly in addressing complex societal challenges like climate change, public health, or economic inequality. Effective governance strategies guided by systemic communication approaches employ continuous feedback loops, adaptive decision-making processes, and transparent stakeholder engagement. Consider governance responses to climate change, where successful initiatives involve adaptive management strategies, continuous environmental monitoring, and ongoing stakeholder dialogue. Countries such as Denmark or New Zealand, known for their progressive environmental governance policies, illustrate this practical application of Luhmann's principles—continuously adapting their climate policies through responsive feedback and meaningful stakeholder interactions, ensuring effective and ethical governance of complex environmental challenges (Dryzek & Pickering, 2017).

The practical implications of Luhmann's theory extend profoundly into educational and organizational leadership practices. Effective leaders employing systemic communication strategies actively encourage continuous reflective dialogue within teams, promoting adaptability, resilience, and innovation. In educational settings, school administrators and educators adopting systemic communication practices foster more responsive, adaptable learning environments, empowering students and teachers alike through ongoing dialogue, reflection, and adaptive engagement. Such practical applications demonstrate how Luhmann's insights into communication and autopoiesis enhance organizational and educational effectiveness, ethical accountability, and responsiveness within complex adaptive systems (Moeller, 2006).

Luhmann's practical applications also encourage a deeper understanding of ethical responsibility, transparency, and adaptability within organizational and governance structures. Organizations and governance systems guided by systemic communication principles remain ethically mindful, adaptive, and transparent, actively aligning internal practices with broader societal values and humanistic goals. By recognizing complexity and communication as integral components of organizational and social systems, these practical applications foster greater ethical awareness, reflective practice, and adaptive leadership, ensuring sustainable, human-centered outcomes.

The practical relevance of Luhmann's autopoietic social systems significantly enhances our ability to effectively manage complexity, communication, and adaptive governance. By embracing systemic communication strategies, continuous feedback loops, and adaptive decision-making processes, organizations and societies become better equipped to respond ethically, effectively, and adaptively to complex social challenges, fostering sustainable innovation, societal resilience, and humanistic well-being.

Philosophical Implications: Complexity, Autonomy, and Ethical Considerations in Social Systems

Niklas Luhmann's theory of autopoiesis presents profound philosophical insights that challenge traditional assumptions regarding the nature and control of social systems. Luhmann's ideas invite us to reconsider social structures as inherently complex, autonomous entities that continuously regenerate themselves through dynamic communication and interaction. This philosophical perspective carries significant implications for understanding the autonomy, ethical accountability, and adaptability inherent within social and organizational governance systems.

Luhmann suggests that social complexity is intrinsic and self-generated, rather than externally imposed or centrally managed. This stance challenges classical views of society as hierarchical, controlled systems. Imagine a bustling city center with diverse interactions among individuals, institutions, businesses, and cultural groups, each entity autonomously engaged in continual dialogue, negotiation, and adaptation. Rather than being centrally coordinated, the vibrant dynamics of the city emerge naturally through countless interactions, dialogues, and self-organizing processes. Similarly, Luhmann emphasizes that societies and social organizations are self-producing systems, continuously creating and re-creating their internal structures, identities, and norms through ongoing communication and adaptive interactions (Luhmann, 1995; Moeller, 2006).

Luhmann's philosophy underscores the essential role of autonomy within social systems, highlighting the significance of independent, self-regulating processes that foster resilience, adaptability, and continuous renewal. Autonomy, in Luhmann's sense, is not isolation or separation but rather the internal capacity of social systems to regulate, adapt, and evolve without external control. This perspective has significant implications for organizational management and governance practices, suggesting that autonomous, self-organizing structures are inherently more adaptive, resilient, and responsive in complex and unpredictable environments. Organizations adopting principles like decentralized teams in innovative companies demonstrate increased creativity, flexibility, and responsiveness, fostering resilience through internal autonomy and continuous communication (Seidl & Becker, 2006).

Luhmann's theory profoundly shapes our understanding of ethical responsibility and mindfulness within social and organizational systems. By emphasizing the self-producing and autonomous nature of social structures, Luhmann highlights the need for continuous ethical reflection, transparency, and accountability in governance practices.

Ethical responsibility, within this framework, involves ongoing reflective dialogue, adaptive responsiveness, and transparent communication that respects autonomy and fosters ethical decision-making. Consider the governance of artificial intelligence systems, where ethical mindfulness requires continuous reflection on social implications, transparency in decision-making processes, and adaptive responses to ethical considerations. Luhmann's perspective provides philosophical foundations for understanding and managing these complex ethical challenges, ensuring technological innovations and organizational practices remain ethically responsible and human-centered (Floridi & Cowls, 2019).

Luhmann's philosophy also challenges us to rethink traditional notions of stability and control, embracing complexity, uncertainty, and adaptability as inherent features of social and organizational systems. Instead of viewing complexity as a problem to be simplified, Luhmann encourages organizations and societies to cultivate adaptive strategies, flexible governance frameworks, and continuous ethical reflection. His philosophy advocates for humility, recognizing our limited ability to predict and control complex social dynamics fully. By embracing adaptive responsiveness and ethical mindfulness, organizations and societies can better navigate complexity, foster sustainable innovation, and ensure meaningful alignment with societal values and humanistic objectives (Moeller, 2006).

Niklas Luhmann's philosophical contributions provide profound insights into the complexity, autonomy, and ethical dimensions of social systems. By recognizing social structures as self-producing and adaptive entities, his approach fosters deeper ethical responsibility, transparency, and adaptive responsiveness. Integrating these philosophical insights ensures that social and organizational governance practices remain resilient, ethically mindful, and genuinely aligned with human dignity, societal well-being, and ecological sustainability.

Synergy and Integration: Linking Social Complexity to Adaptive Governance and Technological Innovation

The integration of Niklas Luhmann's autopoietic social systems theory with contemporary adaptive governance frameworks creates a powerful synergy, enriching our practical and philosophical approaches to managing complexity ethically and innovatively. Luhmann's profound insights offer essential guidance, empowering organizations and governments to navigate social dynamics adaptively, transparently, and responsibly. By understanding social systems as self-generating entities shaped continuously through communication and feedback, adaptive governance practices become more resilient, ethically responsive, and human centered.

To humanize this integration, imagine a vibrant public forum such as a community town hall meeting where diverse voices interact, sharing ideas, concerns, and feedback. Within this forum, communication does not simply transmit information; it actively generates new meanings, perspectives, and possibilities. Luhmann's theory aligns closely with such dynamic interactions, emphasizing that effective governance arises not from rigid hierarchies but from continuous dialogue, reflective communication, and adaptive responses to community input. This concept becomes particularly significant when managing complex societal challenges like climate change, public health emergencies, or social equity issues, where adaptive governance and continuous engagement with community stakeholders are essential (Dryzek & Pickering, 2017).

In practical organizational contexts, integrating Luhmann's insights helps guide effective and ethical governance of technological innovation. Organizations leveraging adaptive governance practices actively solicit stakeholder feedback, regularly adapting technological strategies based on evolving societal needs, market demands, and ethical considerations. Consider organizations managing artificial intelligence development: continuous stakeholder engagement, transparency in decision-making, and adaptive ethical responsiveness are paramount. Such organizations regularly reflect upon and adapt their technological strategies based on continuous communication and societal feedback, ensuring that innovations remain ethically accountable, responsive, and aligned with humanistic values (Floridi & Cowls, 2019).

Adaptive governance frameworks inspired by Luhmann's autopoietic principles also hold practical relevance in public administration, especially during periods of significant complexity and uncertainty. Governments facing public health crises or economic disruptions employ systemic communication strategies, continuously adapting policies, resource allocation, and public engagement practices. For instance, during public health emergencies like COVID-19, governments adopting adaptive governance approaches effectively communicated public health guidelines, adapted policies based on real-time data and community feedback, and maintained transparent, trustworthy communication. This integrative approach demonstrates Luhmann's principles in action, highlighting how systemic communication and adaptive responsiveness foster effective governance, societal resilience, and ethical accountability (Hartley & Jarvis, 2020).

Integrating Luhmann's autopoietic theory with adaptive governance approaches underscores the importance of humility, reflective awareness, and ethical mindfulness in managing complex social systems. Recognizing social systems as continuously self-organizing entities challenges traditional governance paradigms based on rigid control or top-down hierarchy. Instead, Luhmann's insights encourage an adaptive governance approach rooted in continuous learning, reflective practice, and transparent communication. This philosophical perspective fosters ethical stewardship, resilience, and adaptability, ensuring governance practices remain responsive, inclusive, and ethically responsible amidst complexity and uncertainty (Moeller, 2006).

The powerful integration of Luhmann's autopoietic social systems theory with adaptive governance frameworks provides essential practical and philosophical guidance for managing complexity, technological innovation, and ethical governance. By embracing continuous communication, reflective responsiveness, and ethical accountability, organizations and governments can effectively navigate complexity, foster adaptive resilience, and ensure technological and governance practices remain human-centered, ethically mindful, and aligned with broader societal objectives.

To highlight these distinctions, Figure 8.4 juxtaposes Beer's structural subsystems with Luhmann's communicative autopoiesis, offering a comparative perspective on how each framework addresses organizational and social viability.

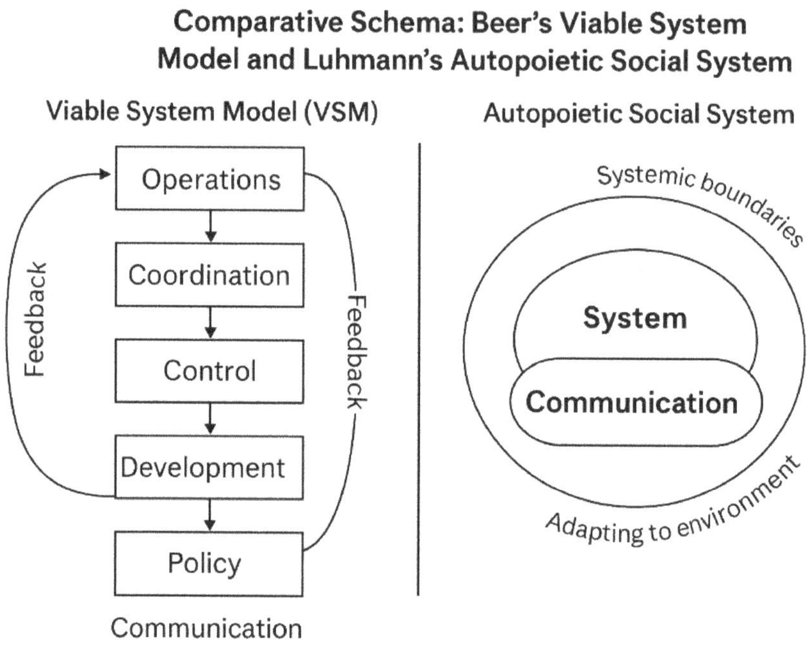

Figure 8.4. *Comparative Schema: Beer's Viable System Model and Luhmann's Autopoietic Social System.*

Note. This schema contrasts Stafford Beer's structural focus on five interlinked subsystems with Niklas Luhmann's emphasis on communication as the self-producing core of social systems. While Beer's model highlights organizational viability through structural feedback and communication channels, Luhmann's framework underscores autopoiesis—systems maintaining identity and coherence through recursive communication within defined boundaries. Beer's Viable System Model outlining five interacting layers, policy, coordination, control, development, and operations, akin to modern city structures with council, administration, finance, innovation, and service delivery.

Conclusion

Through our exploration of Stafford Beer and Niklas Luhmann's pioneering insights, we have greatly enriched our philosophical and practical understanding of complexity, cybernetics, organizational resilience, and social dynamics. Their profound contributions have illuminated the intricacies of managing complexity, highlighting that adaptive flexibility, transparent communication, and continuous ethical reflection are essential in navigating contemporary societal and technological challenges.

Stafford Beer's Viable System Model (VSM) serves as a powerful framework for understanding and managing organizational complexity. By conceptualizing organizations as dynamic, adaptive entities capable of maintaining resilience through continuous internal feedback, Beer encourages leaders and managers to foster adaptable decision-making, decentralized governance structures, and ongoing ethical reflection. This practical philosophy empowers organizations to face external complexities confidently and ethically, ensuring resilience and sustained innovation.

Complementing Beer's organizational insights, Niklas Luhmann's theory of autopoietic social systems deepens our philosophical appreciation of social complexity, autonomy, and adaptive communication. Luhmann's visionary perspective challenges traditional hierarchical governance, emphasizing instead the self-producing and continually evolving nature of social systems. His insights underline the importance of ethical accountability, continuous responsiveness, and transparency in governance and communication processes, equipping organizations and societies with essential tools for effective and responsible adaptive management.

The synergy between Beer's organizational cybernetics and Luhmann's social systems theory significantly enhances our capacity to manage complexity ethically, sustainably, and adaptively. Organizations embracing these insights demonstrate remarkable innovation, resilience, and responsiveness, continuously aligning their technological advancements and governance strategies with humanistic values, ecological sustainability, and societal well-being.

Beer's and Luhmann's contributions encourage us to recognize complexity as an inherent and valuable part of organizational and social life. Their insights advocate humility, adaptability, and ongoing ethical mindfulness, encouraging leaders, innovators, and policymakers to approach complexity not as a challenge to be controlled, but as an opportunity for continuous learning, creative innovation, and ethical stewardship. By recognizing and embracing these principles, we can effectively navigate complexity, foster adaptive organizational resilience, and promote responsible technological advancement.

The pioneering ideas of Stafford Beer and Niklas Luhmann provide profound philosophical and practical guidance for navigating the complexities of contemporary society. By adopting adaptive governance practices, transparent communication, and reflective ethical accountability, we ensure that technological innovations, organizational practices, and social dynamics remain deeply aligned with humanistic values, societal well-being, and ecological sustainability. Their enduring legacy inspires us to engage thoughtfully and adaptively, creating a future characterized by resilience, ethical responsibility, and meaningful human-centered innovation.

Chapter 9: Systems, Rationality, and Sustainability—Insights from Donella Meadows, John von Neumann, and Herbert A. Simon

Introduction

As we continue our exploration into the profound depths of complexity, we are increasingly mindful of the interconnectedness and interdependence of natural, technological, and human-made systems. Complexity does not merely represent a technical or scientific challenge; rather, it profoundly influences our daily lives, informing our decisions, shaping our environment, and determining our ability to adapt effectively. In this context, understanding complexity requires more than scientific insights, it demands a nuanced appreciation of ethics, human rationality, sustainability, and adaptive governance, empowering us to thoughtfully engage with the dynamic world around us.

In this chapter, we turn our attention to three remarkable visionaries whose interdisciplinary insights significantly deepen our practical, ethical, and philosophical grasp of complexity, sustainability, and rational decision-making. Each of these scholars has profoundly reshaped our understanding, offering powerful tools to navigate complexity effectively and ethically. Donella Meadows, a visionary environmental scientist and systems thinker, provided groundbreaking contributions that illuminate pathways for ecological sustainability and systemic resilience. Through her deep insights into leverage points and systemic interactions, Meadows has empowered communities, organizations, and societies to pursue sustainability meaningfully, transforming ecological and social systems toward more harmonious coexistence.

Complementing Meadows' profound ecological insights, we explore the pioneering contributions of John von Neumann, whose groundbreaking work in mathematics, computing, and game theory fundamentally revolutionized our understanding of rationality, decision-making, and computational complexity. Von Neumann's seminal theories, particularly those relating to game theory and computational complexity, offer essential frameworks for navigating strategic interactions, technological innovation, and adaptive decision-making amidst complexity. His insights are crucial for understanding the rationality underpinning economic decisions, computational advancements, and ethical considerations within complex adaptive systems.

Finally, we examine Herbert A. Simon, a Nobel laureate and interdisciplinary scholar who advanced our understanding of human decision-making, organizational complexity, and cognitive limitations. Simon's foundational concept of bounded rationality reminds us that human decisions occur within practical constraints of knowledge, resources, and cognitive capabilities. His innovative approach significantly reshapes how we manage complexity, adaptive governance, and organizational resilience, enabling us to develop decision-making processes that remain ethically aware, reflective, and adaptive to dynamic complexities.

Together, the interdisciplinary insights of Meadows, von Neumann, and Simon illuminate practical pathways toward sustainability, rational decision-making, and ethical responsibility within complex adaptive systems. By integrating their visionary perspectives, we can navigate complexity more effectively, ensuring that our societal decisions, technological advancements, and organizational practices remain profoundly human-centered, ethically responsible, and ecologically sustainable. Their enduring contributions inspire us not merely to manage complexity but to embrace it as a valuable opportunity for ethical stewardship, adaptive innovation, and meaningful human flourishing in a dynamic and interconnected world.

Donella Meadows

Biography and Academic Contributions

Donella "Dana" Meadows (1941–2001) was a visionary American scientist, educator, and pioneering advocate of environmental sustainability whose groundbreaking contributions profoundly reshaped global perspectives on ecological systems, sustainability, and systemic complexity. Born in Elgin, Illinois, Meadows demonstrated from an early age a remarkable passion for understanding the interconnectedness of environmental, social, and economic systems. Her academic journey, marked by rigorous scientific exploration and deep humanistic sensitivity, led her to become one of the most influential voices advocating systemic solutions to global sustainability challenges.

Meadows gained international acclaim primarily through her seminal work with the Club of Rome, co-authoring the influential 1972 report, The Limits to Growth. This groundbreaking study used system dynamics modeling to explore the consequences of unchecked global growth on ecological stability, resource availability, and societal well-being. Published during a critical period of heightened environmental awareness, the report significantly shifted public and policy-maker attention toward the urgent necessity of sustainable practices and ecological stewardship (Meadows et al., 1972).

Throughout her career, Meadows consistently emphasized interdisciplinary scholarship, bridging environmental science, economics, social sciences, and systems theory. She recognized early on that sustainability could not be achieved through isolated approaches, but required a holistic, systemic understanding of the intricate relationships between human activities, natural ecosystems, and socioeconomic factors. Her work transcended traditional disciplinary boundaries, promoting a richer, more integrated appreciation of how complex systems operate, interact, and evolve over time (Meadows, 2008).

In addition to her influential research, Meadows was a deeply committed educator and communicator, dedicated to translating complex scientific insights into clear, engaging narratives accessible to diverse audiences. As a professor at Dartmouth College, she passionately advocated systems thinking and ecological literacy, shaping generations of students, educators, policymakers, and practitioners worldwide. Her accessible writings, public lectures, and influential columns regularly highlighted the interconnected complexity of global systems, inspiring broad societal awareness and meaningful action toward sustainability.

Meadows' contributions significantly enriched the philosophical discourse on complexity, ethics, and adaptive governance. By emphasizing systemic dynamics and interconnectedness, she challenged traditional, reductionist perspectives on environmental management, advocating instead for ethical stewardship, reflective adaptability, and continuous learning. Meadows' philosophy encourages us to embrace complexity and interdependence as fundamental to sustainability, resilience, and ethical responsibility, highlighting that meaningful solutions must be systemic, inclusive, and ethically mindful (Meadows, 1999).

Donella Meadows' legacy is profoundly evident in the ongoing global efforts toward sustainable development, environmental stewardship, and adaptive management strategies. Her concepts of systemic leverage points are specific, strategic areas within complex systems where small shifts produce significant systemic changes and continue to guide innovative practices in environmental management, public policy, and organizational strategy. Meadows' foundational insights remain deeply influential, empowering individuals, organizations, and governments worldwide to address complex environmental and societal challenges through systemic, ethical, and adaptive approaches.

Through her life's work, Meadows provided powerful tools for understanding systemic complexity, ecological resilience, and sustainability. Her profound humanistic vision continues to inspire us to thoughtfully navigate complexity, foster ethical responsibility, and collaboratively strive for sustainable solutions that genuinely enhance human flourishing, ecological integrity, and societal resilience in an interconnected world.

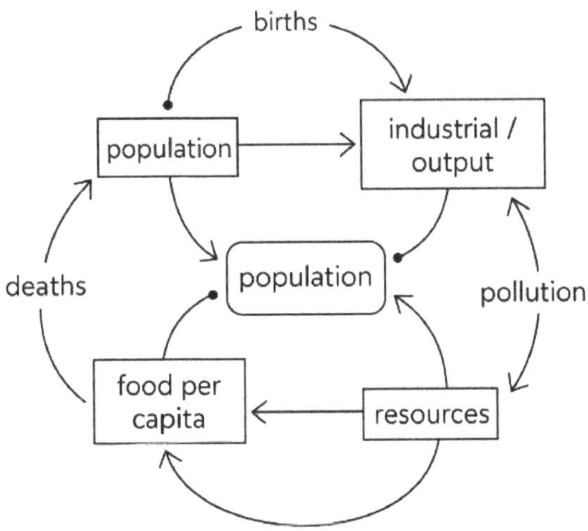

Figure 9.1. *World3 Model of The Limits to Growth.*

Note. This systems dynamics diagram illustrates Donella Meadows' seminal contribution in The Limits to Growth (1972). It shows the interrelationships between population, industrial output, resources, food per capita, and pollution, emphasizing reinforcing and balancing feedback loops that drive ecological and economic sustainability.

Fundamental Concepts: Systems Thinking, Leverage Points, and Sustainability

At the core of Donella Meadows' transformative insights into complexity lies the interconnected philosophy of systems thinking and the strategic use of leverage points. Meadows profoundly understood that sustainability and resilience are not simply achieved through isolated solutions or piecemeal interventions; rather, they emerge from careful, holistic consideration of the intricate interrelationships within complex systems. This systemic view invites us to recognize complexity as inherently interdependent, encouraging thoughtful identification of key leverage points, strategic areas within systems where small interventions yield significant, transformative outcomes.

Systems thinking, as articulated by Meadows, challenges traditional reductionist approaches, advocating instead for understanding the dynamic interactions among various system components and the feedback loops that sustain them. To understand this intuitively, imagine a river ecosystem. Alterations in water quality, fish populations, vegetation, and human activity are deeply interconnected, each influencing the other in intricate, often unforeseen ways. Meadows argues that systems thinking is essential for grasping such complexity, guiding us toward meaningful, holistic interventions that respect systemic interdependencies and promote long-term sustainability (Meadows, 2008).

Central to Meadows' systemic approach is her concept of leverage points. Specific locations within complex systems where modest adjustments can lead to profound, systemic shifts. She emphasized that effectively intervening in complex social, ecological, or economic systems requires identifying high-impact leverage points capable of initiating meaningful, enduring transformations. Leverage points might involve modifying economic incentives, altering regulatory frameworks, adjusting information flows, or reshaping societal paradigms and values. For instance, reorienting economic subsidies from fossil fuels toward renewable energy can significantly accelerate society's transition to sustainable energy sources, exemplifying the transformative potential of strategic leverage points (Meadows, 1999).

Meadows highlighted that leverage points operate at multiple levels, ranging from tangible parameters (such as subsidies or taxes) to deeper systemic layers like societal beliefs, goals, and paradigms. Among these leverage points, Meadows identified paradigm shifts that are fundamental transformations in societal attitudes, beliefs, and values as especially potent. For example, shifting society's underlying paradigm from unlimited economic growth toward ecological sustainability represents a powerful leverage point capable of initiating widespread systemic change. This deeper-level leverage point influences numerous interconnected systems, guiding collective decision-making, technological innovation, and sustainable practices across multiple societal domains (Meadows, 1999; Abson et al., 2017).

Meadows' systems thinking and leverage points significantly impact fields such as sustainable development, environmental policy, and adaptive management. Environmental policymakers leveraging Meadows' insights effectively design strategies targeting key leverage points, promoting sustainable practices such as ecosystem restoration, sustainable agriculture, and renewable energy transitions. Businesses employing systems thinking frameworks systematically identify leverage points within their operational and supply-chain practices, optimizing resource use, reducing environmental impacts, and enhancing resilience. These practical approaches demonstrate the profound effectiveness and real-world relevance of Meadows' systemic contributions to sustainability (Sterman, 2001).

Meadows' ideas profoundly challenge traditional linear thinking, inviting deeper reflection on complexity, interdependence, and ethical responsibility. Her system's thinking approach underscores the necessity of humility, recognizing that effective intervention in complex systems requires adaptive responsiveness, ethical mindfulness, and continuous reflection. This philosophy encourages us to appreciate complexity as a rich source of possibility, creativity, and sustainable innovation, guiding our collective responsibility to steward ecological and social systems ethically and adaptively (Meadows, 2008).

Figure 9.2
Leverage Points in a System

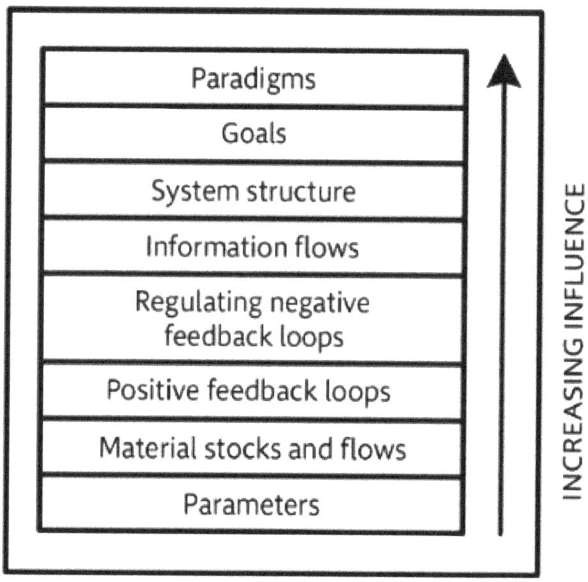

Figure 9.2. *Leverage Points in a System.*

Note. This figure presents Donella Meadows' hierarchy of leverage points within a systemic structure. It illustrates how interventions range from parameters (low leverage) to paradigm shifts (high leverage), showing that small changes at higher levels of systemic influence can lead to profound and transformative outcomes.

Donella Meadows' fundamental concepts of systems thinking, leverage points, and sustainability provide powerful philosophical and practical tools, empowering us to thoughtfully navigate complexity, foster sustainability, and ethically guide societal change. By embracing these systemic insights, we can ensure that our decisions and actions remain deeply interconnected, adaptive, and aligned with humanistic values, ecological sustainability, and societal resilience.

Practical Applications: Environmental Management, Sustainable Development, Policy Making

Donella Meadows' groundbreaking insights into systems thinking and complexity have significant practical applications in environmental management, sustainable development, and policy formulation. By embracing a systemic approach, Meadows' principles enable communities, organizations, and governments to effectively navigate complexity, manage environmental resources sustainably, and create policies that are adaptable, inclusive, and responsive to ecological and societal dynamics.

In environmental management, Meadows' concepts have guided numerous ecological restoration and biodiversity conservation initiatives. For example, restoration projects in damaged ecosystems, such as deforested lands or degraded wetlands, benefit immensely from systems thinking frameworks. Practitioners employing these principles carefully analyze interactions among ecological elements, understanding that interventions must account for interconnected impacts on species, habitats, and local communities. Restoration practices inspired by Meadows' insights frequently include continuous monitoring, feedback loops, and adaptive adjustments, ensuring ecological restoration initiatives are resilient, effective, and sustainable in the long term (Folke et al., 2005).

Meadows' systems thinking significantly enriches sustainable city planning and urban development strategies. Cities worldwide face increasingly complex environmental, social, and economic challenges, from climate change and resource scarcity to urban density and social equity. Systems thinking frameworks enable urban planners to consider how transportation, green spaces, housing, and economic activities are intricately connected. Cities adopting sustainable planning approaches inspired by Meadows, such as Copenhagen or Singapore, integrate renewable energy transitions, urban agriculture, and adaptive infrastructure strategies. These approaches effectively address complexity, fostering urban resilience, ecological sustainability, and community well-being through continuous adaptation and stakeholder engagement (Newman & Jennings, 2008).

In the realm of sustainable development and policy formulation, Meadows' insights profoundly influence adaptive governance strategies and participatory policymaking. Governments and organizations adopting systems thinking frameworks emphasize participatory governance, inclusive stakeholder engagement, and continuous policy adaptation. Participatory budgeting practices in cities worldwide exemplify Meadows' principles that communities actively participate in allocating resources toward sustainable initiatives, ecological conservation, and community development. This approach ensures policies remain responsive, transparent, and ethically aligned with community needs and ecological considerations, highlighting Meadows' systemic emphasis on interconnectedness and adaptive governance (Cabannes, 2004).

Meadows' insights significantly inform adaptive resource management strategies, particularly within sustainable agriculture and natural resource governance. Organizations employing systems thinking principles successfully manage agricultural resources, water management, and fisheries sustainably. Adaptive management approaches involve continuous ecological monitoring, stakeholder collaboration, and flexible decision-making, enabling communities and policymakers to respond dynamically to ecological feedback and environmental changes. Examples include adaptive water governance in drought-prone regions or community-based fisheries management initiatives, demonstrating the practical effectiveness and ecological sustainability achievable through Meadows' systemic insights (Armitage et al., 2009).

Meadows' systems thinking encourages ethical stewardship, humility, and adaptive responsiveness in managing ecological and social systems. Practical applications of her ideas foster continuous ethical reflection, transparency, and community engagement. Organizations, governments, and communities adopting Meadows' principles prioritize ethical mindfulness, ecological sustainability, and societal resilience, ensuring sustainability initiatives remain ethically responsible and adaptive to evolving environmental and societal contexts.

The practical applications of Donella Meadows' systems thinking offer powerful tools for managing environmental complexity, sustainable development, and adaptive policy formulation. By embracing systemic insights, communities, organizations, and governments effectively navigate complexity, foster ecological sustainability, and ensure policies and practices align closely with human-centered values, environmental resilience, and societal well-being.

Philosophical and Ethical Implications: Ecology, Complexity, and Ethical Stewardship

Donella Meadows' profound insights offer significant philosophical and ethical guidance, emphasizing our collective responsibility to manage complex ecological and social systems with humility, adaptability, and ethical mindfulness. Central to Meadows' philosophy is the recognition that environmental sustainability and ethical stewardship are intrinsically interconnected, necessitating continuous reflection, adaptive governance, and transparent communication within complex adaptive systems.

Meadows viewed complexity not merely as a challenge to be overcome but as an integral and meaningful aspect of ecological and social dynamics. She encouraged an approach marked by humility, emphasizing our limited capacity to fully predict or control complex ecological interactions. This philosophical stance challenges traditional hierarchical, reductionist approaches to environmental management, advocating instead for adaptive, responsive, and ethically reflective governance practices. For Meadows, understanding and navigating complexity effectively requires a profound awareness of systemic interactions and ethical responsibilities, fostering a more integrated and holistic approach to sustainability (Meadows, 2008; Meadows & Wright, 2008).

Meadows' philosophy also underscores the essential importance of resilience as a fundamental principle within ecological and social systems. Ecological resilience, in Meadows' perspective, involves a system's ability to maintain stability and adaptive equilibrium in the face of significant disturbances. Mindfully, resilience can be likened to a community that thrives despite economic disruptions or natural disasters, continuously adapting and responding to changing circumstances. Meadows' philosophical insights advocate for building resilience through adaptive strategies, fostering greater flexibility, diversity, and adaptive capacity within ecological systems, communities, and governance frameworks (Walker & Salt, 2006).

Meadows emphasized ethical stewardship as an inherent responsibility in our engagement with ecological and social complexity. Her ethical philosophy challenges us to reflect continuously on how our actions, decisions, and governance frameworks impact the natural environment and future generations. This stewardship perspective highlights our profound responsibility to manage natural resources sustainably, maintain ecological integrity, and ensure societal resilience through transparent and ethically responsible decision-making. Meadows' insights inform practical ethical frameworks for managing environmental resources, guiding adaptive governance, and fostering responsible environmental stewardship (Sterman, 2012).

In organizational contexts, Meadows' philosophy of ethical stewardship encourages transparent communication, adaptive responsiveness, and continuous reflective awareness. Organizations adopting her systemic perspective prioritize ethical responsibility, ensuring sustainability practices align closely with broader societal values and ecological integrity. Ethical organizational governance inspired by Meadows involves ongoing reflection, transparent stakeholder communication, and adaptive decision-making processes. This philosophy empowers organizations to navigate complexity ethically, sustainably, and adaptively, fostering resilience, innovation, and societal well-being (Laszlo, 2003).

Meadows' philosophical and ethical insights offer profound guidance for ethically mindful engagement with ecological and social complexity. By embracing humility, adaptability, and ethical stewardship, we foster greater resilience, sustainability, and humanistic responsibility in our interactions with complex adaptive systems. Meadows' legacy reminds us that effective ecological management, sustainable development, and ethical governance require continuous reflection, adaptive responsiveness, and profound ethical accountability, ensuring that our collective decisions remain deeply aligned with ecological sustainability, human flourishing, and societal resilience.

Synergy and Integration: Connecting Systems Thinking to Complex Adaptive Governance

Integrating Donella Meadows' principles of systems thinking and leverage points into adaptive governance provides a powerful synergy that enhances our capability to manage environmental and organizational complexity with resilience, responsiveness, and ethical accountability. Meadows' systemic insights and the adaptive governance framework come together to create practical tools and strategies, enabling effective navigation of complex, evolving environmental and societal landscapes.

At the heart of this integration is the recognition that complex systems be they ecological, social, or organizational require ongoing adaptive learning, ethical reflection, and strategic intervention. Systems thinking encourages us to perceive challenges not in isolation, but as interconnected dynamics influenced by numerous variables, relationships, and feedback loops. This understanding aligns seamlessly with adaptive governance approaches, which emphasize continuous monitoring, real-time feedback, stakeholder participation, and flexible policy-making processes. When combined, these approaches enable more resilient, adaptive, and ethically mindful responses to complex challenges such as climate change, resource management, and organizational resilience (Folke et al., 2005).

To illustrate this integration clearly, consider adaptive water governance in regions prone to drought and climate variability. Meadows' insights guide policymakers and communities toward identifying strategic leverage points such as water pricing structures, conservation incentives, and community engagement programs. Adaptive governance frameworks, informed by systems thinking, encourage stakeholders to continuously monitor ecological conditions, respond adaptively to real-time data, and adjust policies accordingly. This integration ensures sustainable water management strategies remain responsive, inclusive, and ethically accountable, effectively adapting to changing environmental conditions and community needs (Pahl-Wostl, 2007).

Integrating Meadows' systemic principles into organizational management practices significantly enhances adaptive capacity and ethical accountability. Organizations adopting systems thinking and adaptive governance strategies systematically identify key leverage points such as organizational culture, decision-making processes, and communication channels. For example, companies aiming to enhance sustainability practices actively engage employees and stakeholders through participatory dialogues, adaptive feedback mechanisms, and transparent decision-making frameworks. These strategies foster systemic innovation, continuous learning, and ethical transparency within organizations, ensuring practices align closely with broader ecological values and societal expectations (Senge, Smith, Kruschwitz, Laur, & Schley, 2008).

This integrated approach significantly enriches environmental policy and climate governance initiatives. Policymakers employing systems thinking insights alongside adaptive governance frameworks continuously adapt climate strategies based on ecological feedback, stakeholder engagement, and ethical reflection. For instance, adaptive climate governance initiatives, such as participatory climate adaptation planning or community-based renewable energy programs, exemplify Meadows' systemic principles. These initiatives demonstrate how identifying and acting on leverage points can create transformative shifts toward sustainability, resilience, and societal well-being, addressing complex environmental and societal challenges effectively and adaptively (Termeer, Dewulf, & Breeman, 2013).

Integrating Meadows' systems thinking with adaptive governance frameworks underscores the importance of humility, ethical reflection, and ongoing adaptability within complex adaptive systems. This philosophical stance encourages organizations, communities, and policymakers to approach complexity not merely as a barrier to be overcome, but as a rich source of innovation, adaptive learning, and ethical stewardship. By continuously reflecting on leverage points and adaptive strategies, we can foster greater ecological sustainability, societal resilience, and ethical accountability, ensuring our practices remain responsive, adaptive, and aligned with humanistic values and ecological integrity (Meadows, 2008).

The synergy and integration of Donella Meadows' systems thinking and adaptive governance frameworks provide profound practical and philosophical insights for managing environmental complexity, organizational resilience, and ethical innovation. By embracing systemic interconnectedness, adaptive responsiveness, and ethical mindfulness, organizations, governments, and communities can effectively navigate complexity, foster sustainable innovation, and ensure meaningful alignment with broader societal and ecological objectives.

John von Neumann

Biography and Academic Contributions

John von Neumann (1903–1957) was a visionary mathematician and interdisciplinary scholar whose extraordinary insights fundamentally shaped modern computing, complexity science, economics, and decision-making. Born in Budapest, Hungary, von Neumann's intellectual brilliance was evident early in his life, allowing him to traverse diverse academic disciplines seamlessly. Known for his extraordinary memory and intellectual breadth, von Neumann contributed transformative insights spanning mathematics, physics, economics, computer science, and strategic decision-making, demonstrating his profound interdisciplinary curiosity and capacity for innovative thought.

Von Neumann's academic journey led him to prestigious institutions, including the University of Göttingen and Princeton University's Institute for Advanced Study, where he became a central figure in twentieth-century intellectual life. His landmark 1944 collaboration with economist Oskar Morgenstern, Theory of Games and Economic Behavior, introduced foundational concepts of game theory, significantly transforming our understanding of rational decision-making and strategic interaction within economics and social science. Through game theory, von Neumann provided rigorous mathematical tools to analyze how individuals, organizations, and nations strategically interact, cooperate, or compete—offering profound implications for decision-making within complex adaptive systems (von Neumann & Morgenstern, 1944).

Beyond economics, von Neumann's pioneering contributions to computing significantly influenced technological innovation and artificial intelligence. He played a critical role in the development of modern computer architecture, known today as the von Neumann architecture, establishing core principles such as stored-program concepts and sequential execution. These fundamental insights laid the groundwork for modern computer systems, influencing computing technologies and enabling subsequent advancements in artificial intelligence, deep learning, and complexity science (Aspray, 1990).

Von Neumann's interdisciplinary curiosity also led him into pioneering work on cellular automata, mathematical models demonstrating how simple, local interactions among individual units can lead to complex emergent behaviors. Cellular automata have become foundational tools for complexity theory, illustrating how intricate patterns and behaviors emerge spontaneously from simple, well-defined interactions. Von Neumann's insights into cellular automata have profoundly influenced subsequent research in complex adaptive systems, computational biology, and ecological modeling, providing practical tools and philosophical insights for understanding complexity and emergent phenomena (von Neumann, 1966).

Throughout his career, von Neumann remained deeply involved in practical, real-world applications, contributing significantly to developments in nuclear physics, strategic policy, and systems analysis. His involvement in the Manhattan Project and strategic defense policy during the Cold War reflected his commitment to applying scientific insights toward complex, real-world decision-making processes. While recognizing the potential risks inherent in advanced technology, von Neumann also emphasized ethical responsibility, thoughtful reflection, and adaptive decision-making, acknowledging that strategic policy and technological advancement must remain aligned with broader humanistic values and ethical accountability (Macrae, 1992).

Von Neumann's intellectual legacy endures vividly in contemporary advancements across economics, computing, artificial intelligence, and complexity science. His foundational insights into rational decision-making, computational complexity, and strategic interactions continue to guide contemporary scholars, practitioners, and policymakers. His interdisciplinary curiosity, ethical mindfulness, and innovative spirit serve as ongoing inspirations, reminding us of our profound responsibility to engage thoughtfully, adaptively, and ethically with technological advancement, economic decision-making, and complex adaptive systems.

John von Neumann's remarkable life and scholarship thus offer profound insights into navigating complexity, fostering interdisciplinary collaboration, and promoting ethical innovation within contemporary society.

Fundamental Concepts: Game Theory, Cellular Automata, and Computational Complexity

John von Neumann's intellectual legacy is deeply rooted in his pioneering contributions to game theory, cellular automata, and computational complexity. Each of these fundamental concepts significantly advanced our understanding of decision-making, strategic interactions, and the emergent behaviors that define complex systems.

Von Neumann's ground-breaking work on game theory, particularly through his influential collaboration with economist Oskar Morgenstern, provided a rigorous mathematical framework to analyze strategic decision-making among rational actors. At its heart, game theory explores how individuals, organizations, or nations make choices when outcomes depend on the decisions of multiple interacting entities. To understand this concept, consider everyday strategic interactions such as negotiating a business deal or navigating diplomacy between nations. Each participant must consider not only their own decisions but also anticipate how others will respond strategically. Von Neumann's work illuminated these complex interactions, providing insights into cooperation, competition, and decision-making within diverse economic, social, and political contexts (von Neumann & Morgenstern, 1944; Dixit & Nalebuff, 2008).

Beyond strategic decision-making, von Neumann's pioneering introduction of cellular automata significantly enriched complexity theory and our understanding of emergent phenomena. Cellular automata involve simple computational units arranged in a grid, each cell interacting according to straightforward, predetermined rules. Despite their simplicity, these localized interactions can produce extraordinarily complex and unpredictable patterns and behaviors. To appreciate this intuitively, envision a bustling city street where individual pedestrians follow simple personal navigation rules yet collectively generate complex patterns of movement, adaptation, and interaction. Cellular automata principles, exemplified by von Neumann's theoretical frameworks, profoundly influence contemporary studies in artificial intelligence, ecological modeling, and computational biology, providing essential tools to understand and simulate complex adaptive systems (von Neumann, 1966; Wolfram, 2002).

Moreover, von Neumann's insights into computational complexity underscore the inherent unpredictability and adaptive complexity within computational and decision-making processes. Computational complexity examines how challenging problems are to solve, highlighting why some decisions are inherently more difficult or resource-intensive than others. Von Neumann's early exploration of computational complexity revealed that many real-world problems ranging from resource allocation and economic modeling to strategic planning are inherently complex, requiring adaptive, responsive, and nuanced decision-making approaches. These insights guide contemporary approaches to artificial intelligence, machine learning, and strategic governance, emphasizing the necessity of continuous adaptation, ethical reflection, and responsive innovation in complex environments (Papadimitriou, 2003).

Philosophically, von Neumann's concepts deepen our appreciation of complexity, uncertainty, and the adaptive nature of decision-making processes. Game theory challenges traditional assumptions about individual rationality, emphasizing the nuanced interplay between cooperation, competition, and strategic interaction. Cellular automata demonstrate how complexity emerges spontaneously from simple local interactions, challenging linear, reductionist perspectives. Computational complexity underscores the philosophical importance of humility and adaptability, recognizing that complex problems require continuous learning, adaptive governance, and reflective decision-making strategies (Dixit & Nalebuff, 2008; Wolfram, 2002).

Ultimately, von Neumann's pioneering contributions to game theory, cellular automata, and computational complexity continue to shape contemporary understanding of decision-making, complexity science, and artificial intelligence. By embracing his fundamental insights, we can effectively navigate strategic interactions, manage adaptive complexity ethically, and foster continuous innovation and reflective decision-making. Von Neumann's visionary legacy thus inspires us to approach complexity as a meaningful opportunity for adaptive learning, ethical stewardship, and sustained human-centered innovation.

Choice B	Player B	Choice A1	Choice A2
	Choice B1	(3, 2)	(0, 4)
	Choice B2	(5, 1)	(1, 3)

Player A

Figure 9.3. *Von Neumann's Game Theory Payoff Matrix.*

Note. This figure depicts a canonical 2x2 game theory payoff matrix introduced by John von Neumann and Oskar Morgenstern. The table represents strategic choices made by two players, where the first number in each cell indicates Player A's payoff and the second number indicates Player

B's payoff. It demonstrates interdependent decision-making in competitive or cooperative scenarios.

	Remain Silent	Confess
Remain Silent	−1, −1	−3, 0
Confess	0, −3	−2, −2

Prisoner B

Figure 9.3a. *Prisoner's Dilemma Payoff Matrix.*

Note. This matrix illustrates the Prisoner's Dilemma, one of the most widely studied examples in game theory. Two prisoners must independently decide whether to remain silent (cooperate) or confess (defect). The outcomes show that although mutual cooperation yields a better collective outcome (–1, –1), rational self-interest leads both players to defect, resulting in a worse collective payoff (–2, –2). This paradox captures the tension between individual rationality and collective benefit.

1. The Setup of the Prisoner's Dilemma
   Two prisoners (A and B) are accused of a crime.
   Each has two choices:
   Remain Silent (Cooperate) with the other prisoner.
   Confess (Defect) against the other prisoner.
   The numbers in the payoff matrix represent years in prison (negative values) for each player.
   Example: (–1, –1) means both get 1 year each.
   Example: (–3, 0) means A gets 3 years, B goes free.
2. The Possible Outcomes

Let's walk through each scenario in the matrix:

Prisoner A	Prisoner B	Outcome (Payoffs)	Meaning
Remain Silent	Remain Silent	(–1, –1)	Both serve 1 year (light sentence)
Remain Silent	Confess	(–3, 0)	A serves 3 years, B goes free
Confess	Remain Silent	(0, –3)	A goes free, B serves 3 years
Confess	Confess	(–2, –2)	Both serve 2 years

3. Why (–1, –1) is "Better"
   If both cooperate (remain silent) → (–1, –1).
   Total prison time = 2 years (1 + 1).
   If both defect (confess) → (–2, –2).
   Total prison time = 4 years (2 + 2).
   From a collective perspective, (–1, –1) is better because society (and the two prisoners together) "spend" fewer years in prison overall.
4. Why They End Up at (–2, –2)
   Here's the twist:
   Each prisoner reasons:
   "If the other remains silent, I can go free by confessing."
   "If the other confesses, I get 2 years by confessing, but 3 years if I stay silent."
   So, confessing always seems safer (less personal risk).
   That's why both parties rationally defect → (–2, –2).
   Yet ironically, this leads to a worse collective outcome compared to (–1, –1).
5. The Insight of the Prisoner's Dilemma

Individual rational choices can lead to collectively worse outcomes.

It explains real-world issues like:

Countries over-polluting instead of cooperating on climate change.

Companies engaging in price wars.

Individuals competing instead of collaborating.

To summarize:

(–1, –1) is better collectively because the group spends fewer years in prison.

But rational self-interest drives both players toward (–2, –2), which is worse collectively, but feels "safer" for each individual.

Practical Applications: Economic Decision-Making, Computing, and Artificial Intelligence

John von Neumann's pioneering contributions to game theory, computational technology, and complexity theory have significantly shaped practical decision-making frameworks across economics, computing, and artificial intelligence. By providing foundational insights into how individuals, organizations, and complex systems make strategic decisions, von Neumann's ideas continue to guide practical strategies, innovations, and adaptive responsiveness within contemporary economic, technological, and governance environments.

In economic decision-making, von Neumann's contributions to game theory fundamentally reshaped how businesses, policymakers, and strategic planners approach decision processes under conditions of uncertainty and interdependence. Practical applications of game theory in economics extend widely, from negotiation strategies and market analyses to regulatory policies and international diplomacy. For example, corporations regularly employ game-theoretic principles to anticipate competitor strategies, optimize pricing, and manage market uncertainty. Similarly, policymakers use game theory to analyze trade negotiations, environmental regulations, and resource allocation strategies, guiding adaptive decision-making and strategic responsiveness to complex economic environments (Brandenburger & Nalebuff, 1996).

Von Neumann's foundational contributions to computational technology have had profound impacts, particularly on the evolution and capabilities of modern computing systems. His innovative principles underpin the architecture of contemporary computers, enabling sophisticated computational methods now central to economic modeling, strategic forecasting, and risk management. Organizations widely use computational models informed by von Neumann's principles to simulate complex economic scenarios, assess investment risks, and guide strategic planning. For instance, financial institutions employ advanced computational models for risk assessment, investment decision-making, and adaptive financial planning, effectively managing economic complexity and uncertainty through rigorous computational analysis (Mirowski, 2002).

In artificial intelligence (AI), von Neumann's computational complexity insights and foundational work on algorithms have significantly influenced practical AI decision-making systems. Modern AI frameworks, such as machine learning algorithms and deep learning models, draw heavily from computational complexity principles introduced by von Neumann. Practical AI applications influenced by his insights include predictive analytics, autonomous decision-making systems, and strategic governance frameworks. For example, AI-driven predictive analytics employed by healthcare organizations and public health authorities enable adaptive responsiveness to disease outbreaks, resource allocation, and patient care strategies, reflecting von Neumann's computational principles in practical applications (Russell & Norvig, 2020).

Strategic governance frameworks and policy decision-making processes benefit significantly from von Neumann's game-theoretic and computational insights. Adaptive governance approaches, widely employed by public institutions and governments worldwide, utilize game theory and computational complexity principles to analyze policy interactions, strategic decision-making, and resource management. Adaptive climate governance, for example, uses computational modeling and strategic decision frameworks informed by game theory to effectively manage climate risks, international negotiations, and environmental policies, demonstrating the practical integration of von Neumann's insights into strategic governance and adaptive decision-making (Sterman, 2008).

Philosophically, von Neumann's practical contributions emphasize adaptive responsiveness, strategic rationality, and ethical reflection within decision-making processes. His insights encourage organizations, policymakers, and technologists to thoughtfully engage with complexity, uncertainty, and strategic interactions, fostering ethical accountability and continuous adaptive learning. By integrating von Neumann's game-theoretic principles, computational complexity insights, and strategic governance frameworks, we can effectively navigate complexity, foster adaptive innovation, and ensure decision-making processes remain ethically mindful, transparent, and aligned with broader humanistic objectives (von Neumann & Morgenstern, 1944; Brandenburger & Nalebuff, 1996).

Ultimately, von Neumann's practical applications in economic decision-making, computing, and artificial intelligence provide powerful tools and strategies for effectively managing complexity, uncertainty, and strategic interactions. His visionary contributions continue to guide adaptive governance, strategic decision-making, and technological innovation, ensuring practical decisions and policies remain resilient, responsive, and ethically accountable within complex adaptive systems.

Philosophical and Ethical Implications: Rationality, Complexity, and Ethical Responsibility

John von Neumann's groundbreaking insights carry profound philosophical and ethical implications, particularly regarding rationality, complexity, and ethical accountability within strategic decision-making, technological innovation, and artificial intelligence. Philosophically, his theories invite us to reconsider traditional notions of rationality, highlighting the intricate interplay between strategic complexity, adaptive responsiveness, and ethical mindfulness.

Central to von Neumann's philosophical contributions is the recognition that rational decision-making within complex environments requires more than rigid logic or straightforward calculations. His foundational contributions to game theory suggest that rationality involves a nuanced understanding of interdependent strategies, complex interactions, and adaptive responses. Respectfully, this challenges traditional assumptions that human decision-making is purely rational and predictable. Instead, von Neumann emphasizes that decision-making within complex environments necessitates ongoing adaptation, strategic responsiveness, and ethical reflection, recognizing the profound uncertainty and dynamic complexity that characterize human interactions and technological systems (von Neumann & Morgenstern, 1944; Brandenburger & Nalebuff, 1996).

Von Neumann's philosophical insights into complexity extend significantly to ethical responsibility and governance within advanced technologies, including artificial intelligence and computational systems. He underscored that complexity is not merely a technical issue but a deeply ethical one, demanding continuous reflective awareness, transparent communication, and adaptive decision-making processes. Organizations and innovators developing AI systems, for example, must consider ethical transparency, accountability, and the broader societal implications of their innovations. By emphasizing ethical mindfulness in technological and economic decisions, von Neumann's philosophy encourages us to continuously reflect on the ethical implications of our strategic interactions, technological advancements, and adaptive governance practices (Floridi & Cowls, 2019).

Furthermore, von Neumann's philosophical perspective underscores the necessity of humility in managing complexity. Recognizing that computational complexity and strategic decision-making inherently involve uncertainty and unpredictability, his theories encourage decision-makers and policymakers to approach complexity with humility, acknowledging the limits of human rationality and predictive capability. This philosophical stance fosters adaptive governance frameworks and strategic decision-making processes that remain open, reflective, and responsive to continuous feedback and evolving complexities (Mirowski, 2002).

Von Neumann's insights into rationality and complexity also carry important implications for ethical leadership and organizational responsibility. Leaders and organizations adopting his philosophical approach prioritize transparent communication, continuous learning, and ethical accountability. For instance, strategic leaders utilizing game theory principles ethically consider their decisions' implications on stakeholders, ecosystems, and societal values, ensuring responsible decision-making aligned with humanistic objectives. Such philosophical reflection fosters greater organizational resilience, ethical transparency, and adaptive responsiveness to complex challenges (Brandenburger & Nalebuff, 1996).

Ultimately, von Neumann's philosophical contributions to rationality, complexity, and ethical responsibility provide profound insights for thoughtfully navigating contemporary strategic, technological, and organizational challenges. By embracing adaptive governance, reflective ethical mindfulness, and continuous learning, organizations and policymakers can effectively manage complexity, foster responsible innovation, and ensure their decisions remain deeply aligned with humanistic values, societal well-being, and ecological sustainability. Von Neumann's enduring philosophical legacy thus continues to inspire ethical responsibility, adaptive governance, and thoughtful innovation within our increasingly complex and interconnected world.

Synergy and Integration: Bridging Mathematics, Computation, and Complexity Science

Integrating John von Neumann's foundational insights in game theory, computational complexity, and mathematical principles offers transformative philosophical and practical tools for effectively navigating contemporary challenges in complexity, governance, and ethical decision-making. Von Neumann's interdisciplinary approach bridges mathematics, computation, and strategic decision-making, providing essential frameworks that empower organizations and policymakers to understand and ethically manage the complexities inherent in adaptive governance and technological innovation.

At the core of von Neumann's interdisciplinary integration is the recognition that managing complexity requires more than isolated expertise; it demands the thoughtful combination of mathematical rigor, computational clarity, and strategic responsiveness. Consider the analogy of a well-orchestrated symphony, where individual musicians, each skilled in their instrument, collaborate harmoniously under a conductor's guidance. Mathematics, computation, and complexity science function similarly: each contributes essential insights, and their strategic integration ensures cohesive and adaptive decision-making. Organizations effectively employing these combined insights can better respond to market volatility, technological disruptions, and societal expectations, exemplifying the synergy that von Neumann envisioned (von Neumann & Morgenstern, 1944; Mirowski, 2002).

In practical organizational contexts, integrating game theory and computational insights enables effective adaptive governance strategies and strategic decision-making processes. Organizations facing complex, unpredictable environments frequently use computational models informed by von Neumann's principles to anticipate market dynamics, assess strategic risks, and adaptively manage resources. For instance, companies operating globally utilize sophisticated game-theoretic modeling to understand competitive dynamics and market uncertainties, adjusting strategies responsively and ethically. This practical integration enhances organizational adaptability, ethical transparency, and responsiveness, aligning business practices with broader societal values and humanistic objectives (Brandenburger & Nalebuff, 1996).

The integration of von Neumann's insights profoundly shapes adaptive governance frameworks, particularly within complex public policy and governance environments. Policymakers increasingly employ computational complexity principles and game theory insights to inform responsive, adaptive policy strategies addressing global challenges like climate change, economic volatility, or public health emergencies. Practical governance approaches, such as adaptive climate policy frameworks or dynamic economic strategies, illustrate how mathematical rigor and computational modeling, guided by von Neumann's principles, facilitate strategic responsiveness and ethical accountability within governance systems (Sterman, 2008).

Moreover, von Neumann's integration of mathematics and complexity science provides essential philosophical and practical guidance for responsibly managing technological innovation and artificial intelligence (AI). AI developers employing von Neumann's interdisciplinary insights effectively navigate computational complexity and strategic decision-making challenges, ensuring technological innovations remain ethically accountable, transparent, and responsive. For example, organizations developing AI-driven healthcare diagnostics utilize computational complexity models and strategic decision-making frameworks, ensuring innovations align ethically and responsibly with patient care objectives and societal expectations (Topol, 2019).

Philosophically, von Neumann's integrated insights emphasize continuous reflection, adaptive responsiveness, and ethical stewardship within complexity management and decision-making processes. Organizations and policymakers adopting this integrative approach prioritize ethical mindfulness, transparency, and ongoing reflective learning. The philosophical synergy between mathematics, computation, and complexity science encourages us to embrace complexity as an opportunity for innovation, adaptability, and ethical responsibility, fostering sustained human-centered innovation and responsible governance practices (von Neumann & Morgenstern, 1944; Mirowski, 2002).

The integration of von Neumann's pioneering contributions bridges mathematics, computation, and complexity science, equipping organizations, leaders, and policymakers with powerful practical and philosophical tools for effectively navigating complexity, adaptive governance, and ethical innovation. By thoughtfully embracing this interdisciplinary synergy, we foster resilience, creativity, and humanistic responsibility, ensuring decisions remain adaptive, transparent, and ethically accountable in our interconnected and rapidly changing world.

Herbert A. Simon

Biography and Academic Contributions

Herbert Alexander Simon (1916–2001), an American scholar whose intellectual contributions span economics, cognitive psychology, artificial intelligence, and organizational theory, fundamentally reshaped our understanding of human decision-making, rationality, and complex adaptive systems. Born in Milwaukee, Wisconsin, Simon displayed early intellectual curiosity and versatility, qualities that propelled him toward interdisciplinary scholarship and groundbreaking insights that continue to resonate deeply within academia and practical fields.

Simon's academic journey was characterized by a remarkable blend of curiosity, analytical rigor, and commitment to understanding human behavior and organizational dynamics. Initially trained in political science and economics, Simon soon recognized the limitations inherent in traditional assumptions about human rationality and decision-making. His interdisciplinary exploration eventually guided him toward cognitive psychology and artificial intelligence, fields in which he introduced pioneering insights and innovative theoretical frameworks.

In 1978, Simon was awarded the Nobel Memorial Prize in Economic Sciences for his groundbreaking contributions to understanding human decision-making within organizations, particularly the concepts of bounded rationality and satisficing. Simon challenged traditional economic models that assumed individuals make perfectly rational decisions. Instead, he argued that human decision-making is inherently bounded by cognitive limitations, available information, and practical constraints, leading individuals to seek satisfactory rather than optimal solutions—a behavior he termed "satisficing." This nuanced understanding of decision-making profoundly reshaped modern behavioral economics, organizational management, and cognitive modeling, offering essential insights into how individuals, organizations, and policymakers make adaptive, responsive decisions within complex environments (Simon, 1957, 1996).

Simon's interdisciplinary contributions significantly influenced artificial intelligence research. His pioneering work on problem-solving, cognitive architecture, and human-computer interaction provided foundational principles guiding contemporary AI development. Notably, Simon co-developed early cognitive computing models and computer simulations, such as the General Problem Solver, which sought to replicate human reasoning processes. These innovations helped establish the foundational principles of cognitive science and human-centered artificial intelligence, emphasizing the close interplay between human cognition, computational systems, and decision-making processes (Newell & Simon, 1972).

Throughout his career, Simon maintained a strong commitment to understanding organizational complexity and adaptive behavior. He proposed that organizations function as adaptive systems, continuously adjusting decision-making processes, structures, and strategies in response to complex environmental challenges and uncertainties. Simon's pioneering insights encouraged organizations to embrace adaptive governance, continuous learning, and ethical mindfulness, effectively responding to complexity and ensuring decision-making processes remain transparent, responsive, and ethically accountable (Simon, 1996; Augier & March 2004).

Simon's extensive academic legacy extends significantly beyond economics and cognitive psychology, profoundly influencing fields such as management theory, education, artificial intelligence, and public policy. His interdisciplinary approach provided critical frameworks for adaptive decision-making, organizational learning, and ethical governance, empowering organizations and policymakers to navigate complexity effectively and ethically. Simon's insights into human cognition, bounded rationality, and adaptive responsiveness continue to guide contemporary organizational strategies, cognitive modeling frameworks, and governance practices worldwide.

Simon's contributions challenge traditional assumptions of rationality, emphasizing the profound complexity, uncertainty, and adaptiveness inherent in human decision-making processes. His philosophy encourages ongoing ethical reflection, transparency, and humility within organizational and technological governance, recognizing our limited capacity to predict complex outcomes fully. Simon advocated for human-centered, adaptive governance, highlighting ethical responsibility, continuous learning, and reflective decision-making as essential components for effectively managing complexity and uncertainty (Simon, 1996; Gigerenzer & Selten, 2002).

Herbert Simon's interdisciplinary scholarship provides powerful philosophical and practical tools for understanding complexity, adaptive decision-making, and ethical innovation. His profound insights continue to inspire adaptive governance, responsible innovation, and thoughtful ethical stewardship, ensuring that human decision-making processes, organizational practices, and technological innovations remain deeply aligned with humanistic values, societal resilience, and ecological sustainability.

Fundamental Concepts: Bounded Rationality, Decision-Making, and Organizational Complexity

Herbert A. Simon's groundbreaking concepts of bounded rationality and satisficing significantly reshaped our understanding of human decision-making within complex environments, organizational behavior, and adaptive processes. His insights challenged the classical economic notion of humans as fully rational actors, highlighting instead the realistic and often imperfect conditions under which decisions are made. Simon recognized that human rationality is inherently constrained by cognitive limitations, limited time, incomplete information, and finite computational capacities, leading individuals and organizations to pursue practical rather than theoretically optimal decisions.

What is Satisficing?

Coined by Herbert Simon in 1955, satisficing combines "satisfy" + "suffice."

It describes how real-world decision-makers (humans, organizations) choose options.

Instead of finding the optimal solution (which may require infinite time, information, or resources), they stop once they find an option that is "good enough."

Bounded rationality describes decision-making processes wherein individuals make rational choices within the limits of their knowledge, cognitive capabilities, and available resources. To illustrate this intuitively, consider a person shopping for groceries in a busy market: rather than evaluating every single product available for optimal nutrition and price, they quickly select items that appear "good enough" based on prior experience, familiarity, and time constraints. Similarly, in complex organizational and strategic environments, decision-makers rely on heuristics, intuition, and simplified models to navigate complexity, uncertainty, and limited information effectively (Simon, 1957; Gigerenzer & Selten, 2002).

Simon's concept of satisficing further elaborates on this idea, proposing that decision-makers often seek solutions that are sufficiently good, rather than perfectly optimal given their practical constraints. In real-world scenarios, the pursuit of an optimal solution often becomes impractical due to complexity, cost, and cognitive limitations. For instance, organizational managers tasked with hiring new employees typically do not seek a perfect candidate but rather a candidate who sufficiently meets established criteria. This satisficing behavior acknowledges the complexity, uncertainty, and practical constraints inherent in human decision-making processes, enabling efficient and timely decisions without exhaustive searches for optimal outcomes (Simon, 1996; March 1994).

In organizational contexts, bounded rationality and satisficing significantly influence decision-making, strategic planning, and adaptive management practices. Organizations face continuous complexity, uncertainty, and rapidly changing environments, necessitating decision-making processes that are flexible, efficient, and responsive to evolving contexts. Simon's insights inform adaptive governance strategies, where organizations employ heuristics, continuous feedback, and simplified decision frameworks to respond effectively to complex environmental and market dynamics. This adaptive approach enhances organizational resilience, responsiveness, and innovation, recognizing that effective decision-making requires continuous reflection, adaptability, and ethical responsibility within complex adaptive systems (March 1994; Gigerenzer & Selten, 2002).

Simon's insights into bounded rationality have significant philosophical implications regarding human cognition, ethics, and organizational responsibility. Philosophically, recognizing bounded rationality encourages humility and ongoing ethical reflection within decision-making processes. Organizations guided by Simon's principles prioritize transparency, adaptive learning, and reflective awareness, ensuring decision-making remains ethically accountable, transparent, and responsive to societal expectations. By emphasizing adaptive responsiveness and continuous ethical reflection, Simon's insights provide essential philosophical tools for managing complexity, fostering ethical responsibility, and ensuring decisions align closely with humanistic values and societal well-being (Simon, 1996).

Simon's fundamental concepts of bounded rationality and satisficing offer profound philosophical and practical guidance for navigating complex adaptive systems. By acknowledging cognitive limitations, embracing adaptive heuristics, and fostering ethical reflection, organizations and decision-makers can effectively manage complexity, foster adaptive resilience, and ensure that their decision-making processes remain human-centered, ethically responsible, and responsive to evolving complexities in an interconnected world.

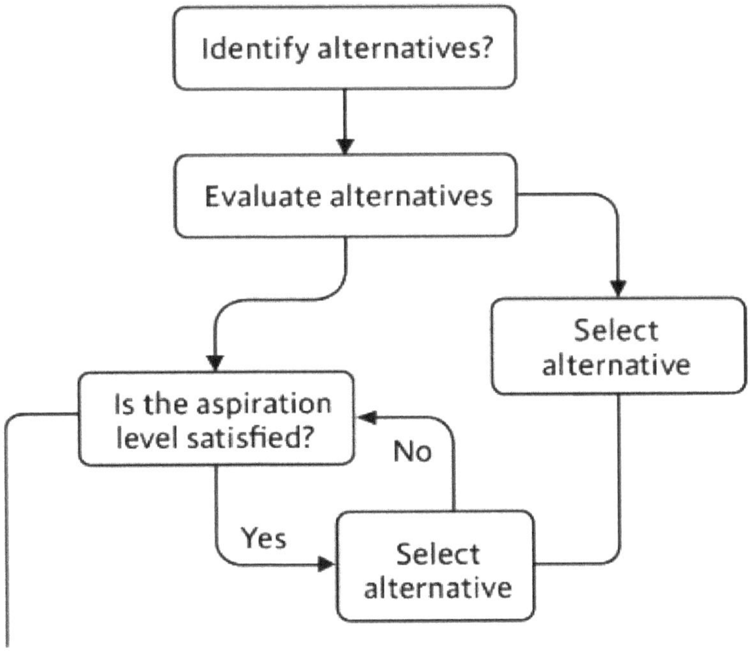

Figure 9.4. *Bounded Rationality and Satisficing.*

Note. This flowchart illustrates Herbert Simon's concept of bounded rationality, showing how decision-makers operate with limited cognitive resources. Rather than searching for the absolute best option, individuals employ a satisficing strategy: they select the first alternative that meets acceptable aspiration levels, balancing rationality with practical constraints.

Practical Applications: Behavioral Economics, Artificial Intelligence, Management Theory

Herbert Simon's groundbreaking insights have profoundly influenced practical fields including behavioral economics, artificial intelligence (AI), and organizational management. By emphasizing bounded rationality and adaptive decision-making, Simon's theories have provided robust frameworks for organizations and policymakers seeking to navigate complexity effectively, ethically, and adaptively.

In behavioral economics, Simon's concept of bounded rationality offers a foundational understanding of how individuals and organizations realistically make economic decisions. Traditional economic models often assumed perfectly rational decision-making; however, Simon highlighted how cognitive limitations, emotional factors, and limited information profoundly shape economic behaviors. Practically, organizations employing behavioral economic insights design interventions, policies, and strategies that align with realistic human behaviors. For instance, businesses adopt choice architectures—such as default retirement plans or sustainable product placements—to encourage ethical decision-making and sustainable behaviors, recognizing that small adjustments within decision contexts can significantly influence economic choices (Thaler & Sunstein, 2008).

In artificial intelligence and cognitive computing technologies, Simon's contributions have deeply informed the development of human-centered AI systems. Modern AI-driven decision-support technologies leverage insights into human cognitive limitations, ensuring that AI interfaces and algorithms align closely with natural human decision-making processes. For example, decision-support systems in healthcare or financial management utilize AI algorithms informed by bounded rationality principles to assist human decision-makers effectively. These cognitive computing systems provide timely, context-sensitive information and recommendations, acknowledging the practical limitations of human cognition and enhancing adaptive decision-making within complex environments (Russell & Norvig, 2020).

Simon's insights significantly shape contemporary organizational management theory and adaptive governance practices. Organizations navigating complex environments frequently adopt adaptive management strategies inspired by Simon's bounded rationality and satisficing concepts. Such practices include decentralized decision-making structures, continuous feedback mechanisms, and simplified heuristic frameworks for strategic decision-making. Companies adopting agile practices or holacratic organizational designs exemplify Simon's insights by managing complexity through adaptive responsiveness, ethical awareness, and continuous organizational learning (Laloux, 2014; March, 1994).

Strategic decision-making frameworks influenced by Simon's theories are widely used by organizations and policymakers facing uncertainty and complex strategic environments. For instance, strategic foresight methodologies, scenario planning, and adaptive policy frameworks effectively incorporate bounded rationality principles, guiding organizational and governance strategies adaptively and ethically. Strategic governance approaches in public policy, sustainable development, and organizational innovation demonstrate how Simon's insights practically enable decision-makers to manage complexity effectively, respond adaptively to emerging challenges, and remain ethically mindful and transparent in strategic decision-making processes (Mintzberg, Ahlstrand, & Lampel, 1998).

Simon's practical applications encourage humility, ethical responsibility, and adaptive reflection within decision-making processes. His insights remind us that practical decision-making and organizational governance must continuously consider cognitive limitations, ethical implications, and adaptive responsiveness. Organizations employing Simon's principles cultivate ethical mindfulness, continuous reflection, and responsive governance, ensuring practical strategies and technological innovations remain closely aligned with broader societal values and humanistic objectives (Simon, 1996; Gigerenzer & Selten, 2002).

Simon's practical contributions to behavioral economics, artificial intelligence, and organizational management provide powerful philosophical and ethical frameworks for navigating complexity effectively and adaptively. By embracing bounded rationality, continuous ethical reflection, and adaptive governance, organizations and decision-makers effectively manage complexity, foster resilient innovation, and ensure ethical accountability within complex adaptive systems.

Philosophical and Ethical Implications: Rationality, Human Behavior, and Adaptive Ethics

Herbert A. Simon's influential contributions extend far beyond economics and artificial intelligence, provoking deep philosophical reflections on rationality, human behavior, and ethical responsibility. At the heart of Simon's philosophical insights lies the recognition that traditional models of perfect rationality do not adequately reflect how humans make decisions. Simon's concepts of bounded rationality and satisficing challenge conventional views, inviting us to reconsider human decision-making processes as inherently shaped by cognitive limitations, emotional factors, and situational constraints.

Simon encourages humility in understanding human rationality, recognizing that our cognitive capacities are inherently bounded, and our decisions are influenced significantly by limited information, psychological biases, and social contexts. This insight highlights the necessity of adaptive ethics, a flexible, reflective approach to ethical decision-making that accounts for the complexities, uncertainties, and cognitive constraints individuals and organizations face. To illustrate this thoughtfully, consider the complexity of medical ethics decisions faced by healthcare professionals, who must continually balance patient care, medical evidence, emotional considerations, and situational contexts. Simon's adaptive ethics encourage reflective awareness and humility, guiding medical practitioners toward ethically mindful decisions responsive to evolving complexities and circumstances (Simon, 1996; Gigerenzer & Selten, 2002).

Simon's philosophical insights deeply enrich our understanding of human behavior, organizational dynamics, and decision-making under uncertainty. By emphasizing bounded rationality and adaptive satisficing strategies, Simon invites us to view human decision-making as inherently adaptive, dynamic, and context sensitive. Ethical decision-making, according to Simon, is not simply about achieving optimal outcomes but involves continuous reflection, adaptive responsiveness, and ethical mindfulness. Organizations guided by Simon's insights actively cultivate environments where ethical reflection, adaptive learning, and responsive decision-making flourish, ensuring organizational actions remain ethically aligned with broader societal values and humanistic objectives (March 1994).

Simon's adaptive ethics also carry significant implications for governance practices and societal decision-making frameworks. Policymakers and organizational leaders adopting adaptive ethics frameworks prioritize continuous reflection, stakeholder engagement, and adaptive responsiveness, recognizing that ethical decisions must remain context-sensitive and continuously evaluated. Practical governance examples inspired by Simon's adaptive ethics include participatory governance approaches, adaptive policy frameworks, and continuous stakeholder feedback mechanisms, ensuring governance decisions remain ethically mindful, adaptive, and responsive to evolving complexities and societal expectations (Thaler & Sunstein, 2008).

Simon's philosophical stance emphasizes the ethical responsibility inherent in managing technological advancements, particularly in artificial intelligence (AI) and cognitive computing technologies. Simon argued that ethical innovation demands continuous reflection, transparency, and adaptability in developing and implementing advanced technologies. Organizations involved in AI development utilize adaptive ethics frameworks, continuously reflecting on potential societal impacts, biases, and ethical implications. By embracing adaptive ethics, technological innovation can remain transparent, accountable, and deeply aligned with human-centered values, societal well-being, and ethical responsibility (Russell & Norvig, 2020).

Simon's philosophical and ethical contributions offer profound guidance for navigating complexity, human decision-making, and adaptive governance. By embracing bounded rationality, reflective awareness, and adaptive ethics, we can foster ethical mindfulness, continuous learning, and adaptive decision-making within complex adaptive systems. Simon's enduring legacy inspires us to thoughtfully engage with rationality, human behavior, and ethical responsibility, ensuring decisions remain responsive, adaptive, and ethically aligned with broader humanistic values and societal objectives.

Synergy and Integration: Linking Human Decision-Making, Complexity, and AI

The thoughtful integration of Herbert Simon's influential insights on bounded rationality, adaptive decision-making, and complexity provides profound philosophical and practical tools for effectively managing complexity, fostering ethical artificial intelligence, and enhancing organizational resilience. By linking Simon's pioneering ideas with contemporary advances in artificial intelligence (AI) and complexity science, we achieve a powerful synergy that enhances our understanding of human decision-making, strategic responsiveness, and ethical responsibility within complex adaptive environments.

At the core of this integration lies Simon's foundational concept of bounded rationality, the idea that human decision-making is naturally constrained by cognitive limitations, available information, and contextual factors. Integrating bounded rationality principles into AI development profoundly enriches decision-support systems, ensuring these technologies align closely with realistic human behaviors and ethical considerations. For instance, advanced AI-driven tools for medical diagnosis or financial management increasingly acknowledge human cognitive limitations, enhancing their capacity to support practical, ethical, and context-sensitive decision-making. By bridging Simon's concepts with AI technologies, organizations foster decision-making practices that remain responsive, adaptable, and ethically mindful in complex real-world scenarios (Russell & Norvig, 2020).

The integration of Simon's adaptive decision-making frameworks significantly impacts organizational governance and strategic management practices. Simon emphasized that effective governance in complex environments requires continuous learning, adaptive responsiveness, and ethical accountability. Organizations employing adaptive governance frameworks inspired by Simon's insights demonstrate enhanced responsiveness to uncertainty and complexity. These organizations strategically integrate human-centered AI technologies and adaptive decision-making processes, facilitating ethical innovation and organizational resilience in rapidly evolving contexts. Companies such as IBM, Google, or Microsoft, known for ethical AI governance frameworks, actively integrate bounded rationality and adaptive decision-making principles into their organizational strategies, ensuring technological advancements align ethically and adaptively with societal needs and humanistic objectives (Floridi & Cowls, 2019).

In societal and governance contexts, Simon's decision-making insights helps guide ethical policymaking, adaptive governance strategies, and resilience-building initiatives. Policymakers employ bounded rationality concepts to inform adaptive policy strategies addressing complex challenges such as climate change, public health emergencies, or economic volatility. Adaptive governance approaches informed by Simon's principles emphasize ongoing stakeholder dialogue, continuous policy adaptation, and transparent decision-making processes. For example, governments adopting participatory governance and adaptive management strategies actively integrate Simon's insights, enhancing policy responsiveness, ethical accountability, and societal resilience in complex adaptive environments (Sterman, 2008).

The synergy between Simon's insights on human decision-making and contemporary advancements in AI and complexity theory underscores the necessity of humility, ethical reflection, and adaptive responsiveness. Simon's philosophy encourages organizations, technologists, and policymakers to recognize complexity as inherent and meaningful, fostering continuous ethical reflection, transparent communication, and responsible innovation. By embracing bounded rationality, adaptive ethics, and ethical stewardship, we can thoughtfully navigate complexity, foster responsible technological advancements, and ensure decision-making practices remain deeply aligned with human dignity, societal well-being, and ecological sustainability (Simon, 1996; Gigerenzer & Selten, 2002).

Integrating Simon's fundamental concepts with contemporary AI and complexity science provides powerful philosophical and practical guidance for managing complexity, fostering adaptive decision-making, and ensuring ethical innovation within artificial intelligence, organizational governance, and societal resilience. By embracing Simon's insights, we cultivate greater ethical mindfulness, adaptive responsiveness, and reflective awareness, ensuring technological innovation and organizational strategies genuinely serve human flourishing, ecological integrity, and societal harmony.

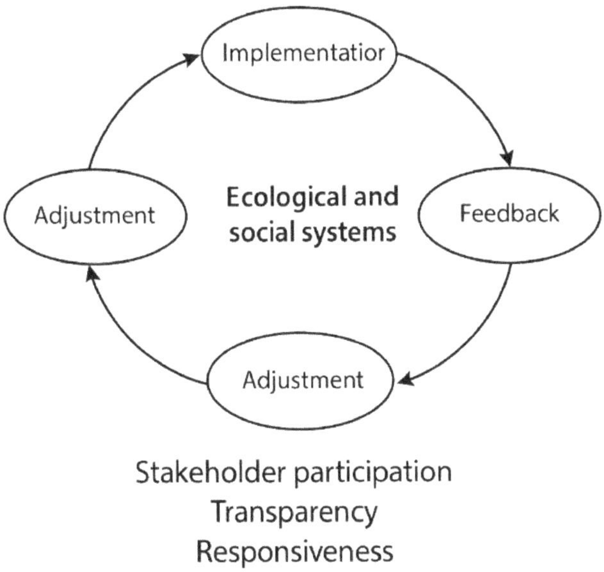

Figure 9.5. *Adaptive Governance Cycle.*

Note. This circular flowchart illustrates the adaptive governance process for managing ecological and social systems. The cycle includes monitoring, learning, adjustment, and implementation, supported by feedback at each stage. It emphasizes stakeholder participation, transparency, and responsiveness, aligning with Donella Meadows' systems thinking and reinforcing resilience in complex adaptive systems.

Conclusion

In our detailed exploration of the visionary insights from Donella Meadows, John von Neumann, and Herbert Simon, we have profoundly enriched our understanding of how complexity, rationality, and ethical responsibility intersect to guide sustainable development, decision-making, and adaptive innovation. Each of these distinguished scholars has illuminated critical aspects of complexity, inspiring us toward a more thoughtful, integrated, and responsive approach to complex adaptive challenges that shape our contemporary world.

Donella Meadows has shown us that achieving sustainability requires more than isolated interventions, it demands an awareness of intricate systemic interactions and carefully identified leverage points. Through her systems-thinking approach, we are encouraged to perceive complexity as interconnected networks of relationships and feedback loops, empowering us to identify strategic interventions capable of transformative societal and ecological change. Meadows' humanistic vision underscores that meaningful sustainability emerges from our collective ability to think holistically, act ethically, and adapt responsively to complex ecological and social dynamics.

John von Neumann has deepened our appreciation of decision-making complexity, computational rationality, and the strategic interplay that characterizes organizational behaviors. His foundational contributions in game theory and computational complexity illuminate inherent unpredictability, strategic considerations, and adaptive reasoning underpinning human interactions and organizational decisions. Von Neumann's intellectual legacy highlights the importance of adaptability, ethical reflection, and strategic responsiveness in effectively managing complexity within economic systems, technological innovation, and adaptive governance frameworks.

Herbert Simon complements this understanding by emphasizing that human decision-making is inherently limited, shaped significantly by cognitive constraints, informational shortfalls, and contextual influences. His concepts of bounded rationality and satisficing encourage us to embrace complexity with humility, acknowledging the limits of our predictive capacities and rational decision-making. Simon's insights equip us with practical and ethical tools for navigating complexity adaptively, fostering continuous learning, ethical responsibility, and reflective awareness within organizational and societal contexts.

Integrating the insights of Meadows, von Neumann, and Simon reveal essential philosophical clarity and practical guidance. Their collective contributions remind us that complexity, adaptive responsiveness, and ethical stewardship are not abstract philosophical concepts. They are practical necessities embedded within daily life, strategic decision-making, organizational practices, and governance frameworks. Their ideas reinforce that true innovation, ecological sustainability, and societal progress depend critically upon our capacity to continuously reflect, adapt, and engage ethically with the complex challenges we face.

Their integrated perspectives invite us toward deeper ethical mindfulness, continuous reflection, and adaptive governance, ensuring our technological innovations, organizational decisions, and policy strategies remain transparent, accountable, and responsive to evolving complexities. Practically, their contributions provide robust frameworks for understanding systemic complexity, decision-making processes, and adaptive governance strategies, empowering us to navigate complexity effectively, ethically, and sustainably.

The enduring legacies of Donella Meadows, John von Neumann, and Herbert Simon inspire us to approach complexity not as a challenge to be feared or avoided, but as an opportunity for continuous learning, ethical responsibility, and adaptive innovation. By integrating their perspectives, we enhance our ability to create solutions that genuinely promote human flourishing, ecological harmony, and societal resilience. Their profound humanistic vision enables us to shape an interconnected world characterized by sustainability, adaptive responsiveness, and ethical stewardship, ensuring meaningful benefits for both current and future generations.

Chapter 10: Integrating Complexity—Navigating the Future through AI and Quantum Computing

Introduction: Reflecting on Our Complex Journey

Throughout the preceding chapters, we have embarked upon a profound intellectual exploration of complexity, embracing insights from visionary thinkers whose contributions illuminate our understanding of adaptive systems, cybernetics, human decision-making, and ethical responsibility. This transformative journey has guided us from the foundational ideas of chaos theory and quantum mechanics to the intricate dynamics of cognitive science, systems thinking, and organizational adaptability. Each chapter has progressively enriched our appreciation of complexity as a vibrant tapestry interwoven with human curiosity, strategic innovation, and ethical mindfulness.

We have drawn inspiration from pioneers such as Henri Poincaré and Edward Lorenz, who revealed the fundamental unpredictability and sensitivity inherent in complex systems. John Holland and Stuart Kauffman further expanded our understanding by exploring genetic algorithms and the spontaneous emergence of complexity through self-organization. Gregory Bateson and Ilya Prigogine emphasized the crucial roles of feedback loops and dissipative structures, helping us appreciate complexity as adaptive, interconnected, and ever evolving. Building upon these insights, we engaged with Murray Gell-Mann and Claude Shannon, whose interdisciplinary contributions to complexity science, information theory, and computational thinking illuminated the profound ways complexity manifests within information systems, adaptive governance, and societal dynamics.

The visionary contributions of Norbert Wiener and Heinz von Foerster deepened our grasp of cybernetics and second-order observation, highlighting the essential role of communication, feedback, and reflective awareness within complex adaptive systems. Donella Meadows, John von Neumann, and Herbert Simon enriched our practical and philosophical insights, emphasizing sustainability, bounded rationality, decision-making complexity, and adaptive ethical governance. Collectively, these visionary scholars have provided an interconnected legacy, fostering a nuanced understanding of complexity, resilience, and ethical responsibility in organizational, technological, and ecological contexts.

As we conclude this journey, we recognize the urgent importance of linking historical complexity insights with contemporary and future advancements in artificial intelligence (AI), deep learning, machine learning (ML), generative AI, natural language processing (NLP), large language models (LLMs), and quantum computing. Today's rapidly evolving technological landscape presents both remarkable opportunities and profound ethical responsibilities. Artificial intelligence, with its powerful capabilities in adaptive learning, pattern recognition, and strategic decision-making, profoundly embodies complexity principles explored by our visionary thinkers. Quantum computing further expands the boundaries of complexity, introducing unprecedented computational possibilities that demand thoughtful reflection, adaptive responsiveness, and ethical stewardship.

This final chapter invites us to integrate historical insights with contemporary advancements, recognizing that effectively managing complexity requires continuous learning, adaptability, and ethical mindfulness. As we venture forward, we acknowledge that our complex journey has not only enriched our intellectual understanding but also profoundly shaped our capacity for ethical reflection, adaptive innovation, and responsible stewardship. By thoughtfully engaging with complexity, AI, and quantum computing through the interdisciplinary wisdom of our visionary scholars, we foster an interconnected future that genuinely promotes human flourishing, ecological sustainability, and societal resilience. This reflection thus marks not an endpoint, but a meaningful beginning and an invitation to navigate complexity ethically, adaptively, and conscientiously in our ever-evolving world.

Complexity as the Foundation of Contemporary AI

From Biological Cognition to Artificial Intelligence

The contemporary landscape of artificial intelligence (AI) has been profoundly influenced by foundational insights drawn from biological cognition and complexity science. Visionaries such as Warren McCulloch, John Holland, and John von Neumann have provided critical philosophical and practical frameworks, bridging biological systems, cognitive neuroscience, and computational theories. Their interdisciplinary contributions illuminate pathways for developing AI technologies that closely emulate natural intelligence, adaptability, and complex interactions characteristic of living organisms.

Warren McCulloch's seminal contributions laid early foundations for the computational modeling of neural networks, demonstrating how simple logical units, modeled after biological neurons, could collectively produce sophisticated cognitive behaviors. McCulloch's neural network framework underscored the interconnected nature of cognition, emphasizing how human intelligence emerges from countless adaptive interactions among individual neurons. This profound insight shaped modern artificial neural networks and deep learning architectures, which similarly rely upon interconnected layers of computational units to learn, recognize patterns, and make adaptive decisions. The enduring impact of McCulloch's insights continues to inform AI research, guiding the design of adaptive algorithms and computational models inspired by biological cognition and neural complexity (McCulloch & Pitts, 1943; Churchland & Churchland, 1990).

John Holland's groundbreaking work on genetic algorithms significantly enriched AI development, providing foundational insights into how complex systems can adaptively evolve and optimize through iterative cycles of selection, mutation, and reproduction. Holland drew inspiration from biological evolution, highlighting that intelligent behaviors and adaptive strategies emerge naturally from simple algorithmic rules and continuous feedback processes. Today, genetic algorithms are widely utilized in machine learning, optimization problems, and adaptive AI frameworks, reflecting Holland's interdisciplinary insights into biological adaptation, complexity, and computational innovation (Holland, 1975, 1992).

John von Neumann further contributed critical insights into computational complexity, decision-making, and cellular automata, emphasizing the adaptive, emergent behaviors arising from simple local interactions. Von Neumann's insights into computational complexity demonstrated how simple computational rules can yield profound, unpredictable outcomes, highlighting the importance of adaptive responsiveness and strategic decision-making within complex adaptive environments. His foundational concepts in computational theory have profoundly influenced AI technologies, from predictive analytics and algorithmic decision-making to cognitive computing and autonomous systems (von Neumann & Morgenstern, 1944; Wolfram, 2002).

To illustrate the integration of these insights, consider the analogy of cultivating a thriving ecosystem. Like an ecosystem, AI development requires careful nurturing, adaptive learning, and dynamic interactions among diverse elements. Ecosystems thrive through adaptive relationships between plants, animals, microorganisms, and environmental conditions, continuously adapting to evolving circumstances. Similarly, contemporary AI frameworks thrive through continuous learning, adaptive interactions among computational nodes, and responsive adjustments to data and feedback. This ecosystem analogy highlights that AI development is inherently dynamic, adaptive, and interconnected, inspired directly by biological complexity and cognitive adaptability.

This integrated understanding encourages ethical mindfulness, adaptive responsiveness, and reflective awareness in AI development and implementation. Recognizing AI as inspired by biological cognition and complex adaptive interactions fosters greater humility and ethical responsibility, ensuring AI technologies remain transparent, accountable, and ethically aligned with broader societal values and human-centered objectives. Organizations and technologists guided by this interdisciplinary philosophy actively embrace continuous learning, adaptive governance, and reflective innovation, ensuring AI technologies genuinely enhance human dignity, ecological sustainability, and societal well-being (Russell & Norvig, 2020; Floridi & Cowls, 2019).

The philosophical and practical integration of biological cognition, complexity theory, and computational principles established by McCulloch, Holland, and von Neumann serves as an essential foundation for contemporary AI innovation. By carefully integrating knowledge from biology, cognitive science, and adaptive systems, we empower ourselves to create artificial intelligence technologies that are ethically responsible, genuinely responsive to human needs, and aligned thoughtfully with human values. This integrated perspective empowers us to navigate complexity effectively, ensuring AI advancements remain responsive, sustainable, and aligned closely with human flourishing, societal harmony, and ecological integrity.

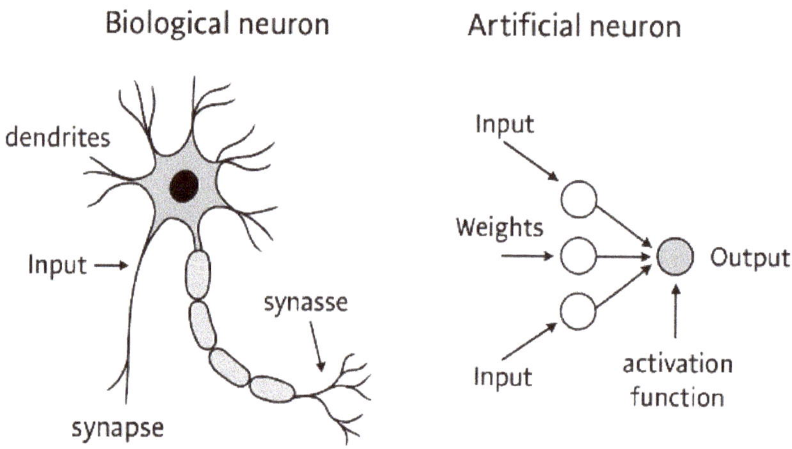

Figure 10.1. *Neural Inspiration: From Biological Cognition to AI.*

Note. The figure illustrates the parallels between a biological neuron, with dendrites, axon, and synapse transmitting signals, and an artificial neuron, where weighted inputs are processed through an activation function to generate an output. This comparison shows how neuroscience inspired the architecture of artificial neural networks.

Generative AI and Complexity Theory

The intriguing intersection between generative artificial intelligence (AI) and complexity theory reveals fascinating insights into how creativity, innovation, and pattern recognition emerge from simple yet powerful self-organizing interactions. Stuart Kauffman's pioneering exploration of self-organization provides valuable perspectives, showing how complexity theory can illuminate the impressive capabilities and potential of generative AI systems.

Kauffman's concept of self-organization where simple elements spontaneously produce intricate and dynamic patterns without central coordination profoundly aligns with the fundamental mechanisms underlying generative AI. To illustrate this concept intuitively, imagine a flourishing garden that emerges naturally through interactions among plants, insects, weather conditions, and soil nutrients, all collaborating and adapting without any central planner. Similarly, generative AI systems operate through interactions among numerous computational elements, algorithms, and data points, autonomously generating novel and creative outcomes without explicit external instructions. Kauffman's insights remind us that creativity and innovation within generative AI arise naturally through adaptive interactions, computational feedback, and iterative learning processes (Kauffman, 1993; Mitchell, 2009).

Generative AI systems inspired by complexity theory have demonstrated remarkable capabilities in creative industries, healthcare diagnostics, and adaptive educational frameworks. For instance, generative models in creative fields such as art, music, and design continually surprise us by autonomously producing original works that resonate deeply with human aesthetics and cultural preferences. In music composition, generative AI algorithms analyze patterns, styles, and musical structures, generating entirely new compositions that creatively integrate diverse musical elements. These AI systems embody principles of self-organization and complexity, reflecting the dynamic interplay and adaptive creativity identified in Kauffman's complexity theory (Boden, 2004).

In healthcare diagnostics, generative AI systems similarly leverage complexity-inspired pattern recognition and adaptive learning to enhance medical decision-making and diagnostic accuracy. Generative models can dynamically interpret complex medical data, generating insightful visualizations, diagnostic predictions, and treatment recommendations. For example, AI-driven diagnostic tools in radiology use generative approaches to identify subtle patterns in medical imaging, adaptively assisting physicians in diagnosing illnesses accurately and promptly. These generative systems reflect complexity principles of adaptive self-organization and innovation, significantly improving patient outcomes and healthcare effectiveness (Topol, 2019).

Adaptive education systems represent another powerful real-world application of generative AI and complexity theory. Generative AI-driven educational platforms dynamically respond to students' learning behaviors, adaptively creating personalized content, assessment tools, and learning pathways. By continuously analyzing interactions among learners, educational materials, and learning objectives, these systems autonomously generate innovative educational experiences tailored specifically to individual needs. Such adaptive educational frameworks embody the self-organizing principles of complexity theory, facilitating more responsive, creative, and personalized learning experiences that significantly enhance student engagement and academic success (Woolf, 2010).

The synergy between generative AI and complexity theory invites us to reconsider our perspectives on creativity, innovation, and adaptive learning within artificial intelligence. Kauffman's insights highlight the spontaneous, emergent nature of creativity within complex adaptive systems, challenging traditional views of creativity as exclusively human-directed. Generative AI systems illustrate that creativity and innovation can arise naturally and adaptively through computational interactions and iterative learning processes, prompting deeper philosophical reflections on human creativity, technological innovation, and ethical accountability. By engaging with generative AI from this complexity perspective, we foster ethical mindfulness, reflective awareness, and responsible innovation, ensuring generative technologies remain aligned thoughtfully with societal values and ecological sustainability (Mitchell, 2009).

Stuart Kauffman's insights into complexity theory provide profound philosophical and practical guidance for responsibly developing generative AI technologies. By embracing principles of self-organization, adaptive learning, and ethical reflection, generative AI can become an invaluable tool for fostering creativity, innovation, and adaptive responsiveness in contemporary society.

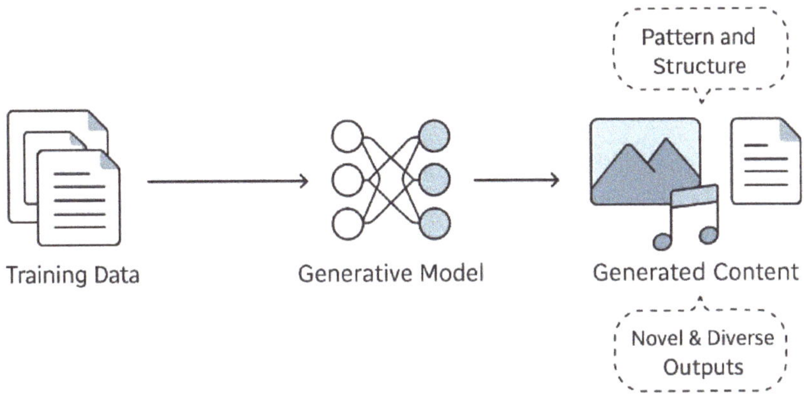

Figure 10.2. *Generative AI and Emergent Complexity.*

Note. This diagram illustrates how generative AI models produce content that exhibits emergent complexity. Training data feeds into the generative model, which generates content that forms novel and diverse outputs. These outputs reflect higher-level patterns and structures that were not explicitly programmed, exemplifying emergence within complex adaptive systems.

Cybernetic Principles in Modern AI Governance and Decision-making

Adaptive Governance and Complexity-Aware AI Systems

In the era of rapidly evolving artificial intelligence (AI), applying cybernetic principles developed by visionaries like Stafford Beer and Ross Ashby offers valuable frameworks to navigate the complexities of AI governance and adaptive decision-making. AI technologies, with their transformative potential and inherent complexities, demand governance strategies that are transparent, responsive, and ethically accountable. Cybernetic frameworks such as Beer's Viable System Model (VSM) and Ashby's concepts of adaptive control provide crucial foundations for effective governance of contemporary AI systems, ensuring these powerful technologies serve broader societal goals and maintain public trust.

Stafford Beer's Viable System Model presents a robust governance framework built upon the principles of adaptability, self-organization, and continuous feedback. Beer advocated for organizational structures that dynamically respond to changing circumstances and complexities, emphasizing that adaptive responsiveness and transparency are fundamental to effective governance. Similarly, AI governance frameworks benefit profoundly from incorporating VSM principles, enabling organizations to respond swiftly and ethically to evolving societal expectations, technological advancements, and regulatory landscapes (Beer, 1972; Espejo & Reyes, 2011).

Ross Ashby's complementary cybernetic insights, particularly the Law of Requisite Variety, further enrich adaptive governance strategies. Ashby argued that effective governance within complex systems requires internal complexity and flexibility sufficient to match external challenges. When applied to AI systems, Ashby's principles guide governance structures toward greater adaptability, responsiveness, and ethical accountability, ensuring AI development remains transparent, responsible, and responsive to societal values and ecological concerns (Ashby, 1956; Pickering, 2010).

Practical case studies from leading technology corporations illustrate the effective integration of these cybernetic principles into AI governance frameworks. Companies such as Microsoft and Google have established AI ethics committees, transparent governance structures, and stakeholder engagement platforms, informed significantly by cybernetic insights. For instance, Microsoft's

Responsible AI Principles and Google's AI ethics framework incorporate adaptive governance, continuous feedback mechanisms, and transparent accountability processes. These frameworks regularly adapt to stakeholder input, societal feedback, and regulatory developments, ensuring AI technologies are developed ethically, transparently, and responsively (Floridi & Cowls, 2019).

Another practical example is IBM's AI Fairness 360, an open-source toolkit designed to address bias and enhance transparency within AI systems. IBM leverages cybernetic principles by implementing continuous monitoring, adaptive feedback loops, and real-time responsiveness, demonstrating the practical value of adaptive governance inspired by Beer's and Ashby's frameworks. Through these initiatives, corporations effectively manage complexity, reduce biases, and improve accountability, fostering greater public trust and ethical responsibility in AI-driven technologies (Bellamy et al., 2019).

Adaptive governance frameworks have significantly influenced policymaking and regulatory environments related to AI. Policymakers increasingly employ complexity-aware approaches, incorporating principles of adaptive governance, stakeholder dialogue, and continuous regulatory adaptation. For instance, the European Union's ethical guidelines for trustworthy AI emphasize transparency, adaptive governance, and continuous stakeholder engagement, reflecting cybernetic principles of feedback loops, requisite variety, and adaptability. These adaptive policy frameworks illustrate practical applications of Beer's and Ashby's insights, enhancing ethical governance, transparency, and societal responsiveness to AI-related complexities (European Commission, 2019).

Integrating cybernetic principles into AI governance underscores the necessity of ethical reflection, adaptive decision-making, and transparent communication. Organizations adopting these principles recognize their profound responsibility in managing technological complexity ethically, adaptively, and transparently. Cybernetic insights encourage governance practices to remain responsive to societal expectations, ethical concerns, and ecological sustainability, fostering continuous learning, reflective awareness, and responsible stewardship in AI innovation (Beer, 1972; Ashby, 1956).

Applying Stafford Beer's Viable System Model and Ross Ashby's cybernetic principles provides robust frameworks for ethical AI governance, adaptive decision-making, and complexity management. By embracing these cybernetic insights, organizations and policymakers can effectively navigate the complexities of modern AI technologies, ensuring transparency, ethical accountability, and adaptive responsiveness remain integral to responsible innovation and societal well-being.

Second-Order Cybernetics and Responsible AI

The integration of Heinz von Foerster's second-order cybernetics into artificial intelligence (AI) development provides a significant opportunity to enhance ethical accountability, foster inclusive decision-making, and improve stakeholder engagement. Second-order cybernetics emphasizes the active and influential role of observers within systems, suggesting that AI development should explicitly recognize the responsibilities and impacts that creators, stakeholders, and communities bear in shaping technological outcomes.

Von Foerster's insights into second-order cybernetics encourage developers, policymakers, and organizations to continuously reflect on how their decisions, assumptions, and ethical values actively influence AI design and deployment. Unlike traditional AI development, which often views creators and users as passive or neutral actors, second-order cybernetics highlights that those involved in AI systems are essential participants, directly shaping the technologies they develop and use. This reflective approach emphasizes ethical transparency, accountability, and active stakeholder participation as foundational components of responsible AI development (von Foerster, 2003; Glanville, 2004).

One practical example of integrating second-order cybernetics into responsible AI involves the implementation of community-driven AI ethics committees. These committees actively involve diverse community members, stakeholders, and ethical experts who continuously assess, provide feedback, and guide AI development processes. Rather than relying solely on technical developers, community-driven committees ensure that AI systems reflect broader societal values, ethical principles, and stakeholder concerns. By explicitly recognizing the observer's active role, these committees foster greater ethical accountability, responsiveness, and transparency in AI development (Floridi & Cowls, 2019; Stilgoe, Owen, & Macnaghten, 2013).

Participatory AI development represents another important practical application of von Foerster's second-order cybernetics. Participatory approaches encourage diverse stakeholders—such as community members, end-users, and ethical experts—to actively engage in AI design, testing, and deployment processes. Participatory AI development ensures that AI systems meaningfully reflect the perspectives, values, and ethical considerations of the broader community. This approach emphasizes inclusivity, transparency, and ongoing ethical reflection, strengthening AI's ability to align with societal expectations and normative standards. Illustrative cases include participatory AI-driven healthcare applications, educational platforms, and community governance initiatives that embed stakeholder engagement throughout the AI development process (Cath, Wachter, Mittelstadt, Taddeo, & Floridi, 2018).

Inclusive governance strategies informed by second-order cybernetics further underscore the importance of continuous reflection, adaptive responsiveness, and ethical responsibility in AI systems. Such governance strategies prioritize stakeholder dialogue, adaptive decision-making processes, and transparent ethical accountability within AI development and deployment. Inclusive AI governance frameworks foster ongoing stakeholder participation, continuous feedback, and adaptive adjustments to evolving ethical and societal contexts. Practical implementations include frameworks adopted by governments and technology companies that ensure AI technologies remain ethically accountable, transparent, and adaptive to societal feedback and ethical reflection (Cath et al., 2018; Stilgoe et al., 2013).

Philosophically, von Foerster's second-order cybernetics profoundly influences responsible AI development by highlighting the inherent complexity, ethical responsibility, and adaptive responsiveness required within technological innovation. Recognizing AI creators and users as active observers and influential participants underscores the necessity for continuous ethical reflection, stakeholder inclusivity, and adaptive governance within complex adaptive systems. This philosophical stance encourages humility, ongoing reflection, and ethical mindfulness, ensuring AI development aligns responsibly with societal values, ecological sustainability, and stakeholder expectations (von Foerster, 2003; Glanville, 2004).

Integrating second-order cybernetics principles into AI development provides practical and philosophical guidance for responsible AI innovation, ethical governance, and inclusive stakeholder participation. By thoughtfully adopting these insights, we enhance the ethical accountability, transparency, and adaptive responsiveness of AI systems, ensuring technologies genuinely reflect community values, societal needs, and ethical principles in our interconnected and rapidly evolving world.

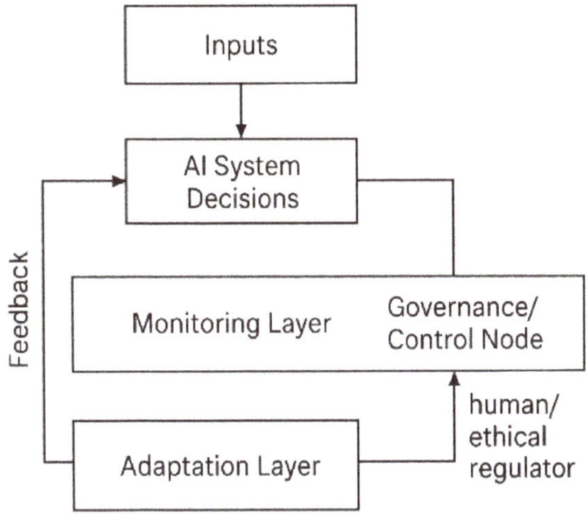

Figure 10.3. *Cybernetic Principles in AI Governance.*

Note. This flowchart illustrates the application of cybernetic principles to AI governance. Inputs enter the AI system, producing decisions that are monitored. Feedback loops enable adaptation, while an external governance/control node provides human or ethical oversight. The model highlights monitoring, feedback, and control as essential for responsible AI governance.

Complexity, Natural Language Processing, and Large Language Models

Complexity and NLP: The Linguistic Self-Organization

Language, fundamentally, is not static; rather, it is a dynamic system that continuously evolves through countless interactions and contexts. Drawing upon Niklas Luhmann's theory of autopoiesis and social systems, we gain profound insights into how language functions as a self-organizing system continuously generating new meanings, evolving patterns, and adapting through perpetual communicative interactions. Just as a living ecosystem adapts to changing environmental conditions through interactions among its components, language similarly adapts and evolves through dynamic interactions among its users, contexts, and societal shifts (Luhmann, 1995; Seidl & Becker, 2006).

From Luhmann's perspective, language itself emerges and adapts through ongoing, recursive processes of communication, meaning making, and interpretation. Each conversational exchange, textual interaction, or communicative encounter contributes to language's ongoing self-production, enabling language to adapt dynamically to new concepts, contexts, and social realities. This systemic view of language challenges traditional linguistic theories that view language as fixed or rule-bound, suggesting instead that language continuously adapts, evolves, and reorganizes itself through social interactions and contextual responsiveness (Moeller, 2006).

In the context of natural language processing (NLP), integrating Luhmann's complexity-inspired insights significantly enhances our approach to language modeling and AI-driven linguistic understanding. NLP systems, particularly large language models such as GPT and its successors, can be viewed as adaptive, self-organizing entities that continuously learn, adapt, and generate new linguistic patterns and meanings through interactions with extensive textual data. These language models, grounded in complexity theory, leverage the dynamics of self-organization to improve linguistic responsiveness, contextual sensitivity, and adaptive communication, enabling more natural, responsive, and contextually appropriate language generation (Brown et al., 2020).

Practical applications of this linguistic self-organization principle within NLP include AI-driven conversational agents, real-time translation tools, and context-sensitive information retrieval systems. Conversational AI assistants, informed by complexity principles, continuously learn and adapt to conversational contexts, user behaviors, and evolving language patterns, demonstrating dynamic, adaptive linguistic responsiveness. Real-time translation systems similarly employ complexity-inspired NLP techniques to adapt translations contextually and culturally, enhancing understanding and communication effectiveness across diverse linguistic communities (Hirschberg & Manning, 2015).

Incorporating Luhmann's autopoietic principles into NLP can enhance AI systems' ethical accountability and transparency. AI developers, recognizing language as a dynamic, context-sensitive system, prioritize continuous ethical reflection, cultural sensitivity, and adaptive responsiveness in NLP technologies. This approach encourages developers and organizations to remain ethically mindful of biases, cultural contexts, and social implications embedded in linguistic interactions, ensuring NLP technologies reflect societal values and ethical principles more fully (Bender et al., 2021).

Integrating complexity theory and linguistic self-organization into NLP inspires deeper reflections on the dynamic relationship between language, cognition, and communication. By recognizing language as a self-organizing, adaptive system, we gain philosophical clarity on how linguistic meaning emerges, evolves, and adapts through continuous human interactions. This insight emphasizes the ethical responsibility inherent in AI-driven linguistic technologies, underscoring the importance of ongoing reflective awareness, adaptability, and transparency within NLP development processes.

The integration of complexity theory, linguistic self-organization, and NLP provide powerful philosophical and practical tools for responsible language modeling and ethical innovation. By embracing complexity, adaptability, and ethical mindfulness within NLP systems, we ensure linguistic technologies genuinely enhance communication effectiveness, cultural responsiveness, and societal understanding, aligning language-driven AI applications with broader human values and societal well-being.

Large Language Models (LLMs) and Ethical Mindfulness

Large language models (LLMs), such as GPT-4.5, represent remarkable advancements in artificial intelligence, transforming how humans interact with technology, share information, and generate knowledge. However, their increasing power and complexity also bring significant ethical responsibilities, especially regarding issues of bias, transparency, accountability, and adaptive responsiveness. Complexity theories and cybernetic principles offer essential frameworks to ethically guide the development and deployment of these sophisticated models, ensuring they align responsibly with societal expectations and broader ethical values.

Complexity theory highlights the interconnected and adaptive nature of systems, reminding developers that biases or ethical oversights within language models can propagate quickly, potentially influencing vast numbers of interactions and users. Large language models learn from extensive textual data, inherently absorbing patterns, biases, and linguistic nuances embedded in the training materials. Consequently, organizations deploying LLMs should remain attentive and reflective, actively working to identify and mitigate potential biases while striving to ensure that linguistic outputs embody fairness, inclusivity, and sensitivity to diverse user contexts (Bender et al., 2021). Cybernetic principles, particularly adaptive governance frameworks inspired by Stafford Beer and Ross Ashby, provide practical guidance for responsibly managing the ethical complexity inherent in LLMs. Cybernetic frameworks emphasize transparency, adaptive responsiveness, and continuous feedback mechanisms, enabling developers and organizations to monitor, assess, and promptly adjust language model behaviors. Adaptive governance approaches informed by cybernetics encourage stakeholder participation, ongoing ethical dialogue, and reflective responsiveness, ensuring that LLMs remain ethically accountable, transparent, and aligned with societal expectations and values (Floridi & Cowls, 2019; Ashby, 1956).

Real-world implications of ethical mindfulness in LLMs are clear in the ethical guidelines and governance frameworks increasingly adopted by organizations. For example, companies such as OpenAI, Microsoft, and Google have established comprehensive ethical guidelines specifically designed to address bias, enhance transparency, and ensure accountability in large language model development. These guidelines typically include continuous monitoring of outputs, stakeholder consultations, regular ethical reviews, and transparent communication regarding model limitations and potential biases (Jobin, Ienca, & Vayena, 2019).

Ethical frameworks employed by organizations involve strategies such as red-teaming—proactively testing language models for biases and harmful outputs—and deploying automated evaluation tools designed to detect and mitigate unintended consequences. Ethical governance of LLMs also includes participatory approaches, involving diverse community stakeholders and ethical experts who offer insights into societal values, cultural contexts, and ethical expectations. Organizations increasingly engage in open dialogue with users, regulators, and community representatives, ensuring language models are ethically mindful, responsive, and adaptive to evolving societal concerns and values (Weidinger et al., 2021).

Integrating complexity theories and cybernetic principles into LLM development fosters continuous reflective practice, humility, and ethical accountability. These principles encourage developers, policymakers, and stakeholders to approach complexity and technological innovation with ongoing reflection, adaptive responsiveness, and ethical stewardship. By explicitly recognizing the complexity of linguistic interactions and the adaptive nature of language models, ethical guidelines encourage continuous improvement, transparency, and accountability within AI-driven language technologies (Bender et al., 2021; Stilgoe, Owen, & Macnaghten, 2013).

The integration of complexity theory and cybernetic insights into the governance and ethical management of large language models provides powerful practical and philosophical tools. Organizations leveraging these insights can effectively navigate complexity, foster ethical innovation, and ensure linguistic technologies responsibly enhance communication, understanding, and societal well-being. Embracing ethical mindfulness, transparency, and adaptive responsiveness ensures that language models such as GPT-4.5 genuinely align with societal values, cultural inclusivity, and ethical responsibility, supporting thoughtful innovation and responsible technological development in our interconnected world.

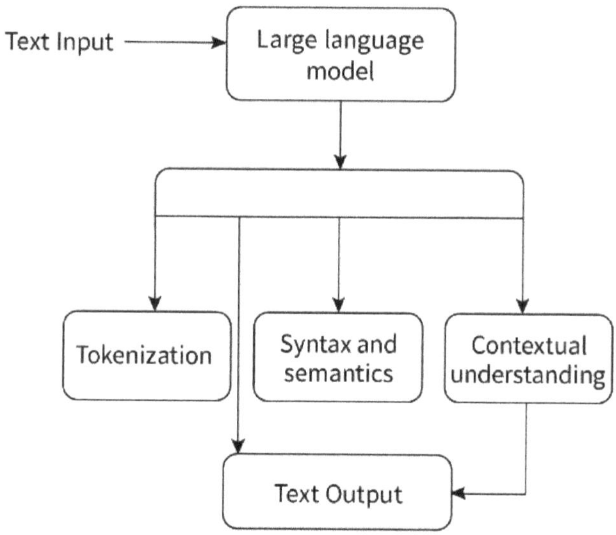

Figure 10.4. *NLP and Large Language Model Complexity.*

Note. This diagram outlines the stages of natural language processing as applied in large language models (LLMs). Text input is transformed through tokenization, syntax and semantic analysis, and contextual understanding, ultimately producing coherent text output. The process highlights the layered complexity and emergent behavior of LLMs.

Quantum Computing: Expanding Computational Complexity and Possibilities

Quantum Complexity and Historical Foundations

Quantum computing stands at the frontier of computational technology, offering profound possibilities for addressing complex problems beyond the scope of classical computing. Its foundational principles—such as superposition, entanglement, and quantum coherence that bring a paradigm shift in our understanding of computational complexity, adaptation, and decision-making processes. Drawing insights from historical complexity theorists like Henri Poincaré, Max Planck, Edward Lorenz, and Claude Shannon provide essential foundations for effectively navigating the intricacies and ethical implications inherent within quantum technologies.

Henri Poincaré's foundational contributions to chaos theory revealed inherent unpredictability and sensitivity in complex systems. Similarly, quantum computing embraces intrinsic unpredictability through quantum superposition, a fundamental principle stating that quantum particles can exist simultaneously in multiple states until observed. This property allows quantum computers to process information simultaneously in various forms, dramatically increasing computational capabilities. Drawing parallels between Poincaré's insights into complexity and quantum computing highlights the importance of adaptive responsiveness, continuous learning, and ethical reflection as we navigate unpredictable quantum landscapes (Nielsen & Chuang, 2010; Gleick, 1987).

Max Planck's revolutionary insights into quantum mechanics emphasized discrete energy states and the probabilistic nature of atomic behavior. Quantum entanglement, a principle that describes the interconnectedness of quantum particles regardless of physical distance, reflects Planck's insights into fundamental interconnectedness and complexity. Entanglement allows quantum computers to achieve exponential computational capabilities, profoundly reshaping strategic decision-making, optimization problems, and adaptive problem-solving processes. Planck's historical insights emphasize interconnectedness and ethical responsibility, reinforcing the necessity of transparency, ethical accountability, and adaptive governance within quantum computing innovation (Planck, 1901; Nielsen & Chuang, 2010).

Edward Lorenz's pioneering work in chaos theory and the butterfly effect further highlights the sensitivity and complexity inherent within adaptive systems. Quantum coherence, the sustained, interconnected quantum state enabling effective quantum processing similarly reflects adaptive complexity and sensitivity. Lorenz's insights underscore the importance of continuously adaptive governance, reflective awareness, and ethical mindfulness in managing quantum complexity. Navigating quantum coherence, much like Lorenz's butterfly effect, requires careful consideration, continuous reflection, and strategic adaptability to effectively harness quantum possibilities while responsibly addressing potential risks and uncertainties (Lorenz, 1963; Gleick, 1987).

Claude Shannon's foundational insights into information theory emphasized uncertainty, communication complexity, and adaptive responsiveness within information systems. Quantum computing significantly expands Shannon's insights by embracing inherent quantum uncertainty, probabilistic decision-making, and adaptive computational capabilities. Shannon's complexity-aware insights inform practical quantum computing strategies—such as adaptive communication protocols, quantum cryptographic frameworks, and quantum decision-support systems—enabling organizations and policymakers to manage computational complexity ethically and adaptively (Shannon, 1948; Nielsen & Chuang, 2010).

To illustrate this concept intuitively, imagine navigating intricate and evolving landscapes rich in possibilities and discoveries yet full of unknown pathways, hidden obstacles, and unexpected interactions. Quantum computing is akin to exploring such a dynamic terrain, requiring continuous learning, adaptive responsiveness, and ethical accountability. Organizations and policymakers engaging quantum computing technologies must thoughtfully balance exploration, innovation, and ethical reflection, ensuring technological advancements remain aligned with broader societal values, human dignity, and ecological sustainability (Floridi & Cowls, 2019).

Integrating historical complexity insights with quantum computing principles emphasize adaptability, ethical responsibility, and reflective mindfulness. Quantum technologies, guided by insights from Poincaré, Planck, Lorenz, and Shannon, encourage humility, continuous reflection, and adaptive governance. This integrated approach ensures quantum computing innovation remains transparent, accountable, and responsive to evolving complexities, enhancing organizational resilience, societal responsiveness, and ethical responsibility within quantum technology development (Nielsen & Chuang, 2010).

Bridging historical complexity theories and quantum computing provides profound philosophical and practical tools for ethically and adaptively managing computational complexity. By integrating these interdisciplinary insights, we foster responsible quantum innovation, adaptive governance, and strategic responsiveness, ensuring quantum technologies serve broader societal well-being, ecological sustainability, and human-centered innovation in our rapidly evolving computational landscape.

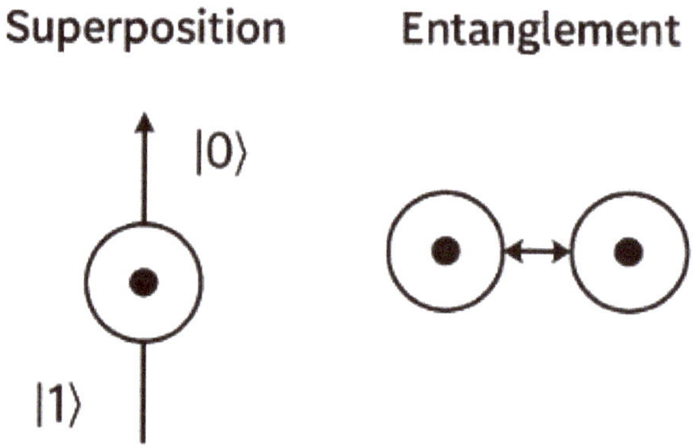

Figure 10.5. *Quantum Complexity: Superposition and Entanglement.*

Note. This diagram illustrates core principles of quantum complexity. On the left, superposition is depicted as a qubit existing in a combination of states |0⟩|0⟩|0⟩ and |1⟩|1⟩|1⟩. On the right, entanglement is shown as two qubits with correlated states, meaning the measurement of one immediately affects the state of the other, regardless of distance. These concepts highlight how quantum systems expand computational possibilities beyond classical logic.

Adaptive Quantum Governance

The rapid advancements in quantum computing present unprecedented opportunities and challenges, requiring thoughtful, adaptive, and ethically responsible governance strategies. Integrating cybernetic insights from pioneers such as Stafford Beer, Ross Ashby, and Norbert Wiener provides robust frameworks for developing governance structures capable of effectively managing the inherent complexity, uncertainty, and transformative potential of quantum technologies.

Stafford Beer's Viable System Model (VSM) serves as a valuable foundation for adaptive quantum governance, emphasizing internal flexibility, decentralized decision-making, and continuous feedback mechanisms. Quantum computing governance, influenced by Beer's insights, requires organizations to establish structures that dynamically adapt to technological advances, societal feedback, and ethical considerations. The VSM enables organizations and policymakers to maintain responsive communication channels, adaptive decision-making processes, and continuous regulatory adaptability, effectively managing quantum computing complexities and technological uncertainties (Beer, 1972; Espejo & Reyes, 2011).

Ross Ashby's Law of Requisite Variety further enriches quantum governance frameworks by highlighting the importance of internal adaptive capabilities sufficient to respond effectively to external complexity and emerging quantum technologies. Quantum computing presents extraordinary complexities, including rapid technological evolution, strategic implications, and ethical concerns regarding privacy, security, and societal impact. Ashby's insights guide policymakers and organizations toward adaptive strategies that ensure their internal decision-making processes and ethical frameworks are capable of effectively addressing these complexities. Adaptive governance informed by Ashby fosters ethical responsibility, transparent accountability, and continuous responsiveness within quantum technology policy frameworks (Ashby, 1956; Pickering, 2010).

Norbert Wiener's foundational principles of cybernetics underscore the crucial role of feedback, communication, and adaptive responsiveness within governance structures, particularly regarding quantum computing advancements. Wiener's insights inform quantum governance frameworks by emphasizing continuous monitoring, stakeholder dialogue, and responsive ethical reflection. For example, organizations and regulatory bodies actively employing Wiener's cybernetic principles engage stakeholders regularly, incorporate adaptive feedback processes, and maintain transparency in their quantum policy development and implementation. These practices enhance organizational preparedness, stakeholder trust, and adaptive responsiveness, effectively navigating quantum complexity and innovation (Wiener, 1948; Conway & Siegelman, 2005).

Practical applications of adaptive quantum governance informed by cybernetic and complexity theories include comprehensive quantum technology policy frameworks implemented by governments, corporations, and regulatory bodies worldwide. Organizations preparing for quantum computing advancements actively employ adaptive governance strategies to ensure technological developments align with ethical accountability, strategic responsiveness, and societal expectations. For example, quantum technology policy initiatives in the European Union and national strategies in countries such as Canada and Australia emphasize adaptive governance approaches, continuous stakeholder consultation, and transparent regulatory adaptability. These frameworks reflect complexity-informed governance principles, ensuring quantum computing innovations remain responsive, ethically responsible, and strategically adaptive to emerging complexities and societal concerns (Fisher & Rip, 2013; European Commission, 2021).

Organizations increasingly integrate strategic decision-making frameworks informed by complexity theory and cybernetic principles to enhance preparedness and responsiveness to quantum computing advances. Strategic frameworks involving scenario planning, adaptive risk assessment, and continuous ethical reflection enable organizations to effectively manage quantum complexity, technological uncertainty, and ethical implications. Quantum preparedness strategies adopted by corporations in finance, healthcare, and cybersecurity demonstrate how integrating cybernetic and complexity principles fosters organizational resilience, ethical mindfulness, and adaptive innovation in the face of transformative quantum technologies (de Wolf, 2017).

Adaptive quantum governance encourages humility, ethical transparency, and continuous reflective awareness. Integrating cybernetic insights into governance strategies highlights the ethical responsibility organizations and policymakers bear in managing quantum computing innovations adaptively and responsibly. Recognizing quantum complexity as an opportunity for ethical reflection, adaptive governance, and strategic innovation ensures quantum technologies genuinely enhance societal well-being, ecological sustainability, and broader ethical values (Floridi & Cowls, 2019; Stilgoe, Owen, & Macnaghten, 2013).

Adaptive quantum governance provides essential philosophical clarity and practical strategies, ensuring quantum computing advancements remain ethically responsible, transparently accountable, and strategically adaptive. By thoughtfully embracing cybernetic principles from Beer, Ashby, and Wiener, organizations and policymakers effectively navigate quantum complexity, fostering adaptive innovation and ethical stewardship that aligns closely with societal values and long-term sustainability.

Ethical Stewardship and Humanistic AI Innovation

Complexity and Ethical Responsibility in AI

In the rapidly evolving landscape of artificial intelligence (AI), addressing ethical responsibility has become not merely beneficial, but essential. Complexity theory provides a profound lens through which we can explore ethical stewardship in AI development, emphasizing transparency, responsiveness, adaptability, and mindful reflection as foundational pillars. By integrating complexity-informed ethical frameworks into AI innovation, we ensure technologies align responsibly with societal values, community expectations, and broader ethical considerations.

Complexity theory teaches us that adaptive systems such as those underlying AI technologies are inherently dynamic and sensitive to initial conditions. Small decisions or oversights in algorithmic development can rapidly propagate into widespread ethical and societal consequences. As AI systems become more complex, the imperative for ongoing transparency, ethical accountability, and continuous responsiveness grows stronger. Ethical AI development informed by complexity theory emphasizes ongoing reflective practice, stakeholder dialogue, and adaptive governance, ensuring AI technologies remain accountable, ethically aware, and responsive to evolving societal concerns (Floridi & Cowls, 2019).

In healthcare AI, complexity-informed ethical frameworks have significantly reshaped decision-making processes and technological innovation. Healthcare organizations employing AI-driven diagnostic tools or treatment recommendation systems increasingly prioritize ethical transparency, adaptive responsiveness, and patient-centered governance. Complexity-aware AI systems continuously monitor patient outcomes, adjust diagnostic algorithms dynamically, and engage stakeholders in meaningful dialogues. For instance, AI systems assisting in radiology and pathology utilize complexity-informed ethical frameworks to manage biases, maintain transparency, and continuously reflect patient values, ensuring healthcare innovation aligns with ethical responsibility and patient well-being (Topol, 2019).

Autonomous transportation represents another practical domain where complexity and ethical responsibility intersect profoundly. Autonomous vehicles must navigate ethical dilemmas, safety considerations, and unpredictable traffic conditions in real-time. Complexity-inspired adaptive governance strategies have guided automotive companies toward transparency, ongoing ethical reflection, and responsive decision-making. For instance, ethical governance frameworks adopted by autonomous transportation companies prioritize continuous stakeholder dialogue, adaptive regulatory engagement, and rigorous ethical monitoring, demonstrating the integration of complexity-informed ethics into responsible AI innovation (Awad et al., 2018).

Generative AI technologies, increasingly prevalent in creative fields, healthcare diagnostics, and education, similarly benefit from complexity-informed ethical stewardship. Generative models dynamically produce content, interactions, or responses, influenced heavily by the initial data and ethical considerations integrated into their development. Complexity-informed ethical frameworks guide organizations toward continuous monitoring of outputs, stakeholder transparency, and adaptive ethical reflection. Practical examples include generative AI systems used in creative arts, music composition, and adaptive education platforms, which integrate ongoing ethical evaluations and community-driven feedback mechanisms to ensure AI outputs align responsively with societal expectations and ethical considerations (Boden, 2004).

Integrating complexity theory into ethical AI development underscores the significance of humility, adaptive reflection, and ongoing ethical accountability. AI systems guided by complexity-informed ethical frameworks recognize the inherent uncertainty and unpredictability within technological innovation. This philosophical stance fosters ongoing reflective practice, stakeholder transparency, and adaptive responsiveness, ensuring AI development remains deeply accountable, ethically responsible, and aligned with broader societal values (Floridi & Cowls, 2019; Stilgoe, Owen, & Macnaghten, 2013).

Complexity-informed ethical stewardship provides essential philosophical clarity and practical guidance for responsible AI innovation. By integrating complexity insights, adaptive governance strategies, and ethical frameworks, we can effectively navigate AI complexities, ensuring technological advancements foster transparency, adaptability, and societal responsibility. The integration of complexity theory and ethical stewardship thus enables organizations, technologists, and policymakers to ensure AI innovation remains adaptive, reflective, and ethically accountable, genuinely enhancing societal well-being, ecological sustainability, and human-centered outcomes.

Philosophical Integration: Complexity, AI, and Human Flourishing

Philosophically integrating insights from complexity theory with artificial intelligence (AI) provides significant guidance for ethical stewardship, adaptive decision-making, and the pursuit of human flourishing. Complexity theories, as articulated by visionary thinkers such as Donella Meadows, Herbert Simon, and Stafford Beer, emphasize continuous ethical reflection, adaptability, and thoughtful responsiveness. These philosophical insights encourage us to thoughtfully consider the implications of AI technologies, ensuring they genuinely enhance human dignity, societal harmony, and ecological sustainability.

Donella Meadows' insights into systems thinking and leverage points underscore the critical importance of considering systemic interconnectedness within AI innovation. Philosophically, Meadows encourages ethical stewardship and continuous reflective practice, recognizing that AI technologies exist within intricate networks of societal relationships, cultural values, and ecological contexts. By identifying strategic leverage points such as ethical transparency, algorithmic accountability, and adaptive governance frameworks, Meadows' insights ensure that AI development remains aligned with broader societal values, ecological sustainability, and human-centered objectives (Meadows, 2008; Abson et al., 2017).

Herbert Simon's philosophical contributions emphasize bounded rationality and adaptive decision-making within complex adaptive systems. Simon's reflections remind us of the cognitive limitations, informational constraints, and contextual factors that shape human decision-making processes. Integrating these insights into AI innovation fosters humility, adaptability, and ethical mindfulness within AI-driven decision-making systems. For instance, AI technologies incorporating Simon's principles prioritize adaptive responsiveness, ethical reflection, and continuous improvement, recognizing that innovation should be realistically grounded in human capacities and ethical responsibilities (Simon, 1996; Gigerenzer & Selten, 2002).

Stafford Beer's cybernetic principles provide additional philosophical guidance for ethical stewardship and adaptive governance in AI. Beer emphasized continuous communication, adaptive responsiveness, and transparent ethical accountability within complex systems. Philosophically, his insights advocate that responsible AI innovation must involve continuous stakeholder dialogue, reflective monitoring, and adaptive decision-making processes. Practically, Beer's cybernetic principles inform governance strategies for AI systems in healthcare, transportation, and organizational management, ensuring technological advancements remain ethically responsible, transparent, and adaptively responsive to societal expectations (Beer, 1972; Espejo & Reyes, 2011).

Practical philosophical integration of complexity theories into AI development is evident in adaptive governance frameworks and ethical guidelines adopted by leading technology companies and policymakers. For instance, the European Union's Ethics Guidelines for Trustworthy AI reflect complexity-inspired principles, emphasizing transparency, stakeholder inclusivity, and continuous ethical reflection. Organizations such as Microsoft and IBM similarly incorporate philosophical insights from complexity theorists, employing adaptive governance frameworks that prioritize transparency, accountability, and continuous stakeholder engagement within AI innovation and deployment (Floridi & Cowls, 2019; Jobin, Ienca, & Vayena, 2019).

The philosophical integration of complexity theories into AI emphasizes continuous ethical reflection, adaptability, and the pursuit of meaningful societal progress. These philosophical insights guide organizations and policymakers toward responsible AI innovation that actively promotes societal harmony, ecological integrity, and human dignity. Practically, AI systems developed according to complexity-informed ethical frameworks actively monitor societal impacts, engage diverse stakeholders, and continuously reflect upon ethical implications, ensuring AI technologies remain aligned with broader human flourishing and ecological sustainability objectives (Stilgoe, Owen, & Macnaghten, 2013).

The philosophical integration of complexity theories with AI innovation provides essential ethical clarity and practical guidance for navigating complexity effectively, adaptively, and responsibly. By thoughtfully embracing continuous ethical reflection, adaptability, and reflective awareness, we foster AI innovation that genuinely enhances societal resilience, ecological sustainability, and the broader pursuit of human dignity and flourishing in our interconnected and rapidly changing world.

Synergy and Future Directions: Navigating Complexity with AI and Quantum Innovation

Integrating Complexity, Cybernetics, and AI for Adaptive Governance

Integrating insights from complexity theory, cybernetics, and artificial intelligence (AI) offers significant opportunities to enhance adaptive governance, ethical innovation, and strategic responsiveness in managing advanced technologies. Complexity and cybernetic principles provide crucial frameworks for developing governance strategies that effectively navigate technological complexity, uncertainty, and rapid innovation in AI, quantum computing, and related fields. This integration fosters ethically accountable governance, adaptive decision-making, and responsive innovation, empowering organizations, communities, and policymakers to effectively manage technological challenges while enhancing societal resilience and ecological sustainability.

At the intersection of complexity theory and cybernetic governance, practical approaches emphasize continuous adaptability, ethical transparency, and strategic responsiveness. Complexity-aware governance strategies recognize that technological ecosystems such as smart cities or quantum-enabled infrastructures are interconnected, dynamic, and sensitive to initial conditions. Cybernetic governance frameworks, informed by insights from Stafford Beer, Ross Ashby, and Norbert Wiener, guide organizations and policymakers toward effective management of these adaptive systems, employing continuous feedback, decentralized decision-making, and transparent accountability processes (Beer, 1972; Ashby, 1956).

Smart city governance strategies provide clear examples of practical integration, emphasizing adaptive responsiveness, stakeholder participation, and ethical transparency. Cities such as Amsterdam, Barcelona, and Singapore incorporate complexity-informed governance practices, leveraging AI and data-driven insights to continuously monitor urban dynamics, resource allocation, and community well-being. Cybernetic governance principles guide these cities toward ongoing feedback mechanisms, participatory governance, and transparent decision-making frameworks, ensuring technological innovations remain responsive, ethical, and aligned with residents' priorities and ecological sustainability objectives (Kummitha & Crutzen, 2017).

Adaptive climate governance represents another real-world example illustrating the synergy among complexity theory, cybernetics, and AI-driven strategies. Climate policies informed by complexity-aware governance emphasize stakeholder inclusivity, adaptive responsiveness, and ongoing reflection in climate decision-making processes. AI technologies facilitate continuous environmental monitoring, real-time data analysis, and adaptive governance responses to emerging climate conditions. For instance, adaptive governance strategies implemented by cities facing climate vulnerabilities incorporate complexity and cybernetic insights, leveraging AI-driven climate analytics to guide responsive, ethical, and transparent climate decision-making and policy implementation (Termeer, Dewulf, & Breeman, 2013).

In organizational decision-making, the integration of complexity theory, cybernetic principles, and AI-driven strategies enhances adaptability, resilience, and ethical responsibility. Complexity-aware organizations recognize the inherent unpredictability and interconnections among strategic decisions, resource allocation, and market dynamics. Cybernetic governance frameworks guide organizational decision-making toward continuous stakeholder feedback, adaptive strategic planning, and transparent accountability processes. For example, leading technology companies, such as IBM and Microsoft, actively integrate complexity-informed AI governance frameworks, continuously adapting organizational decisions based on real-time feedback, ethical reflection, and stakeholder engagement (Floridi & Cowls, 2019; Bellamy et al., 2019).

Integrating complexity, cybernetics, and AI underscores the importance of reflective awareness, ethical mindfulness, and continuous adaptability within governance strategies. This philosophical approach fosters humility, recognizing that effective governance of advanced technologies requires ongoing reflection, adaptive responsiveness, and ethical stewardship. Organizations and policymakers informed by these integrated insights prioritize transparent communication, stakeholder inclusivity, and continuous ethical evaluation, ensuring governance practices remain aligned with societal values, ecological integrity, and responsible innovation (Stilgoe, Owen, & Macnaghten, 2013).

The practical integration of complexity theory, cybernetics, and artificial intelligence provides essential philosophical and practical tools for ethically and adaptively managing advanced technologies. By embracing these interdisciplinary frameworks, organizations, communities, and policymakers effectively navigate technological complexity, foster ethical accountability, and enhance adaptive governance strategies. This integrated approach ensures technological innovations remain responsive, transparent, and ethically aligned with broader societal objectives, ecological sustainability, and community well-being.

Fostering Humanistic AI and Quantum Computing

As we stand at the forefront of technological innovation, particularly in artificial intelligence (AI) and quantum computing, it is increasingly crucial to guide these powerful advancements toward outcomes that genuinely serve societal well-being, ecological sustainability, and ethical responsibility. Ensuring that AI and quantum computing innovations remain centered around human values, ethics, and adaptive governance requires a thoughtful integration of historical insights and contemporary complexity theories.

The philosophical perspectives from complexity and cybernetic theorists, such as Donella Meadows, Herbert Simon, Stafford Beer, Ross Ashby, and Heinz von Foerster, provide critical foundations for developing responsible AI and quantum computing technologies. These thinkers collectively emphasize the importance of continuous reflection, adaptive decision-making, and ethical transparency within complex adaptive systems. Their visionary insights inspire us to carefully design technologies that align with societal values, cultural inclusivity, and ecological integrity, ensuring innovation genuinely enhances human dignity and community resilience (Floridi & Cowls, 2019; Stilgoe, Owen, & Macnaghten, 2013).

Practical strategies for fostering responsible AI innovation include stakeholder engagement, participatory development approaches, and continuous ethical evaluation. Organizations committed to responsible AI practices actively involve diverse community members, ethics committees, and stakeholders in AI development processes. These practices facilitate meaningful dialogue, adaptive responsiveness, and continuous ethical reflection, ensuring AI technologies address biases, remain transparent, and reflect broader societal expectations. Examples include participatory AI-driven healthcare tools, ethically guided autonomous vehicles, and community-responsive AI applications, demonstrating how responsible AI innovation can positively transform communities, organizations, and societal systems (Awad et al., 2018; Topol, 2019).

In quantum computing, fostering responsible innovation similarly requires careful attention to ethical considerations, strategic adaptability, and continuous stakeholder dialogue. Quantum computing's extraordinary computational potential necessitates adaptive governance frameworks capable of addressing ethical challenges, strategic risks, and societal implications. Adaptive quantum governance frameworks, informed by complexity theories and cybernetic principles, guide policymakers and organizations toward transparent regulatory practices, ethical accountability, and continuous responsiveness to stakeholder input and societal values. Practical quantum technology initiatives, such as national quantum strategies and ethical governance frameworks adopted by organizations, illustrate how responsible innovation can effectively balance technological advancement, societal benefit, and ethical responsibility (de Wolf, 2017; European Commission, 2021).

Fostering responsible AI and quantum computing encourages us to view technological innovation as inherently interconnected with broader ethical, ecological, and societal considerations. Complexity-inspired philosophies from Meadows and Simon remind us that technology should support genuine human flourishing, adaptive resilience, and ethical stewardship. Their insights inspire continuous reflective practice, transparency, and ethical mindfulness within innovation processes, ensuring technologies genuinely enhance societal well-being, ecological sustainability, and community empowerment (Meadows, 2008; Simon, 1996).

Fostering responsible AI and quantum computing innovation requires thoughtful integration of complexity theory, cybernetic insights, and ethical governance frameworks. By embracing adaptive responsiveness, continuous stakeholder participation, and reflective ethical accountability, we can ensure that future technological advancements genuinely align with societal values, ethical standards, and ecological integrity. Through this integrated approach, AI and quantum technologies can become powerful instruments for responsible innovation, meaningful societal progress, and sustainable adaptive governance, positively shaping the future of our interconnected world.

Conclusion: Complexity as an Invitation to Ethical Innovation and Adaptation

Through the collective exploration of complexity and the transformative insights of the pioneering thinkers examined in this work, we have deepened our understanding of how to effectively navigate and ethically engage with the profound challenges presented by modern technology. The contributions of visionary scholars such as Henri Poincaré, Edward Lorenz, John Holland, Stafford Beer, Herbert Simon, Donella Meadows, and John von Neumann have provided us with invaluable philosophical and practical tools, enabling adaptive innovation, responsible governance, and reflective awareness in the face of complexity.

Artificial intelligence (AI), machine learning, natural language processing (NLP), generative models, large language models (LLMs), and quantum computing have emerged not only as powerful computational tools but as catalysts of profound societal transformation. These advanced technologies hold the potential to positively reshape our collective future, yet they also demand rigorous ethical accountability, transparent governance, and strategic adaptability to ensure their benefits align genuinely with societal values and ecological sustainability. The interdisciplinary insights from complexity and cybernetic theory have equipped us to approach these technological developments thoughtfully, maintaining vigilance and responsiveness to emerging ethical considerations and societal impacts.

Viewing complexity as a rich and dynamic opportunity, rather than merely as a problem or obstacle, encourages continuous learning, adaptive responsiveness, and responsible stewardship within technological innovation and governance frameworks. Complexity-aware approaches guide organizations, technologists, and policymakers toward reflective strategies, inclusive stakeholder participation, and transparent communication, enhancing adaptability and resilience amid rapidly evolving conditions. Through complexity-informed governance, we can effectively address uncertainty, manage strategic risks, and ensure technological innovations genuinely promote societal progress, ecological harmony, and collective well-being.

Complexity-informed strategies have significantly influenced responsible AI innovation, adaptive organizational management, and quantum computing governance. Organizations incorporating adaptive governance frameworks and ethical accountability practices actively engage stakeholders, reflect continuously on societal feedback, and adaptively respond to emerging challenges and opportunities. Examples range from community-driven AI ethics committees and participatory healthcare innovation to adaptive climate policies and quantum technology governance strategies adopted by forward-thinking organizations and institutions worldwide.

The complexity-informed approach emphasizes humility, transparency, and ethical reflection, underscoring the importance of continuous learning and adaptive governance as essential components of technological innovation. Recognizing complexity as inherent and meaningful inspires us to remain reflective, accountable, and adaptive, fostering innovation aligned closely with human dignity, community resilience, and ecological integrity.

Embracing complexity as an invitation to ethical innovation and adaptation equips us to thoughtfully engage with AI, machine learning, NLP, generative models, LLMs, and quantum computing. Guided by the interdisciplinary wisdom explored in this book, we can responsibly manage technological advancements, ensuring they meaningfully enhance societal flourishing, ecological sustainability, and ethical responsibility. This thoughtful integration of complexity theories and ethical stewardship thus provides an essential foundation for navigating future uncertainties, fostering innovation that genuinely serves the broader well-being of individuals, communities, and ecosystems in our rapidly changing and interconnected world.

Glossary of Key Terms and Acronyms

This glossary provides definitions for key terms and acronyms used throughout the book. It is designed to support readers by offering concise explanations and illustrative examples where helpful.

AI. Artificial Intelligence – Machines performing tasks that usually require human intelligence. *Example: A chatbot answering questions.*

Adaptive Systems. Systems that can learn and adjust in response to changes in their environment. *Example: A business shifting its strategy during an economic downturn.*

Algorithm. A step-by-step procedure for solving a problem. *Example: A cooking recipe is an algorithm for preparing a meal.*

Autopoiesis. The ability of a system to reproduce and maintain itself. *Example: A living cell repairing and regenerating itself.*

Bounded Rationality. The concept that decision-making is limited by available information and time. *Example: Choosing the first restaurant nearby when hungry rather than reviewing all options.*

CAS. Complex Adaptive Systems – Interconnected entities that evolve and adapt. *Example: An economy responding to global events.*

Cellular Automata. Grids of cells that evolve based on simple rules, illustrating complex behavior. *Example: Conway's Game of Life.*

Chaos Theory. The study of how small changes in conditions can lead to unpredictable outcomes. *Example: A butterfly flapping its wings influencing weather patterns.*

Complex Adaptive Systems. Systems of interconnected components that adapt and evolve. *Example: Ecosystems where animals, plants, and climate interact.*

Cybernetics. The study of control and communication in systems. *Example: A thermostat regulating room temperature.*

Dissipative Structures. Ordered systems that arise by expelling energy or matter. *Example: A refrigerator releasing heat to stay cool inside.*

Emergence. The rise of new properties or behaviors from simple interactions. *Example: Ant colonies displaying collective intelligence.*

Entropy. A measure of disorder in a system. *Example: A tidy room naturally becoming messy unless energy is put into cleaning it.*

Feedback Loops. Cycles where outputs of a system influence its inputs. *Example: Microphone feedback causing a loud screech.*

Fractals. Patterns that repeat at different scales. *Example: A coastline that looks jagged whether zoomed in or out.*

Game Theory. The study of strategic decision-making among rational actors. *Example: Two companies deciding whether to compete or cooperate.*

Homeostasis. The ability of systems to maintain stability. *Example: The human body regulating temperature through sweating.*

Information Theory. The study of how information is measured and transmitted. *Example: Compressing a digital photo file.*

LLM. Large Language Model – A type of AI trained on vast text datasets. *Example: ChatGPT generating human-like text.*

Law of Requisite Variety. Ashby's principle that control requires a system to have at least as much variety as its environment. *Example: A manager needs multiple strategies to handle unpredictable challenges.*

Leverage Points. Places within a system where small changes can lead to big shifts. *Example: Changing interest rates to influence an economy.*

NLP. Natural Language Processing – AI methods for understanding and generating language. *Example: Voice assistants like Siri or Alexa.*

Organizational Complexity. The interconnected structures and behaviors that define organizations. *Example: Departments in a company coordinating through formal and informal communication.*

Quantum Computing. A new type of computing using quantum mechanics for efficiency. *Example: Processing many possibilities at once like reading multiple books simultaneously.*

Resilience. The ability of a system to recover from challenges. *Example: A city rebuilding after an earthquake.*

Self-Organization. The process by which order arises without central control. *Example: Birds flocking in coordinated patterns.*

Social Systems. Networks of relationships and communication that form society. *Example: Governments, communities, or corporations.*

System Dynamics. A method for studying complex systems through models and simulations. *Example: Predicting population growth trends.*

Systems Thinking. Viewing problems as part of an interconnected whole. *Example: Managing a forest by considering trees, animals, and climate.*

VSM. Viable System Model – A framework by Stafford Beer for organizational viability.

Viable System Model (VSM). Beer's framework for understanding organizational viability through five subsystems. *Example: A city council with policy, coordination, finance, innovation, and operations.*

References

Anderson, H., & Goolishian, H. (1992). The client is the expert: A not-knowing approach to therapy. In S. McNamee & K. J. Gergen (Eds.), *Therapy as social construction* (pp. 25–39). Sage Publications.

Ashby, W. R. (1956). *An introduction to cybernetics*. Chapman & Hall.

Ashby, W. R. (1960). *Design for a brain: The origin of adaptive behavior* (2nd ed.). Chapman & Hall.

Bateson, G. (1972). *Steps to an ecology of mind*. Ballantine Books.

Beer, S. (1972). *Brain of the firm*. Allen Lane.

Berry, L. L., & Seltman, K. D. (2008). *Management lessons from Mayo Clinic*. McGraw-Hill.

Churchland, P. S., & Churchland, P. M. (1990). Neural worlds and real worlds. *MIT Press*.

Cohen, M. K., Kolt, N., Bengio, Y., Hadfield, G. K., & Russell, S. (2024). Regulating advanced artificial agents: Governance frameworks for AI systems. *Science, 384*(6691), 36–38. https://doi.org/10.1126/science.adn0117

Comfort, L. K. (2007). Crisis management in hindsight: Cognition, communication, coordination, and control. *Public Administration Review, 67*(S1), 189–197. https://doi.org/10.1111/j.1540-6210.2007.00827.x

Conway, F., & Siegelman, J. (2005). *Dark hero of the information age: In search of Norbert Wiener, the father of cybernetics*. Basic Books.

Dennett, D. C. (1991). *Consciousness explained*. Little, Brown & Co.

Dietterich, T. G. (2000). Ensemble methods in machine learning. In *Multiple classifier systems* (pp. 1–15). Springer. https://doi.org/10.1007/3-540-45014-9_1

Doll, W. E., Jr. (2008). Complexity and the culture of curriculum. *Educational Philosophy and Theory, 40*(1), 190–212. https://doi.org/10.1111/j.1469-5812.2007.00404.x

Floridi, L., & Cowls, J. (2019). A unified framework of five principles for AI in society. *Harvard Data Science Review, 1*(1). https://doi.org/10.1162/99608f92.8cd550d1

Frahm, M. (2024). *Complexity: Navigating the intricacies of complex systems*. Independent Publishing.

Galison, P. (1994). The ontology of the enemy: Norbert Wiener and the cybernetic vision. *Critical Inquiry, 21*(1), 228–266. https://doi.org/10.1086/448755

Gell-Mann, M. (1994). *The quark and the jaguar: Adventures in the simple and the complex*. W.H. Freeman.

Gleick, J. (1987). *Chaos: Making a new science*. Viking.

Gleick, J. (2011). *The information: A history, a theory, a flood*. Pantheon Books.

Glanville, R. (2004). The purpose of second-order cybernetics. *Kybernetes, 33*(9/10), 1379–1386. https://doi.org/10.1108/03684920410556016

Goldberg, D. E. (1989). *Genetic algorithms in search, optimization, and machine learning*. Addison-Wesley.

Goodfellow, I., Bengio, Y., & Courville, A. (2016). *Deep learning*. MIT Press.

Harries-Jones, P. (1995). *A recursive vision: Ecological understanding and Gregory Bateson*. University of Toronto Press.

Hartley, K., & Jarvis, D. S. (2020). Policymaking in a low-trust state: Legitimacy, state capacity, and responses to COVID-19 in Hong Kong. *Policy and Society, 39*(3), 403–423. https://doi.org/10.1080/14494035.2020.1783791

Hayles, N. K. (1999). *How we became posthuman: Virtual bodies in cybernetics, literature, and informatics*. University of Chicago Press.

Holland, J. H. (1975). *Adaptation in natural and artificial systems*. University of Michigan Press.

Holland, J. H. (1992). Complex adaptive systems. *Daedalus, 121*(1), 17–30.

Holland, J. H., Holyoak, K. J., Nisbett, R. E., & Thagard, P. R. (1986). *Induction: Processes of inference, learning, and discovery*. MIT Press.

Kauffman, S. A. (1993). *The origins of order: Self-organization and selection in evolution*. Oxford University Press.

Lorenz, E. N. (1963). Deterministic nonperiodic flow. *Journal of the Atmospheric Sciences, 20*(2), 130–141. https://doi.org/10.1175/1520-0469(1963)020

McCord, P. (2017). *Powerful: Building a culture of freedom and responsibility*. Silicon Guild.

Mitchell, M. (2009). *Complexity: A guided tour*. Oxford University Press.

Mitchell, M. (2019). *Artificial intelligence: A guide for thinking humans*. Farrar, Straus and Giroux.

Nielsen, M. A., & Chuang, I. L. (2010). *Quantum computation and quantum information* (10th anniversary ed.). Cambridge University Press.

O'Neil, C. (2016). *Weapons of math destruction: How big data increases inequality and threatens democracy*. Crown Publishing Group.

OpenAI. (2025). *ChatGPT 4.5* [Large language model]. https://chat.openai.com/

Paar, C., & Pelzl, J. (2009). *Understanding cryptography: A textbook for students and practitioners*. Springer.

Papadimitriou, D. B., Nikiforos, M., & Zezza, G. (2013). *The Greek economic crisis and the experience of austerity: A strategic analysis*. Levy Economics Institute of Bard College.

Pickering, A. (2010). *The cybernetic brain: Sketches of another future*. University of Chicago Press.

Planck, M. (1901). On the law of distribution of energy in the normal spectrum. *Annalen der Physik, 4*(553), 237–245. https://doi.org/10.1002/andp.19013090310

Poincaré, H. (1890). Sur le problème des trois corps et les équations de la dynamique. *Acta Mathematica, 13*, 1–270. https://doi.org/10.1007/BF02392506

Potvin, J. Y. (2009). Evolutionary algorithms for vehicle routing. *INFOR: Information Systems and Operational Research, 47*(2), 75–86. https://doi.org/10.3138/infor.47.2.75

Prigogine, I., & Stengers, I. (1984). *Order out of chaos: Man's new dialogue with nature*. Bantam Books.

Preskill, J. (2018). Quantum computing in the NISQ era and beyond. *Quantum, 2*, 79. https://doi.org/10.22331/q-2018-08-06-79

Reason, J. (2016). *Managing the risks of organizational accidents*. Routledge.

Ribeiro, M. T., Singh, S., & Guestrin, C. (2016). "Why should I trust you?": Explaining the predictions of any classifier. In *Proceedings of the 22nd ACM SIGKDD International Conference on Knowledge Discovery and Data Mining* (pp. 1135–1144). ACM. https://doi.org/10.1145/2939672.2939778

Rudin, C. (2019). Stop explaining black box models for high stakes decisions and use interpretable models instead. *Nature Machine Intelligence, 1*(5), 206–215. https://doi.org/10.1038/s42256-019-0048-x

Russell, S., & Norvig, P. (2020). *Artificial intelligence: A modern approach* (4th ed.). Pearson Education.

Shannon, C. E. (1948). A mathematical theory of communication. *Bell System Technical Journal, 27*(3), 379–423. https://doi.org/10.1002/j.1538-7305.1948.tb01338.x

Simon, H. A. (1996). *The sciences of the artificial* (3rd ed.). MIT Press.

Sklar, B. (2001). *Digital communications: Fundamentals and applications* (2nd ed.). Prentice Hall.

Sornette, D. (2017). *Why stock markets crash: Critical events in complex financial systems*. Princeton University Press.

Spejo, R., & Harnden, R. (Eds.). (1989). *The viable system model: Interpretations and applications of Stafford Beer's VSM*. Wiley.

Sterman, J. D. (2008). Risk communication on climate: Mental models and mass balance. *Science, 322*(5901), 532–533. https://doi.org/10.1126/science.1162574

Stilgoe, J., Owen, R., & Macnaghten, P. (2013). Developing a framework for responsible innovation. *Research Policy, 42*(9), 1568–1580. https://doi.org/10.1016/j.respol.2013.05.008

Taleb, N. N. (2012). *Antifragile: Things that gain from disorder*. Random House.

Terhal, B. M. (2015). Quantum error correction for quantum memories. *Reviews of Modern Physics, 87*(2), 307–346. https://doi.org/10.1103/RevModPhys.87.307

Thaler, R. H., & Sunstein, C. R. (2008). *Nudge: Improving decisions about health, wealth, and happiness*. Yale University Press.

Topol, E. (2019). *Deep medicine: How artificial intelligence can make healthcare human again*. Basic Books.

von Foerster, H. (2003). *Understanding understanding: Essays on cybernetics and cognition*. Springer.

von Neumann, J., & Morgenstern, O. (1944). *Theory of games and economic behavior*. Princeton University Press.

Walker, B., Carpenter, S. R., Folke, C., Gunderson, L., Peterson, G. D., Scheffer, M., & Kinzig, A. (2020). Navigating the chaos of the Anthropocene: Complexity and resilience in a rapidly changing world. *Annual Review of Environment and Resources, 45*, 315–336. https://doi.org/10.1146/annurev-environ-012320-083601

Wallach, W., & Marchant, G. E. (2018). An agile ethical/legal model for the international and national governance of AI and robotics. *AI & Society, 33*(4), 551–563. https://doi.org/10.1007/s00146-017-0775-7

Wiener, N. (1948). *Cybernetics: Or control and communication in the animal and the machine*. MIT Press.

Wolfram, S. (2002). *A new kind of science*. Wolfram Media.

Woolf, B. P. (2010). *Building intelligent interactive tutors: Student-centered strategies for revolutionizing e-learning*. Morgan Kaufmann.

Yeganeh, H. (2021). An analysis of organizational responses to the COVID-19 pandemic: Agility, resilience, and flexibility. *Journal of Business Research, 132*, 173–187. https://doi.org/10.1016/j.jbusres.2021.04.005

Zurek, W. H. (2003). Decoherence, einselection, and the quantum origins of the classical. *Reviews of Modern Physics, 75*(3), 715–775. https://doi.org/10.1103/RevModPhys.75.715

Figure References

Figure 1.1. Gleick, J. (1987). *Chaos: Making a new science*. Viking.

Figure 1.2. Goodfellow, I., Bengio, Y., & Courville, A. (2016). *Deep learning*. MIT Press.

Figure 1.3. Sparrow, T. (2025). Graphical representation of chaotic dynamics in quantum and AI computational systems [Author's illustration].

Figure 1.4. Sparrow, T. (2025). Comparing perturbations: Quantum states with decoherence and phase jitter versus ML/DL/GenAI states with fixed scale per step [Author's illustration].

Figure 2.1. Lorenz, E. N. (1963). Deterministic nonperiodic flow. *Journal of the Atmospheric Sciences, 20*(2), 130–141. https://doi.org/10.1175/1520-0469(1963)020

Figure 2.2. Frahm, M. (2025). *Complexity: Navigating the intricacies of complex systems* [Author's illustration]. Independent Publishing.

Figure 2.3. Lorenz, E. N. (1963). Deterministic nonperiodic flow. *Journal of the Atmospheric Sciences, 20*(2), 130–141. https://doi.org/10.1175/1520-0469(1963)020

Figure 2.3a. Nielsen, M. A., & Chuang, I. L. (2010). *Quantum computation and quantum information* (10th anniversary ed.). Cambridge University Press.

Figure 2.4. Sparrow, T. (2025). Quantum ↔ Chaos: Map of reversibility and scale [Author's illustration].

Figure 3.1. Sparrow, T. (2025). Genetic algorithm (GA) workflow with feedback loop [Author's illustration].

Figure 3.2. Sparrow, T. (2025). Applications of genetic algorithms in real-world systems [Author's illustration, adapted from Holland (1992), Goldberg (1989), Potvin (2009), & Mitchell (2009)].

Figure 3.3. Sparrow, T. (2025). NK fitness landscape illustrating adaptive walks toward local and global optima [Author's illustration, adapted from Kauffman (1993)].

Figure 4.1. Sparrow, T. (2025). Recursive levels of learning: Single-loop, double-loop, and triple-loop feedback [Author's illustration, adapted from Bateson (1972/2000)].

Figure 4.2. Sparrow, T. (2025). Dissipative structures: Energy flows, entropy export, and emergent order [Author's illustration, adapted from Prigogine & Stengers (1984)].

Figure 4.3. Sparrow, T. (2025). Conceptual diagram integrating Bateson's feedback loops and Prigogine's dissipative structures into a six-step adaptive governance loop [Author's illustration].

Figure 5.1. Sparrow, T. (2025). Complex adaptive system (CAS) network [Author's illustration, adapted from Gell-Mann (1994)].

Figure 5.2. Sparrow, T. (2025). Complex adaptive system: Triangular network clustering [Author's illustration, adapted from Gell-Mann (1994)].

Figure 5.3. Sparrow, T. (2025). Analogy between Shannon's entropy and risk management [Author's illustration].

Figure 6.1. Sparrow, T. (2025). Price escalation monitoring communication loop in project management [Author's illustration].

Figure 6.2. Sparrow, T. (2025). Observer-participant loop in second-order cybernetics: Participatory urban planning example [Author's illustration, adapted from von Foerster (2003)].

Figure 6.3. Sparrow, T. (2025). Synergy and integration: Wiener, von Foerster, and complexity science [Author's illustration].

Figure 7.1. Sparrow, T. (2025). McCulloch-Pitts logical neuron concept: From biological analogy to modern AI [Author's illustration].

Figure 7.2. Sparrow, T. (2025). From McCulloch-Pitts logical neurons to modern deep learning: Facial recognition example [Author's illustration].

Figure 7.3. Sparrow, T. (2025). Ashby's concept of homeostasis: Enhanced airport feedback loop [Author's illustration].

Figure 7.4. Sparrow, T. (2025). Ashby's law of requisite variety: Dynamic management in complex systems [Author's illustration].

Figure 8.1. Medina, E. (2011). *Cybernetic revolutionaries: Technology and politics in Allende's Chile*. MIT Press.

Figure 8.2. Beer, S. (1979). *The heart of enterprise*. Wiley.

Figure 8.3. Luhmann, N. (1995). *Social systems* (J. Bednarz, Jr., & D. Baecker, Trans.). Stanford University Press.

Figure 8.4. Seidl, D., & Becker, K. H. (2006). *Niklas Luhmann and organization studies*. Copenhagen Business School Press.

Figure 9.1. Meadows, D. H., Meadows, D. L., Randers, J., & Behrens III, W. W. (1972). *The limits to growth*. Universe Books.

Figure 9.2. Meadows, D. H. (2008). *Thinking in systems: A primer*. Chelsea Green Publishing.

Figure 9.3. von Neumann, J., & Morgenstern, O. (1944). *Theory of games and economic behavior*. Princeton University Press.

Figure 9.3a. Axelrod, R. (1984). *The evolution of cooperation*. Basic Books.

Figure 9.4. Simon, H. A. (1955). A behavioral model of rational choice. *The Quarterly Journal of Economics, 69*(1), 99–118. https://doi.org/10.2307/1884852

Figure 9.5. Folke, C., Hahn, T., Olsson, P., & Norberg, J. (2005). Adaptive governance of social-ecological systems. *Annual Review of Environment and Resources, 30*, 441–473. https://doi.org/10.1146/annurev.energy.30.050504.144511

Figure 10.1. Goodfellow, I., Bengio, Y., & Courville, A. (2016). *Deep learning*. MIT Press.

Figure 10.2. Mitchell, M. (2019). *Artificial intelligence: A guide for thinking humans*. Farrar, Straus and Giroux.

Figure 10.3. Wiener, N. (1948). *Cybernetics: Or control and communication in the animal and the machine*. MIT Press.

Figure 10.4. Manning, C. D., Raghavan, P., & Schütze, H. (2008). *Introduction to information retrieval*. Cambridge University Press.

Figure 10.5. Nielsen, M. A., & Chuang, I. L. (2010). *Quantum computation and quantum information* (10th anniversary ed.). Cambridge University Press.

Index

A

Adaptation: 11, 49, 216, 219, 224, 240, 245, 249, 256, 272, 280, 287, 291, 296, 312, 314, 321

Adaptive: 6–7, 9–10, 13, 18, 20, 24, 34, 43–44, 51, 57, 64, 66–67, 71, 74–79, 82, 84–87

Adaptive Governance: 6–7, 9, 11, 15, 22, 24, 33–34, 40–44, 49, 51, 60, 66, 83, 86–87, 94, 97, 262–264

AI: 1, 6, 9, 11, 13–23, 25–29, 31, 295, 303–315, 317–318, 320–321, 324, 326, 328

Algorithm: 35, 39, 78–81, 83, 101, 315, 327

Ashby: 10, 13, 171–172, 294, 300–302, 308, 310, 317, 320, 328

Autonomy: 25, 86, 152, 182, 211–213, 217, 219, 223–225, 229

Autopoietic Systems: 202, 217–223, 225, 227–229, 292

B

Bateson: 10, 13, 95–102, 107–113, 277, 320–321, 327

Beer, Stafford: 5

Bias: 33, 35–36, 38, 44, 46, 100–101, 212, 286, 293–294

Black Box: 323

Butterfly Effect: 9, 17–18, 50, 53, 55, 60, 67, 72–73, 125, 141, 210, 297–298, 316

C

Chaos: 6, 9–10, 15–17, 21–24, 41, 44–46, 48, 50–60, 62–64, 66–76, 84, 89, 93, 95–97, 103–104, 316

Chaos Theory: 6, 9, 15–17, 22–24, 66–67, 70–73, 75, 84, 89, 114, 141, 171, 277, 297

Complex Adaptive Systems: 1, 6, 8, 10–11, 13–23, 25–27, 29, 31, 33–35, 38–45, 48–51, 53–55, 57–60, 62–73, 75–77, 167–171, 174–184, 186–191, 241, 243, 245, 248–249, 255, 265, 268, 271, 274, 278, 280–281

Complex Systems: 16, 53, 55, 69, 73, 75–76, 88–89, 93, 96, 98–99, 102, 104, 145, 148, 161, 164, 169, 186–187, 194, 196, 199

Complexity (General): 1–23, 24, 227, 229–236, 238–243

Cybernetics: 10, 97, 111, 141–144, 150, 288–290, 294, 301, 308–310, 316, 320–321, 324, 328–329

D

Decision-Making: 7, 11, 21–22, 43, 50, 57, 85–87, 111–112, 116, 118, 122–124, 126–127, 129–130, 133, 232, 237, 240, 277–278, 280, 283, 285

Development: 7, 77, 102, 105, 122, 127, 142–143, 150, 152, 157, 160, 162, 167, 174, 176–177, 182–184, 188, 293–295, 299, 301

Dissipative Structures: 7, 10, 13, 58, 60, 68, 84, 86, 88, 92, 95–97, 99, 218–220, 223–225, 228–229, 262, 267, 277, 283, 285–286, 300–301

E

Entropy: 9–12, 42–49, 70–72

Environment / External: 32, 88, 145, 158, 160, 172, 187–192, 194–196, 199, 203, 206, 208–209, 212, 218–219, 224, 229, 283, 286, 291, 300

Ethics / Ethical Governance: 6–7, 9, 11, 15, 22, 24, 33–34, 40–44, 49, 51, 60, 66, 83, 86–87, 94, 97, 99–101, 109–113, 115, 118, 320

F

Feedback: 10, 13, 20, 33–35, 42–43, 51, 70, 78–79, 81–83, 90, 95–101, 108–113, 122–124, 264, 267, 270, 274, 277–278, 280–281, 283, 286–289, 291, 294

Fractals: 317

G

Gell-Mann, Murray: 10, 13, 95, 114, 116–117, 119, 121, 125, 136, 138, 140–141, 277

Genetic Algorithms: 10, 13, 18, 23, 41, 54, 71, 74–79, 84–87, 91–94, 114, 127, 132–134, 137, 141, 167, 214, 254, 267, 277, 279–280, 283, 303, 321, 323, 327

Governance / Governance Applications: 10, 58, 85, 111, 121, 133–134, 176–180, 184, 239, 241, 247, 253–255, 266, 289, 292–293, 301, 311, 321, 323, 327

H

Homeostasis (Ashby): 13, 109, 152–153, 172, 186–187, 189–192, 199, 317, 328

Human-in-the-Loop: 25, 33–35, 38, 42, 44, 48, 51, 68, 79, 81–83, 91, 99–100, 110–111, 120, 145–147, 155–156, 187, 327–328

I

Information: 3, 10, 13, 19, 25, 32, 38, 62, 65, 77, 95, 98–99, 105, 111, 114–115, 122, 126–137, 139, 141, 143–149, 151, 153, 155, 169, 175, 178, 204, 218, 226, 237, 261, 263–264, 267, 269, 271, 277–278, 292–293, 297–298, 315, 317, 320–323, 326, 329

Information Theory: 6–7, 9, 15–18, 22–24, 29, 44–45, 50–52, 54–59, 62–63, 66–67, 302–305, 316–317, 320–321, 329

Interpretability: 19, 22–24, 31–33, 48–51, 64, 68, 87, 109, 111

J

Judgment: 19

Judgment in Governance: 3, 5–11, 13–29, 31–39, 41–42, 44–62, 274–275, 277–281, 283–285, 287–304, 306–318

K

Kauffman, Stuart: 9–11, 52–54, 59–65

Knowledge Systems: 7, 104, 113, 116, 154–155, 158–159, 161, 163, 232, 264, 281, 293, 323

L

Law of Requisite Variety: 172, 186–189, 191–192, 196–199, 202, 206, 286, 300, 317, 328

Lorenz, Edward: 6, 9, 16, 18, 20, 53–55, 59, 62, 66–68, 70, 72–75, 85, 87, 89, 93–96, 141, 277, 296–298, 312, 322, 326

M

Machine Learning: 13–17, 27, 50, 54, 57, 71, 176, 178, 254, 278, 313–314, 320–321

Models: 11, 13, 19, 21–22, 27–28, 37, 47, 49–50, 54, 60, 71, 77, 79, 90–92, 133, 160, 180, 269, 278

N

Natural Language Processing (NLP): 11, 50–54, 137, 143, 168–169, 175–176, 178, 184, 278, 291, 296, 313, 318

Neumann, John von: 10–11, 13, 75–76, 78, 87, 93, 141–142, 153–159, 161–170, 231–232, 246–251, 253–260, 274–280, 312–313, 324, 329

NK Model (Kauffman): 17–20, 28, 32, 34–36, 38, 40, 42, 52, 76, 89–92, 94, 319, 321–322, 324, 327, 329

O

Operations (VSM Subsystem): 27, 31–32, 159–162

Opsroom (Project Cybersyn): 129, 157–161, 205

Orchestra Analogy: 176

P

Planck, Max: 26–27, 39, 323

Policy-Making: 7, 11, 21–23, 28, 43, 57, 59, 64, 85–87, 90, 100, 101, 105, 111–112, 116, 118, 124, 148–150, 155, 188, 196, 206, 208–209, 228, 233, 235, 237, 239–241, 244–245, 300, 302–306

Prigogine, Ilya: 10, 13, 53, 57, 59–60, 68–72, 95–97, 102–113, 277, 323, 327

Q

Quantum Complexity: 1, 5–11, 13–14, 16, 18–23, 102–105, 107–118, 120–123, 125–126, 128, 130–131, 326, 328

Quantum Foundations: 9, 53, 174, 178, 181, 225, 279, 285, 296, 311

Quantum Computing: 1, 6–7, 9, 11, 13–16, 23, 25–26, 62–68, 72, 74, 76, 93–95, 97, 104, 171–176, 182, 253–255, 261, 267, 270, 296–302, 308

Quantum Governance: 6–7, 9, 11, 15, 22, 24, 33–34, 60, 66, 83, 86–87, 94, 97, 262–264, 267–268, 270, 272–275, 278, 281, 291, 297–314

R

Resilience: 45–46, 49–50, 73, 84, 138–140, 142, 145, 167–169, 172, 189–193, 200–205, 207, 213, 215, 219, 221–224

Risk Management: 33, 49, 86, 110, 129–130, 254

S

Second-Order Cybernetics: 10, 97, 111, 142, 150, 153–165, 169, 171–172, 189, 199, 201, 203–205, 229, 288–290, 294, 301, 321, 328

Shannon, Claude: 4–6, 92–98, 112–116, 141–152

Social Systems: 11, 19–20, 57, 60, 72, 84, 101–102, 109–110, 112–113, 117–120, 125–126, 135, 137, 140, 292, 318, 320, 328–329

Systems: 1, 6, 8, 10–11, 13–23, 25–27, 205–206, 208–211, 214–229, 231–249

Systems Thinking: 1, 6, 8, 10, 13, 96, 217, 236–237, 243–245, 274, 277, 305, 319

T

Thermodynamics: 59, 62, 68, 103, 105, 112

Transparency: 7, 19, 22, 31, 33, 41, 44, 86–87, 101, 109, 111, 118, 126, 135, 137–139, 151–152, 155, 160, 297, 301–308

U

Uncertainty: 10, 18–21, 23, 31–32, 37–39, 45, 50, 52–54, 57, 62–64, 66–69, 71–74, 90, 93, 95, 107, 112–113, 115, 249, 298, 300, 302, 304, 308, 313

Upscaling / Scale Effects: 17, 24, 26, 28–29, 32

V

Variety (Ashby): 172, 186–189, 191–192, 196–199, 202, 206, 286, 300, 317, 328

Viable System Model (VSM): 159–162

W

Wiener, Norbert: 6, 10, 13, 141–152, 163–170, 278, 300–302, 308, 320–321, 324, 328–329

X

XAI (Explainable AI): 20–23, 205

Y

Yield Dynamics in Governance: 6–7, 9, 11, 15, 22, 24, 33–34, 40–44, 49, 51, 60, 66, 83, 86–87, 94, 97, 99–101, 109–113, 297–314, 320, 324, 327, 329

Z

Zero-Sum Games: 141–149, 206, 323